Determining Damages

The LAW AND PUBLIC POLICY: PSYCHOLOGY AND THE SOCIAL SCIENCES series includes books in three domains:

Legal Studies—writings by legal scholars about issues of relevance to psychology and the other social sciences, or that employ social science information to advance the legal analysis;

Social Science Studies—writings by scientists from psychology and the other social sciences about issues of relevance to law and public policy; and

Forensic Studies—writings by psychologists and other mental health scientists and professionals about issues relevant to forensic mental health science and practice.

The series is guided by its editor, Bruce D. Sales, PhD, JD, ScD(hc), University of Arizona; and coeditors, Bruce J. Winick, JD, University of Miami; Norman J. Finkel, PhD, Georgetown University; and Valerie P. Hans, PhD, University of Delaware.

* * *

The Right to Refuse Mental Health Treatment
  Bruce J. Winick
Violent Offenders: Appraising and Managing Risk
  Vernon L. Quinsey, Grant T. Harris, Marnie E. Rice,
  and Catherine A. Cormier
Recollection, Testimony, and Lying in Early Childhood
  Clara Stern and William Stern; James T. Lamiell (translator)
Genetics and Criminality: The Potential Misuse of Scientific Information in Court
  Edited by Jeffrey R. Botkin, William M. McMahon, and
  Leslie Pickering Francis
The Hidden Prejudice: Mental Disability on Trial
  Michael L. Perlin
Adolescents, Sex, and the Law: Preparing Adolescents for Responsible Citizenship
  Roger J. R. Levesque
Legal Blame: How Jurors Think and Talk About Accidents
  Neal Feigenson
Justice and the Prosecution of Old Crimes: Balancing Legal, Psychological, and Moral Concerns
  Daniel W. Shuman and Alexander McCall Smith

Unequal Rights: Discrimination Against People With Mental Disabilities and the Americans With Disabilities Act
  Susan Stefan
Treating Adult and Juvenile Offenders With Special Needs
  Edited by José B. Ashford, Bruce D. Sales, and William H. Reid
Culture and Family Violence: Fostering Change Through Human Rights Law
  Roger J. R. Levesque
The Legal Construction of Identity: The Judicial and Social Legacy of American Colonialism in Puerto Rico
  Efrén Rivera Ramos
Family Mediation: Facts, Myths, and Future Prospects
  Connie J. A. Beck and Bruce D. Sales
Not Fair! The Typology of Commonsense Unfairness
  Norman J. Finkel
Competence, Condemnation, and Commitment: An Integrated Theory of Mental Health Law
  Robert F. Schopp
The Evolution of Mental Health Law
  Edited by Lynda E. Frost and Richard J. Bonnie
Hollow Promises: Employment Discrimination Against People With Mental Disabilities
  Susan Stefan
Determining Damages: The Psychology of Jury Awards
  Edie Greene and Brian H. Bornstein

Determining Damages

THE PSYCHOLOGY OF JURY AWARDS

Edie Greene
Brian H. Bornstein

AMERICAN PSYCHOLOGICAL ASSOCIATION
WASHINGTON, DC

Published by
American Psychological Association
750 First Street, NE
Washington, DC 20002
www.apa.org

To order
APA Order Department
P.O. Box 92984
Washington, DC 20090-2984

Tel: (800) 374-2721; Direct: (202) 336-5510
Fax: (202) 336-5502; TDD/TTY: (202) 336-6123
Online: www.apa.org/books/
Email: order@apa.org

In the U.K., Europe, Africa, and the Middle East, copies may be ordered from
American Psychological Association
3 Henrietta Street
Covent Garden, London
WC2E 8LU England

Typeset in Goudy by EPS Group Inc., Easton, MD

Printer: Sheridan Books, Ann Arbor, MI
Cover Designer: Berg Design, Albany, NY
Technical/Production Editor: Kristen R. Sullivan

The opinions and statements published are the responsibility of the authors, and such opinions and statements do not necessarily represent the policies of the American Psychological Association.

Library of Congress Cataloging-in-Publication Data
Greene, Edie.
    Determining damages : the psychology of jury awards / by Edie Greene and Brian H. Bornstein.
        p. cm.—(Law and public policy)
    Includes bibliographical references and index.
    ISBN 1-55798-974-5 (alk. paper)
        1. Jurors—United States—Psychology.   2. Verdicts—United States—Psychological aspects.   3. Damages—United States—Psychological aspects.
    I. Bornstein, Brian H.   II. Title.   III. Series.

    KF8972.Z9 G74 2002
    347.73′77—dc21

                                                                2002074429

British Library Cataloguing-in-Publication Data
A CIP record is available from the British Library.

Printed in the United States of America
First Edition

This book is dedicated first and foremost to Alan, David, and Rebecca
and to Christie, Lillian, and Melissa for their love and support.
It is dedicated second to John Harvard's Brew House
in Cambridge, Massachusetts, where it all began.

"Write that down," the King said to the jury and the jury eagerly wrote down all three dates on their slates, and then added them up, and reduced their answer to shillings and pence.

—Lewis Carroll, *Alice's Adventures in Wonderland*

CONTENTS

Preface xiii

Acknowledgments xvii

   Chapter 1.   Introduction 3

   Chapter 2.   Characterizing Jury Damage Awards 29

I. The Issue of Identity: How Plaintiff, Defendant, and Juror
  Characteristics Influence Damage Award Decisions 47

   Chapter 3.   Who Is the Plaintiff? 51

   Chapter 4.   Who Is the Defendant? 63

   Chapter 5.   Who Are the Jurors? 79

II. The Evidence: How Injury Severity and Litigants' Conduct
  Influence Damage Award Decisions 97

   Chapter 6.   Severity and Nature of the Injury 101

   Chapter 7.   The Litigants' Conduct 127

III. Decision Processes and Reforms: How Jurors Reason About
   Damages and How Damage Award Decisions Might Be
   Improved 147

   Chapter 8.   How Jurors Reason About Damages 149

Chapter 9. Reforming Damage Award Decision Making 175

Chapter 10. Final Remarks and Recommendations 199

References 207

Table of Authorities 227

Index 229

About the Authors 237

PREFACE

This book is about how ordinary people, thrust into the unordinary role of jurors, make decisions about damage awards in civil trials. Damage awards are provided for people who have suffered from the actions (and, on occasion, the omissions) of other people. They are intended primarily to compensate the sufferers for their losses and, sometimes, to exact punishment against the wrongdoers.

Jurors and juries instructed to assess damages must undertake an enormously difficult task. Consider the case of Kimberly Miller, a Colorado woman who was killed in a fiery car accident in January 1999. In 2001, Miller's family, including her 8-year-old son and 9-year-old daughter—who were with her in the fiery crash—filed a wrongful-death lawsuit. The defendant—a man with bipolar disorder who was apparently off his medication and running from devils—had blasted through a city intersection at an estimated 94 miles per hour before plowing into the back of Miller's Jeep Wrangler. She died instantly; her children were left physically burned and emotionally scarred. One wonders how any system of justice could hope to repair the lives of these young children. How could money—no matter its amount—bring solace to the souls of these children?[1]

Although money is probably a mediocre remedy at best, it is the remedy devised by the civil justice system to allay these children's suffering and, more generally, to repay people for their losses. It is no easy task to calibrate a life in dollars and cents, but such is the stuff of damage awards assessed by jurors: judging the value of another's life and its ruination, and determining how much money it would take to repair the ruin.

---

[1] This case example arose from an assignment that Edie Greene gave to her students in an advanced psychology seminar. The assignment was to present a case to the class and discuss its psychological implications. The student who shared these details had been a close friend of the decedent.

How juries decide damage awards is an issue of both theoretical and practical import. Psychologists and other social scientists are interested in the ways that jurors attend to and process information about injuries and losses and the manner in which they reach a consensus about these concerns in the course of jury deliberation. These issues indicate something about the larger question of how people make decisions in the context of uncertain information (a feature that characterizes most, if not all, decisions) and about how they talk about and justify their decisions to others. Policymakers may be interested in how current policy and procedures (and potential changes in policy and procedure) affect decision making about damages. Practicing lawyers may want to capitalize on this knowledge base to enhance their advocacy skills. Members of the general public may simply be interested in understanding how juries make these complex and sometimes controversial decisions. Although we rely extensively on the findings of empirical psychological research studies to evaluate the process of decision making about damages, wherever possible we weave real-life cases and laws into our analysis so that our conclusions can ultimately speak to several audiences. We hope we have succeeded.

How juries decide damage awards is also an issue that engenders great passion and rancorous debate. In fact, there may be no more controversial aspect of jury decision making than jurors' ability to assess damages in a fair and predictable manner. Everyone, it seems, has an opinion about jury damage awards yet, as Neil Vidmar (1995) noted, "the claims about juries are founded, in some instances, solely on thin-air conjecture; in others on misrepresentation of data; and in still others on misunderstanding of data" (p. ix). An important aim of this book, then, is to set the record straight about how jurors and juries make decisions about damages, including both how they (often) rise to the occasion and produce awards that are reasoned and reasonable and how they (occasionally) deliver decisions that seem unpredictable and unfounded. A theme that emerges from our analysis is the role of antiquated trial procedures in hindering jurors' attempts to think logically and to deliver rational verdicts.

Finally, how jurors assess damages is an issue with important legal and policy implications. In recent years, state legislatures across the country have enacted reforms in how the task of determining damages is presented to jurors and in the kinds of responses that are sought from juries. Many of these changes have been introduced with nary a nod to how they will affect jurors' reasoning about damages. Another aim of the book, then, is to lend an empirical foundation to the rhetoric and calls for reform that surround jury decisions on damages.

We have chosen to focus on damage awards as assessed by juries even though, as we note at several points in the book, most awards to deserving plaintiffs are worked out through settlement negotiations. Although we limit our sample size significantly by focusing only on the decisions delivered by juries in the context of a trial, we believe that this narrower focus provides a brighter light on the psychological and legal processes that interest us. The narrower focus enables us to understand the decision-making process in finer detail.

ACKNOWLEDGMENTS

A number of people have facilitated the writing of this book. First and foremost, we thank our families for supporting us throughout this undertaking, which often proved more daunting than we anticipated. They intuitively knew when to ask "How's the book coming along?" and when not to. In addition, we are grateful and indeed indebted to each other for the many ways in which each of us was stretched by the other. By seeking explanation and demanding clarity of each other, we both became better writers and clearer thinkers. We also learned that we had more in common than just our research interests, which made the time we spent working together truly enjoyable.

We are also indebted to several people who assisted us in the process of refining and advancing our ideas. We are especially grateful to Norman Finkel, coeditor of the American Psychological Association's (APA's) book series, *Law and Public Policy: Psychology and the Social Sciences*, who first suggested that we write this book and delighted with us in its completion. Bruce Sales, editor-in-chief of the book series, supported our efforts along the way and read an early draft. Susan Poser provided a "lawyerly" perspective on drafts of several chapters. During the time that this book was being written, Edie Greene's research was supported by grants from the National Science Foundation (Grant 9617270) and from the University of Colorado Committee on Research and Creative Works, and Brian Bornstein was supported by a training grant from the National Institute of Mental Health (Grant 5 T32 MH16156-21) and a leave of absence from Louisiana State University, during which time he was fortunate to be invited to be a visiting professor and postdoctoral fellow at the University of Nebraska.

We are grateful to APA acquisitions editor Susan Reynolds, who kept us to a timetable; our development editor Phuong Huynh, who oversaw revisions; and our production editor Kristen Sullivan, who made it all come together. We are also most appreciative of the comments from anonymous reviewers. In the end, of course, responsibility for accuracy and level-headed analysis (or any lack thereof) rests with us.

Determining Damages

1

INTRODUCTION

Injuries diminish people. Some people learn to or choose to live in their reduced state, going about their lives, opting not to seek recompense for their injuries. Others take a different course, choosing to pursue formal legal claims against the person or entity that they believe has wronged them.[1] Sometimes, the resolution of those claims rests with a group of ordinary citizens, thrust into the distinctly unordinary role of jurors. One of the tasks these jurors might be asked to undertake is to determine how much money, termed *damages*, should be assessed against the wrongdoer for purposes of compensating the victim and, on occasion, to punish the wrongdoer.[2] So, in simple terms, if injuries diminish people, then juries, in a sense, reconstruct them, at least to the extent that money is able to do so. This book is about how juries do just that.

We have a specific objective. As psychologists, we are more interested in exploring *how* jurors and juries decide damages than in *what* they decide. (Economists and policymakers would likely have a different orientation and

---

[1]Why some injured people sue and others do not is an interesting and little-researched topic (see, e.g., Felstiner, Abel, & Sarat, 1980–1981; Kritzer, Bogart, & Vidmar, 1991; Sloan & Hsieh, 1995; Vidmar, 1995).

[2]Legal scholars recognize other, secondary goals of damage awards, including encouraging safety, promoting justice, allocating the costs of accidents to those who can best afford them, educating offenders and society in general, and deterring future misconduct. As these secondary objectives are typically not within the purview of juries, we have little to say about them.

interest.) Accordingly, throughout this book we rely extensively on our own scholarly work and the work of other psycholegal researchers to describe the processes by which jurors assess damages. We take into account a variety of contextual factors, such as characteristics of the jurors themselves, the nature of the case, the evidence adduced at trial, and the decision-making abilities of laypeople who must reason about the law.

A simple, familiar conundrum provides a good starting point for our observations. Two people, gazing at the same quantity of liquid in a glass, might attach different labels: One might call the glass half full, the other, half empty. Just as people differ in their descriptions of the contents of the glass, so too do people differ in their depictions of the jury in damage cases. Some liken jurors to irrational, overly sympathetic purveyors of bad judgment who, more often than not, force the exchange of money from modestly errant defendants to overly greedy plaintiffs. Others, looking at the same circumstances, see largely defensible decisions made by people who are largely untrained in the law and often unaided by the system.

Whereas a metaphorical glass can simultaneously be half empty and half full, one wonders how an objective entity—in this case, the ability of jurors to assess damages fairly—can be both. Why is there such disagreement about the role of jurors in the setting of damage awards?

We argue that this contrariety stems in part from the divide between rhetoric and data—that the half-empty folks, often critical of jurors, tend to rely on rhetoric and less on data, and that the half-full folks, who see jurors more favorably, tend to embrace the opposite perspective.[3] Let us set the record straight from the outset and acknowledge that, as empirical scientists, our allegiances are with the latter crowd. Indeed, one important aim of this book is to steer away from rhetoric and provide an empirically based treatment of how jurors and juries assess damages. Also, we argue, when one moves beyond rhetoric and anecdote and in the direction of empiricism and data, the conundrum begins to disappear.

Indeed, a theme that pervades this book is that, in many respects, jurors charged with the complex task of compensating the injured and punishing the wrongdoers do a commendable job of it. As we show, theirs is no easy task. Yet they are usually deliberate and thoughtful about their decisions (Hans & Vidmar, 1986) and, more important, are often right (or at least within the ballpark; Kalven & Zeisel, 1966).

However, we do not purport to argue that the system is flawless. Indeed, jurors sometimes make outlandish decisions. As a result, some plaintiffs walk away from jury trials with windfall profits, while others are left undeservedly bereft and ruined. Some defendants are savagely and unfairly deprived of their property, while others weasel their way out of paying what they rightfully owe.

---

[3]Saks (1989) argued that, for most of its life, the law has muddled along without the backing of data and could surely benefit from its use. We agree.

Rather than lay blame at the feet of the men and women who step out of their everyday lives and into the unfamiliar domain of a courthouse to resolve disputes among adversaries, we prefer to question a system that expects jurors to perform a Herculean task with little know-how. Jurors are routinely confronted by confusing presentations of evidence (Sanders, 1998) and needlessly complicated recitations of the law (Lieberman & Sales, 1997). When their decisions diverge from what we expect (or from what experts might decide), the difficulty of the decision-making context may be at least as much to blame as any moral or intellectual failings on their part (Feigenson, 2000).

A second aim of this book, then, is to show the ways that jurors' decision-making processes are sometimes impaired by structural and procedural elements of civil jury trials. There has been a historical lack of attentiveness to the ability of jurors to consider the evidence fairly and understand the law in damage cases. Courts assume, often incorrectly, that jurors will understand complex evidence, discern the truth from contradictory facts, and apply the instructions to these facts in legally appropriate ways.

Some hopeful signs are on the horizon, however. Many judges and legal commentators have begun to recognize that jurors and juries can be helped to do better; that their decision making can be made more logical and predictable by the addition of a few twists to the typical civil jury trial. So, for example, some judges are providing pretrial instruction about what jurors are expected to do, and others are streamlining jurors' decision making by focusing it on smaller, easier issues. Still others are offering a narrower range of options involving damages. (We discuss these reforms—and others—in detail in chapter 9.) Although not all of these remedies (or others like them) will be beneficial in every case, they acknowledge something that scholars of the jury have been saying for some time: namely, that if jurors are provided with better tools for decision making, their decisions will be both more rational and more predictable.

We begin this chapter with a brief historical look at a system that extracts money from people who have acted wrongly and delivers it to those who have suffered as a result. We then describe the role of jury damage awards in the larger context of the civil justice system and detail the legal objectives and practical issues that are encompassed by various kinds of damage awards. We outline the procedures in a civil damages trial (focusing on those procedures that are relevant to the jury) and pay particular attention to concerns related to the ambiguity of jury instructions on damages. We end the chapter by describing some popular views about jurors' abilities to assess damages in an equitable fashion and detail several concerns and critiques about whether jurors are up to the task. This coverage sets the stage for chapter 2, in which we describe what damage awards actually look like, whether jurors' damage decisions accord with legally derived normative expectations, and whether and how jurors can be helped to make better decisions.

HISTORICAL ROOTS OF DAMAGE AWARDS

The notion of paying money to people to compensate them for their injuries is a very old one (O'Connell & Bailey, 1972). Roman laws from as far back as 450 BCE provided for specific amounts of money to change hands when someone was injured. These laws factored the status of the victim into the equation: If a free man suffered a broken bone, he was to receive 300 *asses*, or copper coins, from the injurer. A slave got only 150 *asses*.

Punitive damages also have deep roots in the law. They were provided for in Babylonian law nearly 4,000 years ago and were recognized in Hittite laws from approximately 1400 BCE, in the Hebrew Covenant Code of Mosaic law dating from 1200 BCE, and in the Hindu Code of Manu of about 200 BCE (Owen, 1994). Roman laws from 450 BCE were primarily punitive in nature, providing for double, triple, and quadruple damages in some cases.

In medieval England, a payment known as a *bot* was appropriated for people who had sustained injuries (including injuries to feelings), and a separate payment, known as a *wite*, was paid to the king for breaking the peace. Amounts varied according to the type of injury. So, for example, the loss of a thumb was worth 20 shillings, loss of a shooting (i.e., index) finger was worth 8 shillings, and loss of a little finger was worth 3 shillings. "Exposure of the bone" also resulted in payment of 3 shillings.

It was only after the jury system evolved in England during the 12th century that the victim of injury was required to provide proof of harm and damage before receiving compensation. However, then, as now, no statutes existed to dictate how much money should be exchanged for various kinds of injuries.

The first mention of "exemplary damages" comes from a false-imprisonment case brought by a journeyman printer against agents of the King (*Huckle v. Money*, 1763). The jury awarded the printer £300 (an impressive sum at the time). On appeal, the court found the award not to be excessive and stated its reluctance to second-guess the jury's assessment, characterizing the damages as "exemplary" (i.e., making an example of the defendant).

The notion of awarding damages for pain and suffering made its first appearance in 1773 when *Scott v. Sheperd*, the famous squib case, was decided. The defendant had thrown a small firecracker, or squib, into a crowded marketplace. It burned the plaintiff and blinded him. According to the pleading, the plaintiff experienced "great excruciating pain" and torment. He was awarded £100 in damages (Chitty, 1809).

To our founding fathers, the right to trial by jury, as instituted in England, was an integral part of the judicial system. The original Constitution of 1787 guaranteed the right to a jury trial only in criminal cases, but concern about the absence of constitutional protections in civil suits resulted in the drafting of the Seventh Amendment (C. P. Murphy, 1993): "In suits at common law, where the value in controversy shall exceed twenty dollars, the right of trial by jury shall be preserved." As in English common law, civil juries in the United States also had the authority to assess a remedy (e.g., a damage award) in civil cases (C. P. Murphy, 1993). Also, as early as 1797, the Supreme Court recognized that determining damages was an appropriate task for a jury: "Wherever matters of fact can be separated from matters of law, it will be agreed to be a general and favorable practice, to allot the assessment of damages to a jury" (*Brown v. Van Braam*, 1797, pp. 348–349).

During the 19th century, as transportation became more rapid, and use of the railroads increased, the number of personal injury lawsuits alleging negligence grew dramatically (O'Connell & Simon, 1972). In these cases, liability was often very clear, so the only real issue, both at trial and on appellate review, was the size of the damage award.

In 1886, the Supreme Court reiterated its reliance on juries to make these decisions while at the same time acknowledging that there were few rules to guide their conduct: "Where no precise rule of law fixes the recoverable damages, it is the peculiar function of the jury to determine the amount by their verdict" (*Barry v. Edmunds*, 1886, p. 565). In a later case, the court again declared that determining damages is a question of fact for the jury, not the judge (*Dimick v. Schiedt*, 1935).

By the mid-1800s, punitive damages had also become a fixture of American law. In 1851, in *Day v. Woodworth*, the Supreme Court asserted that the doctrine of punitive damages was supported by "repeated judicial decisions for more than a century" (p. 371). So even this cursory review shows strong support in the judiciary for the role of jurors in determining compensation for individuals who have sustained injuries and punishment for those who have done wrong.

During the post-World War II period, the size of damage awards soared. This spectacular rise in verdicts is attributable not to any changes in the law itself but rather to contextual factors: a more affluent society, the use of new and more sophisticated trial techniques by plaintiffs' lawyers, and an increasing awareness by lawyers and judges of large verdicts awarded in other parts of the country (O'Connell & Bailey, 1972).

The recent history of damage award decisions by juries has been heated and contentious. As we describe, the civil jury was soundly and roundly criticized throughout the last quarter of the 20th century, especially in the 1980s and early 1990s (Vidmar, 1998). The most frequently voiced concerns about civil juries and damage awards are as follows:

- Jury damage awards are too large and highly variable. Because of this variability, they are hard to predict.
- In assessing damages, jurors fail to consider the social and economic consequences of their awards.
- Jurors are biased against wealthy defendants and in favor of relatively poorer plaintiffs.

Beginning in the early 1980s during President Ronald Reagan's administration, and continuing undaunted through the tenures of Presidents George Bush, Bill Clinton, and (thus far) George W. Bush, reform proponents have supported legislation that, among other things, would make it harder for plaintiffs to recover damages from defendants and would limit the amount of money that defendants would be required to pay. Business concerns, led by members of the insurance industry, have fueled this debate with wide-ranging efforts to vilify the civil jury, claiming that jurors side with unworthy plaintiffs and line their pockets with money that is not deserved (Hans, 2000).

Although legislative efforts to reform federal standards have been largely unsuccessful, reformers have had notable victories in statehouses across the country, and the judiciary has begun to weigh in on this matter as well. Legislatures in approximately 30 states have imposed restrictions on civil juries, often limiting the size of monetary awards (Bonanti, 2000). Also, the Supreme Court, in *BMW of North America v. Gore* (1996), placed new constraints on a jury's decision about punitive damages by deeming the $4 million punitive award in a case involving a car that was repainted prior to sale (with compensatory damages totaling only $4,000) to be "grossly excessive" and striking it down.[4] So the ground has begun to shake under the surface of the civil liability system, and the juries who decide these cases are finding themselves near the center of the storm.

Now, at the beginning of the 21st century, some new trends have begun to emerge. In 1996, the number of personal injury lawsuits in this country began to decline and has continued in that downward direction ever since. In California, the number of big-money personal injury lawsuits is now half what it was in the early 1990s (Rohrlich, 2001).[5] Some of the jury bashing has begun to abate as well.

To what should one attribute this decline? Economist Stephen Carroll of the RAND Corporation's Institute for Civil Justice suspects that the drop in personal injury lawsuits in California is related to a 1988 state Supreme Court decision that changed the rules for personal injury lawsuits,

---

[4]The Alabama Supreme Court had already reduced the award to $2 million.
[5]In that same period, though, punitive damage awards increased dramatically in California (Livingston, 2001).

essentially removing the threat of punitive damages against insurers (Rohrlich, 2001). Other, nationwide changes may have contributed as well. Corporate- and insurance-sponsored tort reform packages may have reduced the incentive for plaintiffs' lawyers to press their clients' claims in court. Improvements in product safety may have reduced the incidence of serious injuries. The advent and increased reliance on arbitration and mediation may have allowed more cases to settle short of trial.

However, many people still sue, and many jurors still determine damage awards. To understand the role of jurors and juries in resolving these disputes, we describe the place of damage awards and jury trials in the larger civil justice system.

THE DISPUTING PYRAMID

To understand fully the role of damage awards and trial by jury in the civil justice system one needs to understand the bigger context in which damages are awarded. The civil liability system has been likened to a "disputing pyramid" (see, e.g., Galanter, 1983; Sanders & Joyce, 1990). Jury verdicts, in general, and damage awards, in particular, usually constitute the most visible part of the process and rest at the pinnacle of the pyramid. Below them reside a number of processes that determine whether a dispute emerges in the first place and whether it rises to the level of a jury trial. These processes include the perception of an injury, the decision to file a claim against the wrongdoer, and attempts at resolution of those claims (Daniels & Martin, 1997).

The pyramid metaphor graphically demonstrates that the great majority of civil lawsuits filed each year are not resolved by a jury. Most are settled outside of the confines of a courtroom. Even among cases that do not settle, many are dismissed by the plaintiffs or by the courts; only a small fraction are tried before a jury (Galanter, 1990; Gross & Syverud, 1996; Hensler et al., 1991).[6] So, in quantitative terms, all of this means that less than 2% of cases resolved in state courts (where most civil cases are heard) and just over 2% of cases handled by federal courts involve jury trials (Galanter, 1990).

Given these statistics, one might reasonably wonder why anyone would really care much about jury damage awards (and why two otherwise reasonable academics would devote so much of the past few years of their lives to studying and describing these awards). Harry Kalven, writing about the influential University of Chicago Jury Project of the 1950s—one of the first large-scale studies of juror decision making, said simply: "Jury han-

---

[6]It is also probably true that juries may not hear cases with the largest losses due to injuries. Cases that involve monumental damages, clear liability, or grossly negligent conduct by a defendant are most likely to settle short of trial (Saks, 1992).

dling of damages is an extraordinarily interesting topic" (Kalven, 1958, p. 159). But is inherent interest enough?

There are several, complementary reasons that the study of jury decision making regarding damages is important, provocative, and indeed, necessary. The first is simple: There are approximately 50,000 civil jury trials each year in the United States. Assuming that half end in verdicts for the plaintiff and discussions about damages, then 25,000 juries (approximately 150,000 individual jurors) must determine damage awards each year. (This number is approximately 10 times the number of people in our country who succumb each year to AIDS [Centers for Disease Control, 2001], and 3-1/2 times the number who die in automobile accidents [National Highway Traffic Safety Administration, 2000]—both social conditions that command a great deal of public attention.)

In that same vein, juries dole out billions of dollars in damages each year, although not all of this money lands in the laps of plaintiffs. (Verdicts are often modified on appeal or by means of posttrial settlement negotiations. In fact, Marc Galanter [1990] suggested that it might be most accurate to think of the jury as providing the winner with a powerful bargaining chip, but one that may be significantly altered after trial.) However, here is the main point: We, and others, wonder how those billions are assessed.

There are other reasons that jury damage awards should be studied. Galanter (1990) argued eloquently that the impact of jury trials (and of jury awards) is vastly disproportionate to their incidence. He contended that the civil jury casts a shadow across a wide spectrum of claims and settlements by communicating what a future jury might do and by helping to value future disputes. Jury decisions set standards that influence a broad array of social behaviors, including claiming, negotiating, and settling. These behaviors, in turn, affect the mix of cases that future juries will face. In essence, data on jury verdicts and awards convey valuable information to attorneys and potential claimants that affect the course of their future conduct.[7]

The study of jury damage awards provides a unique forum for psychologists and other behavioral scientists to probe a number of intriguing psychological issues. These cases ask people to place a monetary value on precious yet priceless items that have been taken from others: good health, good name, and good business opportunities. How do jurors translate these intangibles into dollars and cents? What contribution do their senses of justice, fairness, equity, even outrage, lend to the equation? How are they

---

[7]Not all legal scholars see the same impact of jury verdicts on future litigants. Saks (1992) argued that because attorneys are not particularly sensitive to the nuances of jury behavior, neither are their settlement negotiations so informed. He argued further that if negotiators are able to derive a realistic sense of what a case is worth, it is because they are familiar with the culture of negotiation, not because they are especially well attuned to the behavior of juries.

able to make judgments about uncertain situations, and what role do biases and heuristics play in directing their thoughts? How do they process complex information? What role do emotions play in jurors' cognitive evaluation of the evidence? How are individual jurors with different priorities and objectives able to merge their contrasting desires in order to agree on an award? What role do judicial procedures have in facilitating (and, in some instances, discouraging) the use of rational decision-making strategies? What could be done to improve jury decisions regarding damages?

Finally, scientific scrutiny of damage award decision making is important because many jurors say that arriving at a monetary award is the most daunting aspect of their jury service (Hans, 2000)—more difficult than agreeing on the "facts" of the case, understanding expert testimony, judging the credibility of witnesses, or assessing liability. How, they ask, are they expected to place a monetary value on someone's losses if they are given only limited guidance on how to do so? Careful analysis of the ways that jurors grapple with this task can illuminate the difficulties they encounter along the way and can suggest mechanisms that will improve their performance in the future.

Now that we have placed these awards in the context of the larger system that compensates some people for their losses and extracts payment from others for their wrongdoing, we need to provide more detail about the various kinds of damage awards and the objectives of each. This information will set the stage for understanding the complexities inherent in determining damages and for examining the concerns related to jurors' abilities to make these complicated decisions.

DAMAGE AWARDS DEFINED

Damages may be *compensatory* or *punitive*.[8] The former are generally intended to compensate the injured person for the injury, to return that person to pre-injury levels of functioning, or to replace the loss caused by the injury or wrong (to the extent that money is able to do so). If jurors determine that the defendant is liable, for example, then they are expected to compensate the plaintiff fully for his or her losses by means of compensatory damages. Punitive damages, which we discuss later, are intended to punish the defendant for outrageous conduct and to deter future transgressions. Punitive damages usually are awarded only if compensatory damages have also been awarded, and appellate courts usually expect there to be a reasonable relationship between the two (*BMW v. Gore*, 1996). We next discuss each of the forms of damage awards in more detail.

---

[8]The law also recognizes nominal damages—awarded to vindicate a right in situations where no real loss or injury occurred or was proven. We do not focus on these awards.

Compensatory Damages

Compensatory damages can be either *economic* or *noneconomic* (sometimes referred to as *pecuniary* and *nonpecuniary*). *Economic damages* refers to the financial costs incurred by the plaintiff as a result of the injury. In personal injury cases, for example, these losses typically include past and future income and past and future medical expenses. In commercial cases, losses may include the cost of lost earnings and business opportunities or the inability to expand into new markets or product lines. In libel cases, economic losses typically involve damage or harm to one's reputation or character (Sunstein, Kahneman, & Schkade, 1998).

One might suspect that some of these losses—particularly those associated with quantifiable dollar values—should be relatively easy to measure. Past medical expenses generally fall into this category. One typically knows, for example, the medical costs incurred from the time of an injury to the present, including, among other things, hospital and doctors' bills, medicine, rehabilitation, and therapies. Past income is also relatively easy to quantify, at least for wage earners. One usually knows, for instance, how long the plaintiff has been out of work as a result of an accident and what his or her salary was prior to being injured. (Matters get quickly complicated, however, when the claimant is self-employed or a stay-at-home spouse.)

In the realm of future losses, debate is more contentious. The calculations in personal injury cases, for example, must take into account forecasts about future medical care needs, available job opportunities and advancements, and projected life expectancies, not to mention anticipated rates of inflation. These projections are obviously fraught with uncertainty and can be made in a variety of ways (*O'Shea v. Riverway Towing Co.*, 1982).

Imagine a hypothetical plaintiff who is injured in an automobile accident. Some of the questions that jurors assessing damages in this case might have to confront are: Will the plaintiff need rehabilitative services for 2 years or 5 years? As a result of physical therapy, will the plaintiff's health improve, remain the same, or perhaps even degenerate? To what extent will pre-existing problems be exacerbated by the new injury? What will happen, in the long run, regarding the costs of expensive prescription drugs that the plaintiff will need? For how long will the plaintiff need skilled nursing assistance? For how long will the plaintiff manage to live on his or her own, and when will he or she need the assistance of a full-time caregiver or the confines of an assisted-living facility? Who will care for the injured plaintiff's children, and at what expense?

On the job front, there will be other hard questions: What would the plaintiff have earned over the course of his or her working life? What raises and promotions might he or she have secured? For how many years might he or she have worked? Can the plaintiff successfully retrain to work in a field that involves less wear and tear on his or her body? What will the new career portend in terms of future earnings? For how long will he or she work at the new job? How will a change in careers affect the plaintiff's ability to save for retirement? If the plaintiff is a child, would a college education have been likely, and should his or her loss of earning capacity be measured against that of college graduates?

Noneconomic damages are awarded to compensate the plaintiff for injury to the "intangible, subjective state of the plaintiff's life" (Vidmar, 1995, p. 186). Noneconomic injuries, sometimes referred to by the generic term *pain and suffering* can entail physical pain and disfigurement; emotional distress, including fear, anxiety, and depression; and loss of enjoyment of life, including limitations on lifestyle options. They can also include loss of consortium or companionship (marital or otherwise) and loss of mental faculties.

These losses involve obvious social and psychological components (Wissler, Evans, Hart, Morry, & Saks, 1997) and, because they are frequently hidden from plain view, are especially difficult to quantify. Imagine having to determine how much a person's pleasures were worth and how much of that pleasure was lost when the injuries occurred. Imagine having to attach a price tag to a partner's companionship, affection, aid, and comfort. Imagine having to figure out how much the infliction of embarrassment, or anxiety, or depression, should cost. Or, in a slightly different context, imagine trying to decide the cost of losing one's reputation or good name.[9]

By any standard, these are tough questions. Because of the enormous uncertainties involved in answering them, many critics of civil juries focus their attention on the noneconomic aspect of the damages calculus as the one most fraught with problems. In fact, we suspect that more than a few jurors faced with these daunting questions have wished they could simply gaze into a crystal ball and divine the future. The power of fortune telling would have simplified their task considerably.

To guide jurors through this maze of uncertainty, each side in a civil damage lawsuit is likely to call on its own cadre of experts. These may include economists, accountants, actuaries, doctors, therapists, rehabilitation specialists, vocational counselors, human resource specialists, organi-

---

[9]Some researchers have suggested that a person's good name may be priceless (Bezanson, Cranberg, & Soloski, 1987), a sentiment expressed eloquently by Shakespeare's Iago:

> Good name in man and woman, dear my lord,
> Is the immediate jewel of their souls;
> Who steals my purse steals trash; 'tis something, nothing;
> 'Twas mine, 'tis his, and has been slave to thousands;
> But he that filches from me my good name
> Robs me of that which not enriches him,
> And makes me poor indeed. (*Othello*, Act III, Scene 3)

zational consultants, and other professionals who may attempt a little fortune telling of their own by describing how the plaintiff's future would have unfolded but for the claimed injury and what the forecast looks like now.

Determining compensatory damages is problematic for a variety of other reasons. Jury damage awards are typically discounted to present value; that is, the plaintiff is awarded a certain amount at trial that will, over time, theoretically grow to equal the amount the jury has deemed appropriate compensation. Thus, there may be rancorous debate—spurred by the conflicting forecasts of dueling experts—about prospects for future inflation and interest rates that obviously affect calculation of the reduction (*O'Shea v. Riverway Towing Co.*, 1982). Simply stated, jurors have no inside track on figuring how much a dollar will be worth in 5, 10, or 20 years.

Even with discounting to present value, compensatory damage awards can sometimes amount to hundreds of thousands or even millions of dollars. Herein lurks yet another problem. On occasion, the monetary figures being bandied about in the deliberation room—however well documented and justified by the evidence—are sums that seem exorbitant to laypeople. As a result, jurors may advocate for an award that is, to their minds, more reasonable. Here is one example: One of us had the opportunity to view alternate jurors assessing damages in a trademark infringement lawsuit tried in federal district court.[10] During closing arguments, the plaintiff's attorney had shown why his client was entitled to a $1 million-plus award, but this figure did not sit well with one of the jurors who, during deliberations, dismissed it as outrageous. She argued for something in the range of $100,000, quipping that she could not "relate to" $1 million and was having a hard enough time paying her $8 parking fee at the courthouse.

Or, consider this real world example of jurors assessing damages in light of their own financial situations: In 1998, a jury in Dutchess County, New York awarded $345,000 to Steven Pagones, a White former prosecutor who had been defamed by three advisers to Tawana Brawley, an African American teenager who said Pagones abducted and raped her 10 years before. Although the sum was significantly lower than the $150 million that Pagones had requested, even the much smaller number was problematic for some jurors. According to juror Glen Heinsohn, who earned about $20,000 per year, he and fellow jurors thought they were being generous to Pagones, given what they (i.e., the jurors) earned (Glaberson, 1998).

There are other difficulties inherent in calculating compensatory damages. Because jurors are notoriously poor at understanding the influence of

---

[10] A set of alternate jurors sat through the entire 6-week trial with the expectation that they might be among the jurors who would actually deliberate to a verdict in the case. At the end of the trial, however, they were designated as alternates and were asked to deliberate as a jury for purposes of research. Their multi-day deliberations were videotaped and analyzed as part of a larger project on jury comprehension in complex cases (American Bar Association, 1991).

exponential growth factors such as inflation, investment potential, or earnings growth, they tend instead to use a more linear approach in calculating damages that advantages defendants (Goodman, Greene, & Loftus, 1989). Underscoring all of these other difficulties is the requirement that jurors engage in detailed thinking about the long run—something that most of us are not particularly well equipped to do.

The oft-quoted Harry Kalven aptly summarized the complexities of figuring compensatory damages:

> To price a punch in the nose or a broken leg is at first blush a difficult value judgment. But the law appears to avoid the impossible here by breaking the loss components down into subordinate questions of fact as to medical expense, economic loss, and pain and suffering. Medical expense and economic loss do have some object reality but the warrant to add pain and suffering gives the jury immediate freedom to price the injury subjectively. And where, as is often the case, there is an issue not only of accrued loss but of loss in the future the facts as to medical expense and economic loss become enormously more ambiguous. (Kalven, 1958, pp. 160–161)

As Anderson and MacCoun (1999) noted, the rationale behind compensatory damages—both economic and noneconomic—is plaintiff focused: The jury is to focus exclusively on the needs of the injured party and attempt to return him or her to a pre-injury level of functioning. The second kind of damage award—the punitive damage award—is based on a wholly different rationale. We turn to that now.

Punitive Damages

Plaintiffs may also request another kind of damages, namely, punitive damages (sometimes referred to as *exemplary damages*). This award is designed to punish the defendant for egregious conduct and to deter the defendant and others from engaging in similar conduct in the future (Owen, 1994). Jurors are generally instructed that they may award punitive damages if they find that the defendant acted in a malicious, willful, or wanton manner. These awards serve several secondary purposes as well, including education, retribution, and law enforcement. They may also serve to reimburse the plaintiff for losses that are not recoverable as traditional compensatory damages (Owen, 1994). Nearly all states allow punitive damages, and approximately 60 federal statutes permit the awarding of punitive damages (e.g., 7 U.S.C. § 18 (a)(1)(B), 1994; 10 U.S.C. § 2207 (a)(2), 1994).

In some states, punitive damage amounts are loosely tied to the amount of the compensatory award. In other states, punitive damages are unlimited. In reality, though, punitive damages can be many times larger than the compensatory award and can be imposed in multiple lawsuits arising out of the same alleged misconduct by the defendant. Critics claim that such inherent unpredictability causes defendants to settle cases even when the plaintiff's claims are perceived as inflated or lacking merit, rather than risk a large punitive damage award (Polinsky & Shavell, 1998).

In theory, punitive damages are defendant focused (Anderson & MacCoun, 1999): Without regard to the plaintiff's needs, the jury is to determine what amount of money will effectively punish and deter the defendant. Although, as we note in the next chapter, punitive damages are granted infrequently in civil cases generally, and even less frequently in ordinary tort cases (Daniels & Martin, 1990; Moller, 1996), they have captured a great deal of media attention (Bailis & MacCoun, 1996).

To round out the picture of what damage awards are intended to do and how they are—or should be—determined, we now provide a highly simplified description of how a trial involving damages typically proceeds. We give special attention to concerns related to the ambiguity of the judge's instructions regarding damages. Knowing how damages-related evidence and instructions are presented to jurors, and the problems inherent in that presentation, will help readers piece together jurors' reactions to the trial information.

PROCEDURES IN TRIALS THAT INVOLVE DAMAGES

In this section we focus on tort cases, because they are the most common type of damages-related case tried to a jury and because procedures in other civil damage cases are, for the most part, similar to those in tort cases (although the causes of action are obviously different). Among tort cases, automobile personal injury is very common. Here, in highly simplified form, is what such a trial would look like.

Assume that a woman has been injured in an automobile accident, that she has reason to believe that the defendant was primarily at fault, and that she files a claim against him.[11] Further assume that she has already received some money from her own insurance company to cover some of her medical costs, but that money was insufficient to pay all the bills (and was not intended to compensate her for noneconomic losses). Although her attorney probably met with an attorney for the defendant's insurer to attempt to settle the dispute short of trial, they were unable to resolve their differences, and the case proceeded to trial. A variety of procedural and substantive rules govern the conduct of this sort of a jury trial.

---

[11]The defendant might also file a claim against the plaintiff, alleging injury as a result of the plaintiff's action. In such a counterclaim, the roles are reversed so the "plaintiff" becomes the "defendant" and vice versa. Counterclaims are not uncommon in automobile accident litigation but would not occur in most other torts, such as products liability or medical malpractice.

At trial, the jury will first hear opening statements in which the lawyers present summaries of what they expect the evidence to show. Various witnesses for the plaintiff—both lay and expert—testify next and are cross-examined by the defense lawyer. Expert witnesses would likely be asked to offer opinions about the medical and economic circumstances of the plaintiff and make predictions about what the future will hold. The defense goes next and may counter with its own experts and arguments. In actions for punitive damages, the jury will also probably hear testimony about the financial status of the defendant. At the conclusion of the presentation of evidence, the lawyers deliver closing arguments in which they try to tie the facts adduced during the trial to the relevant legal claims. The plaintiff's attorney will argue that the facts support the alleged claims; the defense attorney will argue that they do not.

Jurors then get instructions from the judge about the applicable law. They are instructed to decide whether the plaintiff, who bears the burden of proof, has persuaded them by a preponderance of the evidence that the facts satisfy the elements of the claims raised. ("Preponderance of evidence" is the standard required for a verdict in a civil lawsuit and is generally assumed to mean that more than 50% of the evidence is in one's favor.) Jurors are instructed that if they find the defendant liable, they may assess damages against the defendant. In so-called *comparative negligence* cases, in which the plaintiff is also partially at fault, the jury will be instructed to apportion the blame between the parties and told that their damage award will be reduced in proportion to the plaintiff's level of responsibility. In most cases, all of these instructions are formulaic and replete with legal terminology that is unfamiliar to many laypeople (Greene & Johns, 2001). In addition, as we show in the next section, the instructions on damages are notoriously imprecise. After receiving instructions, jurors then retire to deliberate until they reach a verdict on whether, for each of the claims raised, the defendant is liable to the plaintiff and, if so, for what amount of damages.

Although televised depictions of jury trials usually end at the climactic moment that the verdict is announced, in fact, at that point the case is far from over. Several things can happen after the trial, including ongoing attempts at negotiated settlements (Feigenson, 2000). In addition, the trial judge may reject the jury's verdict if it is contrary to the law (in which case the putative losing party may become the winner). The judge may also determine that the verdict is against the greater weight of the evidence (in which case he or she will order a new trial).

Even if the judge accepts the jury's verdict on liability, he or she may reject the damage award as either too high or too low, given the evidence presented at trial (Baldus, MacQueen, & Woodworth, 1995). This happened in a contract case filed by stripper Vanessa Inman against a Georgia nightclub, the Pink Pony, and its owner. Inman charged that the managers of the nightclub and promoters of the 1997 Miss Nude World International pageant effectively banned her from the pageant on false cheating charges and then slandered her to other club owners.

The jury awarded Inman $335,000 for tortious interference with a contract, $500,000 for slander, $100,000 in attorneys' fees, and $1.6 million in punitive damages, but the judge "peeled away" (Eustis, 2001) the entire punitive award. According to Judge L. A. McConnell, the punitive damage award was so excessive as to be inconsistent with the preponderance of the evidence. Jurors thought otherwise and were upset that the judge had over-turned their verdict. According to juror Lisa Kagan, she and fellow jurors were trying to be careful about the money they awarded Inman because they were concerned that their judgment would be set aside.

The judge in a racial discrimination case against Wonder Bread also trimmed the punitive award, this time from $121 million to $24.3 million, much to the disappointment of jurors (Opatrny, 2000). In his opinion, San Francisco Superior Court Judge Stuart Pollack wrote "In the court's inde-pendent judgment, these amounts should be adequate to ensure that the defendant takes the jury's findings to heart and acts promptly and forcefully to correct the conditions which gave rise to these verdicts." At least one juror disagreed: "I don't think that $24 million is going to have a deterrent effect on a company with a net worth of $3 billion," stated juror Eric Noble. "It's going to be only a pin prick ... you do the math" (Opatrny, 2000).

Unless the plaintiff accepts a downward adjustment to an overly gen-erous award (termed a *remittitur*), or the defendant accepts an upward ad-justment (termed an *additur*) to an excessively stingy award, the judge may order a new trial. Finally, the losing party may appeal the verdict, and an appellate court may modify that verdict and, in doing so, may add to or subtract from the damage award. In cases in which the verdict is not over-turned on appeal, awards are often adjusted, occasionally upward but more often downward (Shanley & Peterson, 1987).

AMBIGUITY OF JURY INSTRUCTIONS ON DAMAGE AWARDS

We alluded earlier to concerns about the vagueness of the instructions regarding damages provided by the judge to the jury at the conclusion of the trial, just prior to the jury's deliberations. Jury instructions are crucial to the assessment of damages, yet there is a significant consensus that these directives are neither precise enough nor clear enough to be of real assis-tance to jurors (e.g., Greene & Bornstein, 2000). Is that so?

Consider this example of a typical instruction on assessing compen-satory damages in a personal injury case:

If you find in favor of the plaintiff, you shall award as actual damages, insofar as they have been proved by a preponderance of the evidence and insofar as they were caused by the defendant's negligence, an amount which will reasonably compensate the plaintiff for his injuries, if any. In determining such damages, you shall consider the following:

1. Any noneconomic losses or injuries incurred to the present time, or which will probably be incurred in the future, including: pain and suffering; inconvenience; emotional stress; impairment of the quality of life; and
2. Any economic losses incurred to the present time, or which will probably be incurred in the future, including: loss of earnings or impairment of earning capacity; reasonable and necessary medical, hospital and other expenses. (*Colorado Jury Instructions 3d: Civil*, 1989, p. 31)

This instruction informs jurors about the components of economic damages (including past and future economic losses and past and future noneconomic losses) but does not provide definitions of various terms (e.g., pain and suffering, emotional stress) or information on how to consider and weigh these components or translate them into an aggregate award. Although jurors will probably be instructed to discount the assessed damages to present value, they will not be given explicit guidance on how to do this. Neither will they be told how to evaluate any conflicting expert testimony related to damages. Thus, judicial instructions on compensatory damages are relatively vague and ambiguous.

Instructions on punitive damages are even less clear. Courts usually admonish jurors simply to assess punitive damages sufficient to punish and deter and, in so doing, to consider the character of the defendant's conduct and the defendant's wealth. Some courts supplement these instructions with criteria used by appellate courts in a posttrial review of awards. These considerations may include the requirement that the award bear some reasonable relationship to compensatory damages, that it not bankrupt the defendant, and that the jury not be motivated by passion or prejudice. Here is a typical instruction on punitive damages:

If you find in favor of the plaintiff and award her actual damages, then you shall consider whether exemplary (or punitive) damages should be assessed against the defendant. If you find beyond a reasonable doubt[12] that the injury complained of was attended by circumstances of willful and wanton conduct, then in addition to actual damages, you may also assess a reasonable sum as exemplary damages. Exemplary damages, if assessed, are to be assessed as punishment for the defendant, and as an example to others. (*Colorado Jury Instructions 3d: Civil*, 1989, p. 14)

---

[12]The standard for proving punitive damages is lower in other jurisdictions (e.g., by a preponderance of the evidence or by clear and convincing evidence).

Even the U.S. Supreme Court has expressed concerns about the effectiveness of instructions on punitive damages. Suggesting that arbitrariness, caprice, passion, bias, and even malice can replace reasoned judgment and law as the basis for jury decision making about punitive awards, Justice Sandra Day O'Connor noted that juries receive only "vague and amorphous guidance" about punitive damages (*TXO Production Corp. v. Alliance Resources Corp.*, 1993, p. 474). Justice William Brennan voiced a similar concern:

> Without statutory (or at least common-law) standards for a determination of how large an award of punitive damages is appropriate in a given case, juries are left largely to themselves in making this important and potentially devastating decision.... The typical instructions given to jurors, advising them to consider the character and wealth of the defendant and the nature of the defendant's conduct, provide guidance that is scarcely better than no guidance at all. (*Browning–Ferris Industries, Inc. v. Kelco Disposal, Inc.*, 1989, p. 281)

Commentators have noted other problems with instructions related to punitive damages. Some have suggested that juries frequently misunderstand their instructions in complicated cases (where claims for punitive damages are most likely to arise) and experience such confusion that they neglect their instructions altogether and attempt to reach a verdict on the basis of their common sense ("The civil jury," 1997). Others believe that because a typical punitive damages case involves a series of complicated issues, even juries that apparently understand the full legal intent of their instructions may still go astray because they do not correctly assess the social costs and benefits of the defendant's conduct. Melsheimer and Stodghill (1994) reasoned that by providing juries with broad discretion and little guidance, the common law allows jurors' biases and judgmental deficiencies to operate in an unrestrained manner.

The problem may not reside solely with the jury instructions themselves, of course (Greene & Bornstein, 2000). Instructions about damages are notoriously vague because the law of damages is notoriously, and purposefully, vague. In most jurisdictions, standards for defining when a certain kind of damage award (e.g., for pain and suffering, loss of consortium, or punitive damages) is appropriate have not been articulated, in part because it is difficult to identify the particular circumstances in which these damages may be relevant. As a consequence, this vagueness may be an inherent (and, in fact, necessary) aspect of standards for determining damage awards. Unfortunately, jurors often want more direction.

There are, of course, advantages that inhere in vague standards. Such ambiguity allows the trier of fact to apply the doctrine flexibly and, theoretically, to achieve justice based on the individualized facts of a particular case. On the other hand, imprecise standards may allow jurors to subvert justice by relying on their biases, prejudices, and whims. Furthermore, vague direction may legitimize fused decision making by allowing discussions of liability to merge with damage award determinations (Bornstein, 1998). In other words, jurors, lacking clear guidance on what evidence they can legitimately use to assess damages, may factor into their calculation of damages elements of the evidence on liability (Greene, Johns, & Smith, 2001). We return to some of these themes later in this book. For now, it suffices to say that along with the benefits that issue from indefinite standards come difficulties for jurors in placing monetary values on losses that are often intangible and difficult to assess.

Some critics have alluded to an even more fundamental problem than the lack of clarity in jury instructions. These writers suggest that to focus attention on the vagueness of the instructions is to miss an important point: that people have difficulty mapping normative judgments, including those of outrage and punishment, onto an unbounded dollar scale (Kahneman, Schkade, & Sunstein, 1998; Sunstein et al., 1998). According to this team of researchers, people of diverse backgrounds show substantial agreement in judgments of the outrageousness of a defendant's actions and about the appropriate punishment. The same people falter, though, when they are required to map these judgments onto dollar amounts. An implication of this thinking is that punitive damage awards should be reformed so that juries are charged with the tasks that they can perform well (such as judging behavior and suggesting appropriate levels of punishment) and relieved of the tasks on which they perform poorly (such as making decisions about dollar amounts). We revisit these ideas in chapter 9.

THE POPULAR VIEW OF DAMAGE AWARDS

As Valerie Hans (2000) correctly noted, little of the debate about jurors' abilities to assess damages has been informed by careful study and analysis. Rather, flashy anecdotes about whining and undeserving plaintiffs, who seem eager to sue anyone with (or without) a heartbeat, including God[13] and themselves,[14] have prevailed. Rather than recite more horror

---

[13] According to the American Tort Reform Association, a Pennsylvania man sued God for taking "no corrective action" when the USX Corporation fired him after 30 years of employment. The man apparently also demanded that God compensate him by returning his youth and granting him guitar-playing skills. The American Tort Reform Association (ATRA) did acknowledge that a federal judge rejected the lawsuit (see ATRA, 2000).

[14] The group Citizens Against Lawsuit Abuse (CALA) tells of an inmate who filed a $5 million lawsuit against himself, claiming that he violated his own civil rights by getting arrested. He then asked the state to pay because he had no income in jail. Apparently unimpressed by the inmate's ingenuity, a judge dismissed the lawsuit as frivolous (CALA, n.d.). Admittedly, neither of these two aforementioned cases relates to juries' decision making as neither case resulted in a trial.

stories, we instead borrow the words of *Detroit News* columnist Jon Pepper, who was able to skewer several jury decisions in one fell swoop:

> It could have been worse for General Motors Corp. The company got nicked for $150 million by an Alabama jury for producing an allegedly defective door latch on a 1987 Chevrolet S-10 Blazer. That supposedly led to the paralysis of a man named Alex Hardy.
>
> But suppose Hardy's Blazer had a bad paint job, too. According to another Alabama jury, a crummy finish is worth at least $4 million. That's how much it awarded Dr. Ira Gore when his BMW was delivered with an inferior paint job. It cost the good doctor $600 to get his problem glossed over, but Alabamans figured $4 million would teach BMW a lesson.
>
> Or suppose GM promised Hardy, who is black, a car dealership. That might have cost the company anywhere from $7 million to $23 million. That's the going rate for the failure of a minority dealership, according to the *American Spectator* magazine. One Alabama jury, for instance, ordered Ford Motor Co. to give $6 million in punishment, $1 million in economic losses and $700,000 in "mental anguish" for failing to tell a minority dealer "that he was more likely to fail than the 'average' Ford dealer," the magazine reported. . . . [A]nother jury ordered beleaguered GM to pay $23 million to another dealer for similar reasons.
>
> And what if Hardy cut his hand because of GM's alleged carelessness? The carmaker might be out another $23 million or so. A butcher in Mobile County was awarded that much when he caught a wicked slice from an allegedly defective saw.
>
> Had Hardy's Blazer contained a used battery, Fort Knox might not have enough gold. An Alabama battery distributor caught selling previously owned goods was ordered to pay $86,000 in compensatory damages and $10 million in punishment to an aggrieved consumer. That jury apparently had kicked around awards from $100,000 and $8.5 million before deciding on $10 million. "Quite honestly," a juror said later, "I think it had to do with sounding like a round figure," the *Legal Times* reported.
>
> Apparently, the jury settled on "million" because it couldn't spell "kajillion" or "gazillion," which is what GM might have paid if it had financed Hardy's vehicle and overcharged him by mistake. *American Spectator* reports that Mercury Finance Co. of Northbrook, Ill., overcharged an Alabama resident $1,000 on a loan. The jury awarded punitive damages of $50 million, which makes perfect sense. After all, that's a nice round figure. (Pepper, 1996)

Obviously, recitations such as this nourish the public's appetite for litigation horror stories. Notice, though, that this portrayal, like most, is heavy on attention-grabbing news about big monetary awards and has nothing to say about the tedious details of the lawsuits themselves or about the ultimate awards (after reductions and renegotiations). Also missing is any context, including some discussion of the nature of the evidence, that would help one understand the appropriateness (or lack thereof) of these awards. As stated in Pepper's (1996) article, readers have no way of knowing whether, in fact, the evidence supported any of these verdicts or whether the verdicts were later reduced or set aside by a judge.

The media feature descriptions of high-profile cases and big jury awards because people want to know about them. Just as stories about airplane crashes outrank reports of death by diabetes or heart disease in terms of newsworthiness and interest, jury trials outrank settlements, large awards outrank more modest figures, and accidents involving "malfunctioning professionals or products" outrank run-of-the-mill fender benders. However, these stories distort people's perceptions of the civil justice system (Bailis & MacCoun, 1996). So although much of the empirical evidence suggests (a) that jury awards are closely tied to the severity of the injuries and type of case, (b) that these awards not infrequently fall far short of the economic losses sustained, and (c) that jurors' decisions about damages are usually quite rational, this is not what one learns from the media.

Some members of the business community are only too happy to portray jurors as enigmatic and illogical, of course. According to Stephen Daniels and Joanne Martin (1997), the description of disarray in the civil justice system persists despite its lack of empirical verification because it serves a useful political purpose. The image persists because it allows various interest groups to get a place on the policy agenda for their preferred version of reform. According to Daniels and Martin, industry leaders have been more successful in gaining policy changes by appealing directly to the emotions of consumers and voters than by relying on reason and data.

Flashy anecdotes and political rhetoric aside, however, we now take a more detailed look at what some legal commentators, including law professors and judges, have said about the abilities of jurors to determine damage awards fairly and impartially. In the next chapter—and indeed, throughout this book—we return to these themes as we present a picture of what jury awards really look like and how jurors really make these decisions.

CONCERNS AND CRITIQUES ABOUT JURY DAMAGE AWARDS

The critics are vocal on three points: First, that jury damage awards, especially for noneconomic and punitive damages, are too large, highly variable, and unpredictable; second, that jurors fail to consider the social and economic consequences of their awards; and third, that jurors are biased against wealthy defendants and in favor of relatively poorer plaintiffs. We focus only on the criticisms at this point and later provide some data to address these concerns and to offer another perspective on the role of the civil jury in determining damages.

Damage Awards Are Too Large, Highly Variable, and Unpredictable

It is not hard to find examples of enormously large jury-determined damage awards. The mother of all damage awards, at least at the present time, came from a class-action lawsuit against the tobacco industry in which a jury awarded a whopping $144.8 billion in punitive damages to some 500,000 Floridians who were made sick by smoking cigarettes. Observed Judge Robert Kaye shortly after he read the verdict on July 14, 2000, "That's a lot of zeroes" (Bragg, 2000).

However, examples of less extreme (yet still very large) awards abound as well, and some studies point to a recent increase in the size of jury awards. For example, according to LRP Publications, a group that tracks the results of cases in several states each year,[15] jury awards in cases involving defective products have risen sharply in many industries, from cars and tools to appliances and toys (Winter, 2001). According to these data, the median award in 2,751 products liability cases more than tripled between 1993 and 1999. To what extent this trend is characteristic of other awards decided by juries is a point to which we will return.

In terms of variability, damage awards have sometimes been likened to a lottery: "Damage verdicts are damaging when they are as random as lottery numbers. That quality, more than any other, brings the system into disrepute" (Satter, 1990, p. 135). The focus here is primarily on awards for noneconomic and punitive damages, because they both seem so subjective. In fact, although the magnitude of awards correlates positively with the severity of the injuries (termed *vertical equity* by Michael Saks and his colleagues), within categories of severity there is still significant variance in awards (so-called *horizontal inequity*; Saks, Hollinger, Wissler, Evans, & Hart, 1997). *Horizontal inequity* means that plaintiffs whose injuries appear to be of roughly equal severity and who sustained them in a similar manner may walk away from a jury trial with vastly different sums of money. Large-scale studies of awards in cases involving products liability (Viscusi, 1988), medical malpractice (Sloan & Hsieh, 1990), and tort cases in general (Bovbjerg, Sloan, & Blumstein, 1989) have documented this variability. It goes without saying that the system is unfair if similarly situated people— plaintiffs and defendants alike—are not treated similarly. As we show, though, the analogy between damage awards and lotteries is inaccurate.

According to Cass Sunstein and his colleagues, the most troubling aspect of this problem is the unpredictability of punitive damage awards (Sunstein et al., 1998). The potential for unpredictability in punitive dam-

---

[15]We describe concerns related to verdict tracking and reporting services in chapter 2.

age awards leads us to the second main critique about juries and damages, namely, that jurors fail to consider the broader societal consequences of their verdicts, especially in the realm of punitive damages.

Jurors Fail to Consider the Social and Economic Consequences of Their Awards

Here is the argument: If awards are unpredictable, some too low and others too high, then corporate resources are wasted on calculating the expected value of various risks. So, for example, the risk of an extremely large punitive damage award is likely to produce excessive caution in risk-averse companies and may cause them to forego marketing a product that has obvious health and safety benefits for many people.

Consider the case of the popular antinausea drug Bendectin, prescribed for pregnant women to counteract morning sickness. A set of animal studies initially appeared to implicate Bendectin as a cause of birth defects, leading to a massive number of lawsuits against the manufacturer, and even though the weight of scientific studies concluded that there was no causal link between Bendectin use and birth defects, still juries tended to hold the manufacturer, Merrell Dow Pharmaceuticals, responsible (Sanders, 1998). The company eventually removed the drug from the market, apparently concerned that it would otherwise be left in an overly vulnerable position.

In general, corporate leaders complain that the inability to anticipate how much they might have to pay for causing injury makes it exceedingly difficult to know whether they can afford to market a new product (MacCrimmon & Wehrung, 1986). For similar reasons, insurers contend that if they cannot calculate their potential risks with any degree of certainty, then they must charge more or offer less coverage.

Jurors Are Biased Against Wealthy Defendants and Tend to Favor Poor Plaintiffs

Yet another common criticism of the civil jury in the realm of damages is that jurors award more when they perceive that the defendant can afford more and that they empathize with individual plaintiffs as opposed to corporate defendants. The argument is that jurors take from the deep pockets of wealthy defendants and use the money to compensate undeserving plaintiffs. Peter Huber (1988) claimed that juries in civil damages cases are committed to running a generous sort of charity—a portrayal that Hans (2000) likened to the story of Robin Hood, as jurors apparently redistribute money from wealthy anonymous defendants to poor and injured identifiable plaintiffs.

So what do the data really say about the deep pockets of wealthy defendants, the size and variability of damage awards, and corporations' concerns about their inability to forecast risk and their hesitation to market potentially useful products for fear of exposure to monumental damage awards? In chapter 2 we provide a conceptual framework to organize our thoughts about these issues and some preliminary data to address these questions. We return to these themes at various points throughout the book.

A WORD ABOUT METHODOLOGY

Most of the studies on which we rely throughout the book involve experimental methodology (usually jury simulations) as opposed to analyses of verdicts compiled by jury verdict reporters (although we do describe some of the latter in chapter 2). As such, they eliminate the problem of confounds and the difficulty of interpreting differences in behavior. For example, studies that attempt to make comparisons of the verdicts in actual cases and ascribe any disparities to differences in the ways that juries treat plaintiffs (or defendants) are plagued by confounds (Vidmar, 1994b). The cases differ on multiple dimensions (e.g., skill and experience of the attorneys, testimony of lay and expert witnesses, evidence that is admitted, idiosyncrasies of the judge, and demonstrable economic losses). As Vidmar (1994b) noted,

> Any of these dimensions, singly or in combination, may be the plausible cause of the observed differences in verdicts. Rather than jury biases, the verdict differences may result from the fact that the juries are hearing very different evidence or responding to different substantive law. We are comparing apples and oranges. (p. 605)

Jury simulation studies, although they have their own inadequacies, as we note in the next paragraph, nonetheless provide a way to understand the effects of various independent variables (e.g., the plaintiff's gender) on jury damage awards without concerns about confounding variables.

It has long been acknowledged, however, that simulation studies of the impact of isolated features of a trial (e.g., the defendant's attractiveness) may highlight those extralegal factors as salient features of the trial and may present them in a manner that underlines their importance and encourages their uncritical reception (Diamond, 1997). Their prominence may suggest that they should be taken into account (Wasserman & Robinson, 1980). According to a meta-analysis of 78 criminal jury simulation studies (Linz & Penrod, 1982), the effects of extralegal factors are apparently diminished in studies that use more realistic case materials or that encourage more active role involvement among mock jurors. More recent research by Geoffrey Kramer and Norbert Kerr (1989) and by Brian H.

Bornstein (1999) suggests, however, that these variables may exert similar effects in simplified jury simulations and in more realistic settings. Also, although extra-evidentiary issues may matter to individual jurors, the process of jury deliberation has long been suspected to reduce or even eradicate their effects (Izzett & Leginski, 1974). Finally, a study that used data from courtroom observations and posttrial interviews with jurors who served in 38 sexual assault trials found that jurors' extralegal attitudes toward crime and their sentiments toward victims and defendants influenced their verdicts only in cases where the prosecution's evidence was weak (Reskin & Visher, 1986). So the real significance of these legally irrelevant considerations is a question of some debate.

PLAN OF THE BOOK

This book is divided into three parts. Prior to the three parts, however, we aim to set the scene by broadly detailing the issues that confront jurors in damages trials and providing some data on how well jurors do their jobs in this chapter and the next. In particular, in chapter 2 we present a theoretical model of decision making that allows us to assess what jurors actually do, the extent to which they do what the law expects them to do, and whether they can be aided to make decisions that are more in line with those expectations.

The heart of the book is presented in the following three parts, as we describe the scholarly work on jury decision making regarding damages. Here, we move beyond the "what" of jury damage awards (what juries award to whom and from whom) and delve into the "how" and "why." In Part I we focus on how the identity of the players, including the plaintiff (chapter 3) and the defendant (chapter 4), and attributes of the jurors themselves (chapter 5) can influence damage award decisions. In Part II we examine how the evidence that comes out at trial, including evidence regarding injury severity (chapter 6) and the litigants' conduct (chapter 7), affects jurors' judgments on damages. Finally, in Part III we describe the decision-making strategies that jurors use to make sense of this evidence (chapter 8). We then cast our gaze into the future and describe the likely effects of various reforms of the jury system that are being implemented now and that will continue to be explored in order to assist jurors in performing this complicated task (chapter 9). In the concluding chapter (chapter 10), we return to some of the themes that we set out in this chapter.

2

CHARACTERIZING JURY DAMAGE AWARDS

How much do jurors typically award in compensatory damages? In punitive damages? Do their awards vary by the type of case? Do they conform to the evidence, or are they far out of line? Are they highly variable and growing in size? In this chapter we provide a picture of what jury damage awards generally look like in terms of their size and frequency. We also ask whether they conform to legally derived expectations of damage awards and ponder what can be done to bring them in line with those legal dictates.

To provide a theoretical framework within which we can address these issues, we borrow some ideas from David Bell, Howard Raiffa, and Amos Tversky who, in an important treatise on decision making (D. E. Bell, Raiffa, & Tversky, 1988), articulated a three-part model to analyze human judgment and decision making. Elements of their model, aimed at conceptualizing choices that involve uncertainty, are useful for our purposes, because decisions regarding damages are based on uncertain or probabilistic information.

According to these theorists, decisions can be examined from three points of view: (a) descriptive (asking how decisions *are* made), (b) normative (asking how decisions *ought to be* made), and (c) prescriptive (asking how better decisions *might* be made). We briefly detail these different perspectives here and then rely on them to organize much of what we have to say about characterizing damage awards in the remainder of this chapter.

A *descriptive analysis* of decision making purports to describe behavior. It seeks to explain the ways that people actually make decisions, including how they perceive uncertainties, accumulate evidence, talk about their perceptions and choices, resolve internal conflicts, decompose complex problems into separate components, and then reintegrate these separate parts. It includes concerns related to individual biases and predilections, differences in thought patterns among people of different backgrounds, and the influence of various social factors on decision making. This perspective is highly empirical. For our purposes, it is informed by a data-based analysis of damage award decisions (as opposed to, say, a moral or ethical perspective, which is relevant to the normative approach). Also, because much of the psychological literature on damage awards has been concerned with how and why people think about damages and decide as they do, this perspective is the one on which we rely most heavily. However, there are other ways to think about these decisions, too.

The *normative approach* is somewhat harder to characterize. It focuses on how things ought to be. For our purposes, it anchors decisions about damages in a broader view of justice and the objectives of the civil justice system. This perspective actually has several facets and includes notions of how idealized, rational people should think and act. Gone are concerns about actual behavior, including cognitive abilities and disabilities, limited attention span, conflicting values, and postdecisional regrets and reconsiderations. In their place is an emphasis on coherence and rationality in decision making.

The vast legal literature on damage awards, particularly in the realm of punitive damages, tends to take a normative perspective. It focuses on the ethical and social functions of damage awards and the legal criteria for granting them. Legal treatments of punitive damages, for example, emphasize notions of retribution and economic efficiency rather than how these decisions actually get made.

An important question with which we attempt to grapple throughout this book is the extent to which people act in a way that the law believes is proper in assessing damages. To what extent do jurors' decisions conform to legally defined norms? How close (or far) is the description of actual decision making from the normatively prescribed model? Answers to these questions may be especially elusive because there are no universally agreed-on definitions, in the law or elsewhere, about what constitutes appropriate decision making.

The *prescriptive viewpoint* asks how real people (as opposed to the idealized, perfectly rational sort) can be helped to make better decisions. This perspective focuses on ways to overcome the inherent limitations of decision makers to improve their judgments and make their decisions more normatively correct. In essence, it strives to bring the descriptive (what is) in line with the normative (what ought to be).

For our purposes, increasing jurors' chances of making a normatively appropriate decision may involve changing their task. So, for example, some commentators and legislators would place precise dollar limits on how much money a jury can give for pain and suffering so that the resulting award bears some reasonable relationship to the extent of the harm incurred and fulfills the socially agreed on role of noneconomic damages. (This example suggests that norms are derived not only from legal dictates but also from widely shared social concerns, an idea to which we return later in this chapter.) A different prescriptive approach may involve the more radical solution of handling damages cases administratively, much like workers' compensation cases are now dealt with—that is, by assigning monetary values for injuries based on preset formulae. However, as Stephen Adler (1994) correctly noted, both of these approaches are long on promoting predictability and consistency in jurors' judgments and short on preserving the jury's role as an independent arbiter of the facts and law. Wrote Adler (1994), "They reflect the dispiriting trend toward making jurors less harmful by limiting their power to go wrong rather than making them more useful and effective by giving them the tools to do right" (p. 174).

Like Adler, we prefer a different prescriptive direction, namely, helping jurors make better decisions by providing them with more education, simplified decisions, and clearer instructions about how to do their jobs. Specific examples include pretrial instruction, minisummations during the course of trial, clearer instructions at the conclusion of trial, and permitting the jurors to ask questions and discuss the case as it is progressing.

What makes this situation fairly complicated is that jurors obviously come to the courthouse outfitted with differing cognitive capabilities, needs, and emotional makeups, so that there will be no one-size-fits-all prescription for better decision making. Decisional aids, conceptual assistance, and restructuring of the evidence may be useful for one person but not for another. We touch on various attempts to reform the jury's task to bring it closer to rationality later in this chapter and focus extensively on these ideas in chapter 9.

JURIES AND DAMAGE AWARDS: A DESCRIPTIVE ANALYSIS

A descriptive analysis is data driven. Just as the name implies, it describes the decisions that people make (the "what") and the ways in which they do so (the "how"). In this chapter we focus on the *products* or *outputs* of those decisions (the "what"), namely, in what kinds of cases jurors award damages and in what amounts. However, our intent here is neither to offer a complete picture nor to linger, as the focus of this book is really on the processes of decision making (the "how")—describing, from a psychological perspective, how the decisions get made. Indeed, we use this orientation in the remaining chapters of the book.

Still, it is useful to know in what situations jurors are typically asked to award damages, how often they do so, and in what amounts. In part, this coverage will help us address claims that over the past 25 years juries have become more favorably disposed toward plaintiffs and now routinely give awards that are much larger than they were in the past (Danzon, 1990; Huber, 1988; Priest, 1987).

We first ask: What do these cases and resulting awards look like? An important caveat is that we cannot answer this question with absolute authority. Because there is no national reporting system for civil jury verdicts or damage awards, and because reports of awards tend not to be representative of the universe of jury awards, the precise numbers are, at this point, unknown and probably unknowable. Still, it is useful to infer trends and patterns from the information that is available.

The Look of Compensatory Damage Awards

The data that we rely on here come primarily from four relatively recent large-scale studies of compensatory damage awards across a broad spectrum of cases. Ostrom, Rottman, and Hanson (1992) examined all tort cases[1] that reached a bench or jury trial verdict during a 3-month period in 1989 in 27 general jurisdiction trial courts (n = 762 cases). (We focus exclusively on 353 cases that were decided by juries.) Moller (1996) used the RAND Corporation Institute for Civil Justice database to track trends in jury verdicts from 1985 to 1989 and from 1990 to 1994 in 15 state courts of general jurisdiction scattered across California, Illinois, New York, Texas, Washington, and Missouri. Finally, the Bureau of Justice Statistics (DeFrances & Litras, 1999; Litras et al., 2000) conducted a study of more than 15,000 tort, contract, and real property cases decided by trials in the 75 most populous counties in the United States in 1996. About 70% of these trials (n = 10,616) were decided by juries.

On the basis of these studies we know, for example, that 98% of all civil cases are tried in state court and that in most states the civil jury is essentially a tort institution. Of the more than 10,000 state court jury trials examined by DeFrances and Litras (1999), 83% were tort actions, 16% were contract cases, and less than 1% were real property disputes. Even in federal courts, tort cases predominate, although a variety of nontort civil

---

[1]In tort cases, plaintiffs claim injury, loss, or damage as a result of the negligent or intentional actions of the defendant. These cases represent a large proportion of all civil trials decided by juries.

matters—including civil rights, antitrust, and contracts—are increasingly likely to be heard by federal juries.

When one looks only at the state tort cases, further images develop. Automobile personal injury and property liability matters dominate. (In property or premises liability cases, the plaintiff alleges harm as a result of the defendant's failure adequately to maintain property, e.g., by not cleaning up spills on the floor of a grocery store.) Medical malpractice, products liability, and toxic substance disputes each constitute a small fraction of cases tried before juries, despite their prominence in the media. The balance of cases involves contract issues such as fraud, employment discrimination, and landlord–tenant disputes. A large majority of plaintiffs (94% in DeFrances & Litras's [1999] study) are individuals, and slightly fewer than half of defendants are businesses (DeFrances & Litras, 1999). Jury trials that involve corporate plaintiffs are infrequent.

What about verdicts? How often do plaintiffs win? One interesting note to preface this discussion is that trial rates—as measured by the number of verdicts per capita—are generally flat or decreasing (Moller, 1996), suggesting either that filing rates are stable or decreasing or that litigants are more likely to settle than they had been in the past.

Plaintiffs win about half the time (i.e., 49% according to DeFrances & Litras [1999], and 56% according to Ostrom et al. [1992]) although, in tort cases at least, success rates vary by the type of case. Plaintiffs are most successful in automobile personal injury and fraud cases, winning approximately two thirds of the time (Ostrom et al., 1992). Plaintiff win rates are considerably lower in products liability cases (approximately 44%) and medical malpractice cases (approximately 33%; Moller, 1996). Litigant status also seems to matter. In cases pitting individuals against each other, plaintiffs succeed approximately 60% of the time. The rate is approximately the same when an individual sues an insurance company. Plaintiffs are significantly less likely to prevail in cases against the government, winning only 40% of the time (Ostrom et al., 1992).

Finally, we examine the size of jury damage awards. How much do winning litigants get? In this section we answer that question in terms of compensatory awards. In the next section we describe punitive awards.

Concerns about the size of damage awards are at the very core of current controversies surrounding the civil justice system. As we noted, critics of civil juries cite large, high-profile awards as proof that the system is out of control and that reforms are necessary to rein in wildly extravagant jurors. In fact, discerning the truth about the size of damage awards is a complicated undertaking. As Vidmar (1994b, 1995) noted, part of the problem is that the data relied on by some authors to document "spiraling jury verdicts" (Weiler, 1991, p. 48) come from jury verdict reports that may not be representative of the universe of damage awards.

For example, one reporting service, Jury Verdict Research, apparently relies on court clerks, newspaper clipping services, local verdict reporting services, and attorneys who report on verdicts from their trials to provide data about the size and scope of damage awards. Obvious concerns about unrepresentative data arise. However, even if the verdict data were more representative, they would still be representative of only a small, atypical subset of self-selected cases. As Vidmar (1994b) correctly noted, the verdict reports contain no information about how or why a particular case was selected for trial or about how or why a jury decided on the damage award it assessed. Thus, using data derived from jury reporters to argue that awards are excessive and that variability in comparable cases is attributable to jury bias and caprice misses the mark. According to Vidmar,

> These other sources of variance are not documented in the verdict statistics. . . . The apples and oranges problem does not allow us to conclude that juries are free from bias or caprice, but it also does not allow us to conclude the contrary. (1994b, p. 608)

Even when one relies on studies that use more representative samples (e.g., those we have cited in this section), the truth of the matter is not so clear. However, culling from various reports of various aspects of this topic, we are certain of the following conclusion: Although the size of the average award appears to have increased in the past 25 years, it is also true that the distribution of damage awards is dramatically skewed, with a very large number of small awards and a very small number of large awards.

To explain these facts fully, we must take a slight detour into the territory of statistical measurement. There are multiple ways to measure things, and how one measures damage awards, in particular, dramatically affects what one learns about damage awards. Many laypeople are familiar with the notion of averages: An average, or mean, is computed simply by summing the individual pieces (for our purposes, individual awards) and then dividing by the number of items that were summed. If one uses this method to describe the central tendency of a group of damage awards, then awards at the very high end, especially those that are extremely large, will have a disproportionate impact on the resulting average. (The same thing would happen if a kindergarten class computed its average height, and then added Michael Jordan to the mix.)

So it is not surprising that average compensatory awards have risen sharply since the 1980s. Nearly all of the growth in the average is undoubtedly due to a whopping increase in the size of the very largest awards. According to Galanter (1990), a few very large awards account for most of the money awarded by juries.

A better way to gauge the size of damage awards, we argue, is to examine the median, or the point in a distribution of awards that falls in the middle: Half of the awards are for amounts less than the median, and half are for amounts greater than the median. Using this measurement technique reduces the impact of extreme items on the resulting answer.

If one examines median compensatory awards, one finds that they are relatively modest in size. The median awards calculated in the three studies described earlier in this chapter were in the range of $25,000 (Ostrom et al., 1992) to $35,000 (DeFrances & Litras, 1999) and varied by type of tort. Juries in medical malpractice and products liability cases gave, on average, higher awards than did juries in automobile torts or other personal injury cases.[2] In fact, the median award in automobile tort cases was only $19,000 (Ostrom et al., 1992). In DeFrances and Litras's (1999) analysis of some 5,000 cases won by plaintiffs and decided by juries, only 19% of damage awards exceeded $250,000, and a mere 7% topped $1 million.

The picture that emerges from this condensed survey is of juries that are anything but extravagant or unpredictable. Their awards are generally modest, stable, and predictable. Indeed, using just a small number of predictor variables, several studies have been able to account for half or more of the variation in awards in sampled cases (Baldus, MacQueen, & Woodworth, 1995; Peterson, 1984; Sloan & Hsieh, 1990). This means that by knowing something about the evidence with which jurors were confronted, one can make fairly good guesses about the largest of the awards. In particular, as we note in chapter 6, evidence about the severity of plaintiffs' injuries and the extent of their losses is especially useful, because more severe injuries generally result in higher awards. Contrast this picture of moderation and predictability, then, with the media's attention to rare, but exceedingly large damage awards that we described in chapter 1. It is clear that the media have distorted the public's sense of what is common.

Before we pass over that point completely, though, we pause to consider the relatively rare but very large awards that do occur in some cases and that tend to run up the average. Saks (1992) asked a provocative question in a slightly different context, but we borrow its essence for the present purposes. If there has been a large increase in the size of the average damage award, then the proper inquiry is not "Was there an increase?" but rather "Was there an *unjustified* increase?" Saks (1992) suggested a number of reasons that an increase in the size of damage awards might be completely justified. These include (a) changes in the substantive law of torts that increase the number of actionable injuries and that allow plaintiffs' lawyers to be more selective about the cases they bring to trial; (b) changes in the cases themselves to reflect more serious injuries, more expensive medical costs, or the fact that medical treatment is now more effective, allowing people to survive accidents that earlier would have killed them; (c) a growing tendency to settle smaller, less serious cases; or (d) a practice

---

[2]Recall, though, that plaintiffs are less likely to win in medical malpractice and products liability cases than they are in automobile and other personal injury cases.

effect whereby plaintiffs' lawyers are getting better at proving the damages portion of their cases by involving better experts or selecting more financially sophisticated jurors. As Saks (1992) pointed out, no one knows whether these hypotheses are supported by the evidence. They all imply, though, that juries are being asked to consider more serious matters than they had in the past and that increases in award size can arise from various social, economic, or technological developments that have occurred outside of the legal system.

The Look of Punitive Damage Awards

Just as we can describe some patterns related to compensatory awards, so too can we describe trends in punitive awards. In chapter 1 we articulated a variety of criticisms that have been directed at the concept of punitive damages in general and at jurors' abilities to assess punitive damages in particular. It is fortunate that data now exist that allow us to address many of these criticisms.

We rely on the findings from several empirical studies to provide factual grounding. In particular, we use findings from the U.S. General Accounting Office (1989) report on verdicts in products liability cases between 1982 and 1985, Rustad and Koenig's (1995) study of punitive damage awards in medical malpractice cases from 1963 to 1993, the RAND Institute for Civil Justice study of trends in civil verdicts since 1985 (Moller, 1996), and a Cornell University survey of 1992 verdicts collected by the National Center for State Courts (Eisenberg, Goerdt, Ostrom, Rottman, & Wells, 1997). We also use some of the studies described in The Look of Compensatory Damage Awards section.[3] Although the studies used data from different case types, jurisdictions, and time periods, their findings tend to converge on the following generality about the awarding of punitive damages: These awards are neither routine nor mind-boggling in size.

The first thing to note about punitive damage awards is that, contrary to popular belief, they are quite rare. According to a Bureau of Justice Statistics study of civil trials in large counties, punitive damages were awarded in only approximately 4% of jury trials in which the plaintiff won on liability (DeFrances & Litras, 1999). The second fact is that these awards are generally small. According to DeFrances and Litras (1999), half of the punitive damage awards in their study were for $50,000 or less, and punitive damages accounted for only about 21% of all money awarded to the plaintiffs. According to Ostrom et al. (1992), nearly half of the punitive damage awards were for less than the compensatory damages, and the other half were for approximately the same amount. Very rarely were they larger than the compensatory award.

---

[3]Our thinking on this topic was aided by the excellent review of studies of punitive damages provided by Michael Rustad (1998).

Critics claim that the determination of punitive damages is essentially random and that these awards bear no reasonable relationship to the severity of harm. Regarding that question, data tend to show a high correlation between the size of the punitive award and the compensatory award ($r = .71$ in the U.S. General Accounting Office [1989] study) that, in turn, correlates with the severity of injury to the plaintiff (U.S. General Accounting Office, 1989). Combining data from several studies, Theodore Eisenberg et al. (1997) concluded that "far from being randomly related, the punitive damages awards increase monotonically with compensatory damages. . . . The hypothesis that punitive damage awards are randomly plucked out of the air, and bear no relation to compensatory damages, can be firmly rejected" (p. 639).

We can dismiss the concerns of some critics, then, that punitive damages are awarded with regularity and provide a windfall recovery for plaintiffs (see, e.g., Schwartz, Behrens, & Mastrosimone, 1999). We also must acknowledge, though, that the largest punitive damage awards are indeed very large and, according to Moller (1996), increasing. In fact, these large punitive damage awards represent up to half of the total damages awarded in some jurisdictions examined by the RAND Institute for Civil Justice. So the picture that begins to emerge from these data mirrors the snapshot of compensatory awards: Most punitive damage awards are small, but a few punitive damage awards are very large.

Punitive damages are more likely to be awarded in some kinds of cases than in others. In particular, cases that involve financial injuries are more likely to receive punitive damages than are cases that entail personal injuries (Moller, Pace, & Carroll, 1999). The former typically involve fraudulent or contractual misconduct or intentional wrongdoing. Plaintiffs in cases with more familiar causes of action, such as products liability, medical malpractice, and automobile personal injury, are unlikely to receive punitive damages.

We also must acknowledge that punitive damages in business litigation have apparently grown in both number and size in the past 25 years, as these damages are increasingly awarded for the financial harm caused by opportunistic business practices (Rustad, 1998). Thus, the target of a punitive damage award is likely to be a business or corporation that has: (a) engaged in deceptive, unscrupulous, or opportunistic conduct in contractual arrangements or (b) engaged in or condoned wrongful termination or sexual harassment with blatant disregard for others' well-being.

In most states, the financial circumstances of the defendant can be factored into the calculation of punitive damages. This fact is of special concern to proponents of tort reform who, according to Rustad (1998), want everyone, whether a drunk driver or a Fortune 500 company, to be treated equally. We discuss various reform proposals that effectively remove wealth from the punitive damages equation—including limiting punitive damages to a fixed dollar amount or to a multiple of the compensatory award—in chapter 9. For now, though, we assess the concern that punitive damages are unpredictable because they vary according to the wealth of the wrongdoer.

Corporate defendants are indeed likely to be assessed larger punitive awards than individual defendants. For example, Eisenberg et al. (1997) found that the mean punitive damage award in cases in which the defendant was a business was $817,000, as compared to $279,000 in cases where the defendant was an individual. In her interviews of jurors in business-related cases, Hans (2000) gleaned that jurors followed the instructions that punitive damages should be large enough to hurt the defendant financially. One juror noted that "If somebody hit me up for ten dollars, it's gonna hurt me. But these corporations, you give them a five-thousand dollar fine, that's nothing to them" (Hans, 2000, pp. 196–197). Another juror likened the awarding of punitive damages to disciplining a child: "If you tap its hand, then it's not going to bother him but if you smack him hard then they're going to feel it" (Hans, 2000, p. 197).

One might argue that corporate entities, especially those defending against actions requesting punitive damages, should be required to pay more, because they have more. Unless punitive damages are calibrated to wealth, one might argue, the remedy is ineffective at deterring the malicious actions of wealthy defendants. By this reasoning, punitive damages are not really unpredictable if they are tied to the financial circumstances of the defendant.

We tackle one final concern about punitive damages. Popular thinking is that juries redistribute wealth from rich, largely blameless defendants to poor, greedy plaintiffs. (Hans [2000] aptly likened this concern to the age-old story of Robin Hood.) The fact of the matter is that punitive damages are rarely awarded unless the defendant's conduct is truly egregious. In their analysis of punitive damages in medical malpractice cases, Rustad and Koenig (1995) concluded that punitive damages were generally appropriate, based as they were on (a) health care providers' extreme departure from accepted professional standards, (b) abject neglect and abandonment of patients, and (c) failure to secure informed consent and to diagnose obvious medical conditions. In this example, as in others, reality and rhetoric seem to be riding different trains.

Before we leave this topic we must acknowledge that despite the striking similarity in the findings from these empirical studies, there is ongoing debate over the scope and scale of punitive damages. Proponents of tort reform have been fueled by their own studies, conducted primarily for purposes of litigation or to advocate for changes in punitive damages doctrine and practices (Rustad, 1998). We opt not to delve into those studies here but simply acknowledge the lingering controversy about whether a crisis in punitive damages really exists, with each side insisting that the other is motivated by some sort of political agenda.

JURIES AND DAMAGE AWARDS: A NORMATIVE ANALYSIS

We take as a starting point the axiom that the legal system provides a set of norms, or standards, for how damage awards are to be assessed. It is beyond the scope of this book to examine how, or from where, those norms were derived. For our purposes it will suffice to ask whether jurors' decisions conform to, or diverge from, these legally derived dictates.

In his influential book entitled *Commonsense Justice: Jurors' Notions of the Law*, Norman Finkel (1995) hinted at an answer. The term *commonsense justice* refers to ordinary citizens' notions of what is just and fair. Finkel and others (e.g., Haney, 1997; Horowitz, 1997; Olsen-Fulero & Fulero, 1997) have provided compelling evidence that community sentiment (and hence, jurors' verdicts) may differ from the "black letter" law on the books in predictable ways.

One divergence concerns the context in which an act is viewed and a judgment is made. Jurors may intuitively contemplate a wider context of circumstances than the law would allow. Reasoning that a narrower perspective will result in a cleaner and more precise judgment, the law asks jurors to make compensatory damages assessments, for example, by focusing primarily on the severity of the plaintiff's injuries. Many jurors might prefer to focus on the bigger picture, including the actions of the defendant in causing those injuries. For these jurors, considering only the consequences does little to reveal the entire drama or to deliver justice.

How well do jurors' decisions comport with norms derived by the civil justice system for paying people for their losses? To answer that query, we start with an example regarding jurors' use of evidence on the defendant's financial well-being (a topic we cover in considerably more detail in chapter 4).

Consider how the resources of a defendant in a civil damages lawsuit are to be heeded. The normative standard, articulated (although not always explicit) in the jury's instructions, is that a defendant's financial wealth should not be considered in judgments of compensatory damages but should be considered in determining punitive damages. Suppose, for example, that a plaintiff is injured in an accident because his car's brake pads—ostensibly repaired by the defendant—had failed. In the realm of compensatory damages, it should not matter whether the defendant is a small locally owned automobile repair shop or the Ford Motor Corporation: Jurors should award compensatory damages that fully and fairly repay the plaintiff for his losses.

Matters are different for punitive damages because, as we noted in chapter 1, they serve a different purpose. In theory, for punitive damages to function as an effective deterrent and source of punishment they must be calibrated to the resources of the defendant. More money would be required to punish and deter a financially well-endowed defendant than one that is less wealthy.

One can ask whether jurors' compensatory award decisions reflect this normative standard. At first blush, the answer is "no" (although, as we later point out, the story is somewhat more complicated). Early studies used archival and jury simulation research to compare the treatment of corporate and individual defendants and found that wealthier defendants were made to pay more in compensatory damages than were less wealthy defendants.

More recent work (e.g., Hans, 2000; MacCoun, 1996) has clarified this idea and casts doubt on the so-called "deep-pockets" phenomenon, however. In a series of carefully crafted interviews that Hans (2000) conducted with jurors who had served in business-related cases, she asked about the evidence that had been presented regarding the finances of each party in the lawsuit and whether jurors considered this information in assessing monetary awards. In terms of compensatory damages, the results were impressive in the extent to which they showed jurors adhering to the legal norms: Only a small minority of jurors acknowledged that financial disparities between the plaintiff and defendant influenced their judgment of damages. When asked what facts they considered in arriving at an award, most jurors mentioned issues of plaintiff need, fairness, and proof of negligence, rather than the financial well-being of the defendant.[4]

Hans's (2000) jurors, when questioned about their use of financial evidence in discussions about punitive damages, also said that the defendant's financial status was important. More than 60% of jurors said that their juries had considered what the defendant could afford to pay, and another one third said that their juries had discussed but not used evidence of the defendant's financial status.

It is interesting that these discussions did not always have the effect of increasing the punitive award. Some jurors said that they considered the defendant's wealth only to assure themselves that their preferred damage award would not bankrupt or financially destroy the defendant. They were concerned about emptying the pockets of certain corporate defendants. The norm of equity is apparently at work here, as jurors rendered awards that varied according to the relative resources of the parties.

This urge to decide the lawsuit in a way that is fair to all parties, termed *total justice* by Feigenson (2000), may produce a result that does not comport with legal norms. Hans (2000) suggested that undercompensation of some very severely injured plaintiffs could be attributable to jurors'

---

[4]These findings might simply reflect jurors' failure to attend to the financial worth information, although that explanation is made untenable by Hans's discovery that jurors *had*, in fact, been attentive to this evidence.

resistance to compensate fully if that would mean digging to the bottom of the defendant's pocket. As Finkel (1997) pointed out, the widening of the context by laypeople may lead to better justice, but then again it may make for worse justice.

Here is another example that allows us to evaluate whether jurors' sentiments comport with legal norms. This time the results are less positive. Juries in virtually all civil negligence trials are expected to abide by the principle of independence regarding their determinations of liability and damages. In other words, each of these decisions is, theoretically, to be informed by a unique set of evidence. For example, judgments about the defendant's liability are to be based on the actions that led to an accident and not on the outcome of the accident. Judgments about the plaintiff's compensation are to be based on the extent of the plaintiff's injuries (the outcome) and not on the defendant's actions.

Harry Kalven, writing in 1958 about the University of Chicago Jury Project, stated the rule:

> If the trier [of fact] is persuaded that a preponderance [of evidence], however narrowly, favors liability he is then to award the full damages proved. He is not, that is, to discount damages because of his doubts as to liability. And equally . . . he is not to increase damages because of his view of the degree of fault in the defendant's conduct. (p. 165)

The rules of damages assume that compensation will be related to the extent of the plaintiff's injuries and not to the manner in which he or she was hurt, or to sentiments about the defendant's behavior.

However, a series of studies conducted by Edie Greene over the past few years has documented considerable distance between legal expectations and psychological reality (Greene, Johns, & Bowman, 1999; Greene, Johns, & Smith, 2001). Jurors' judgments regarding both liability and damages in a negligence case were not as narrowly construed as the law intends; rather, judgments of negligence were influenced, to a certain extent, by evidence regarding the severity of the plaintiff's suffering, and judgments of damages were influenced, to a certain extent, by evidence regarding the reprehensibility of the defendant's conduct. In chapter 7 we discuss the psychological mechanisms by which this fusion apparently occurs.

For now, though, it is fruitful to consider whether this "misuse" of evidence, although normatively inappropriate, might serve other ends. In fact, jurors' use of extra-evidentiary information—although legally improper—may produce verdicts that are, in jurors' minds, more equitable or fair. The norm of equity, in apparent conflict with the legal norm of independence, may be at play here. Thus, laypersons may use evidence of the defendant's conduct to set damages because it somehow seems intuitively appropriate to do so. (This reasoning also reflects the *just world belief* that people who behave worse should be punished more severely.)

This example suggests that there may be competing norms at work when jurors gauge damages; some (e.g., verdict independence) are derived from the legal system itself, and others (e.g., equity) emanate from shared social beliefs. Other normative considerations weigh in here, as well, for example, jurors' reluctance to saddle a tortfeasor with a monumental payment, their skepticism about the capacity of money to assuage harm, and their sense that an accident victim should bear some of the cost of his injuries and recovery.

Kalven (1958) put it well when he wrote:

> The jury is the most interesting of the critics of the law . . . for the truth seems to be not that the jury is at war with the law but that its views are somewhat askew the traditional legal norms. The jury agrees wholly with much of the law, but at times it makes distinctions the law chooses to ignore and at times it ignores distinctions the law chooses to make. (pp. 164–165)

JURIES AND DAMAGE AWARDS: A PRESCRIPTIVE ANALYSIS

In 1993, Craig Haney wrote that data-based social sciences could be used to close the gap between psychological reality and legal fiction. Although not sanguine that the social sciences had done a good job of gap-narrowing, Haney urged researchers to press for "psychologically-initiated and inspired—or at least, aided and abetted—legal change" (Haney, 1993, p. 372).

Following Haney's (1993) call, we ask what psychologists have learned about damage award decisions that could prompt legal change and make those decisions more rational, more predictable, and, ultimately, more fair. Earlier in this chapter we discussed favoring an approach that kept jurors at the center of these decisions because damages considerations seem especially within their purview. However, we also favor modifying the ways that jurors are asked to award damages so that these decisions can be aided and abetted by their knowledge of how real people think, reason, and ultimately decide.

In chapter 9 we describe and evaluate many reform proposals. For now, though, we take a look at modifications related to the nonindependence problem (e.g., in judgments of liability and damages in negligence cases). We evaluate two variations: one involving a change in jury instructions (a pragmatically simple but legally complicated solution) and the other involving bifurcation (a pragmatically complicated but legally feasible solution). Both may offer modest success in restoring some decisional independence to jurors' judgments.

First, consider the possibility that simply reminding jurors to think independently about liability and damages will have the intended effect:

Jurors would be told to rely only on evidence concerning the defendant's actions in their judgments of liability and only on evidence concerning injury severity in their judgments on damages. Wissler, Rector, and Saks (2001) evaluated the impact of this sort of instruction in a jury analogue study. They found that instructions that told jurors not to discount awards for compensatory damages to reflect uncertainty about the defendant's liability were effective in reducing those tendencies. Instructions not to increase awards to reflect the defendant's egregious conduct were similarly effective. Wissler et al. (2001) suspected that when the law explains to jurors both *how* to treat the evidence and *why they should do so*, jurors are more likely to comply with the law's intentions.

Next consider a procedure termed *bifurcation*. In a bifurcated trial the presentation of some evidence is separated from the presentation of other evidence, and jurors are asked to make decisions about only one set or another. It seems an obvious remedy for the nonindependence problem. Although the results of jury simulation studies are mixed (see chapter 9), bifurcation may be effective in reducing the impact of injury-related information on judgments of liability for compensatory damages (Greene & Smith, 2002), because in bifurcated proceedings, jurors typically have little detailed knowledge about the extent of the plaintiff's injuries when they make decisions regarding liability. Bifurcation is apparently less effective at reducing the impact of liability-related evidence on monetary awards, because even in most bifurcated trials, the liability phase comes first, so jurors have that evidence in mind when gauging damages.

FROM PRODUCT TO PROCESS

This is all we have to say about what damage awards look like. Now we turn our attention away from the *products* of decision making about damages and focus instead on the *processes* of decision making. How is it that jurors, individually and collectively, put a dollar value on another person's losses? We start by looking at how jurors' decisions are influenced by the personal attributes of the plaintiffs and defendants in these courtroom dramas. We also examine the role of attitudes, experiences, and biases that the jurors themselves may bring to the courthouse. Woven throughout this analysis—and indeed, throughout the rest of this book—are the threads of the descriptive, normative, and prescriptive formulations.

I

THE ISSUE OF IDENTITY: HOW PLAINTIFF, DEFENDANT, AND JUROR CHARACTERISTICS INFLUENCE DAMAGE AWARD DECISIONS

INTRODUCTION

THE ISSUE OF IDENTITY: HOW PLAINTIFF, DEFENDANT, AND JUROR CHARACTERISTICS INFLUENCE DAMAGE AWARD DECISIONS

In the next three chapters we ponder the extent to which the identities of various players in the civil justice system—plaintiffs, defendants, and jurors—can explain horizontal inequities in damage awards, the large differences in awards for similar injuries. It may be that different kinds of plaintiffs—men and women, old and young, Black and White—engender in jurors different kinds of thought processes that explain why they receive different sums as awarded damages. It may also be that different kinds of defendants—individuals and corporations, large and small businesses—activate different sets of expectations and beliefs in jurors that, in turn, explain why they are assessed different sums as damages. Finally, it may be that the characteristics and beliefs of jurors themselves—their gender, political beliefs, educational attainments, similarity to the litigants, thoughts about the civil liability system—can facilitate understanding of why there are apparently large horizontal inequities in damage award assessments.

These possibilities exemplify the impact of *extralegal factors*—characteristics of a case that have no legal relevance to the decision at hand (Kalven & Zeisel, 1966). More than 50 years ago, Judge Jerome Frank fueled critics of the jury by suggesting that "Mr. Prejudice and Miss Sympathy are the names of witnesses whose testimony is never recorded, but must nevertheless be reckoned with in trials by jury" (Frank, 1945, p. 122). Indeed, there is considerable evidence that jurors in criminal cases may be susceptible to the effects of extralegal factors.[1]

David Wasserman and J. Neil Robinson (1980) wrote articulately about the impact of extralegal influences in criminal cases. We extend their ideas into the realm of civil juries who must grapple with the difficult issue of assigning a monetary value to various losses sustained by a plaintiff and payable by a defendant.

Wasserman and Robinson (1980) described, in ascending order of subtlety, several ways in which jurors could be swayed by irrelevancies. At its most blatant, the extralegal factor related to the plaintiff's or defendant's identity may be explicitly considered by jurors and treated as having probative value equal to that of other pieces of evidence. The plaintiff's age and gender may be especially important to jurors' assessments of damages, because age- and gender-related stereotypes guide people's judgments of others' injuries, suffering, hardiness, and recovery. There are situations in which these considerations are legitimate, rather than forbidden, concerns, of course. However, even when largely irrelevant, a plaintiff's age and gender may be given some prominence (and perhaps even articulated) in decisions regarding compensation.

Somewhat less blatantly, an extralegal factor (e.g., gender) may affect the probability that a jury will find in favor of one party or another. This burden-of-proof argument is essentially that jurors may need less evidence to be convinced of the merits of the plaintiff's case when, for reasons largely unrelated to the evidence, the plaintiff is relatively more sympathetic than the defendant. Conversely, jurors may require more evidence before they decide that the plaintiff is entitled to compensation when he or she is less sympathetic than the defendant, again for reasons related to identity and not to the dispute in question.

At its most subtle, the extralegal influence may distort either the weight or the probative value of the evidence. One effect of the plaintiff's identity may be a selective marshaling of evidence that favors one side or the other and that, in the end, affects the outcome of the case. In some instances, jurors may be motivated to distort the probative value of the evidence, as, for example, when they decide that the plaintiff's gender really explains some of the other evidence presented in the case. On other occasions, the largely irrelevant information may inflate the value of ad-

---

[1]For example, a meta-analytic study of the effects of physical attractiveness, race, socioeconomic status, and gender of criminal defendants and victims on mock jurors' decisions found that in general defendants were advantaged when they were attractive, female, and of high socioeconomic status and disadvantaged when their victims were White (Mazzella & Feingold, 1994).

mitted evidence by making it appear more informative. Factors related to the plaintiff's and defendant's identities may make a particular outcome appear more likely and the evidence related to that outcome seem more important. Either way, decisions about whether to award compensation and in what amount may be affected.

3

WHO IS THE PLAINTIFF?

In this chapter we focus on the role of plaintiffs' characteristics in influencing damage awards. We begin with the good news: The severity of the plaintiff's injury is the most consistent and potent predictor of jury damage awards. As we detail in chapter 6, more seriously injured plaintiffs are more highly compensated (Bornstein, 1998; Bovbjerg, Sloan, & Blumstein, 1989; Taragin, Willet, Wilczek, Trout, & Carson, 1992). So, in general terms, jurors seem attentive to the appropriate criterion for assessing damages. And yet plaintiffs with seemingly comparable injuries sometimes receive different sums as assessed damages. Might juror sensitivity to the identities of the parties in a lawsuit explain some of this variation?

A significant body of work, which we describe in chapter 4, suggests, at least on its face, that jurors appear to take the identity of the *defendant* into consideration when assessing compensatory damages. The focus of this chapter is the extent to which juries give different awards in similar cases as a function of characteristics of the *plaintiff*. We concentrate on the identity of the plaintiff and examine how jurors weigh this factor (both implicitly and explicitly) in their computations of compensation.

A disclaimer is in order: We know less about the effects of plaintiffs' features on damage awards than we know about the effects of defendant factors. One explanation for the paucity of data is that plaintiffs are a decidedly diverse lot: In personal injury cases they are likely to be individuals or a class of similarly situated individuals, whereas in commercial cases (e.g., commercial transactions, employment cases, real estate cases) they may be individuals, small or large businesses, or governmental entities (Gross & Syverud, 1996). It is obvious that diverse plaintiffs will bring different characteristics with them into the courtroom, so global hypotheses about the impact of these factors (e.g., something akin to the deep-pockets hypothesis concerning defendant wealth) are lacking.

Data are especially paltry on the effects of plaintiff characteristics on noneconomic damages (related to intangibles such as the plaintiff's physical and mental distress, pain and suffering, loss of consortium, etc.) despite the fact that there are significant horizontal inequities in compensation for these losses. As Wissler and her colleagues noted, no studies have examined how jurors perceive the amount of pain and suffering experienced by different kinds of plaintiffs and how they translate those perceptions into a judgment about compensation (Wissler, Evans, Hart, Morry, & Saks, 1997). As a result, little is known about the extent to which characteristics of the plaintiff influence noneconomic damage awards and the extent to which other factors, such as case type or severity of injury, might matter.

WHO IS THE PLAINTIFF?

Before we review the data on the impact of various socioeconomic characteristics of the plaintiff on jurors' damage awards, we briefly turn our attention to describing these plaintiffs. We attempt here to answer the question "Who seeks compensation in jury trials?" This review sets the stage for our analysis of the ways that the identity of the plaintiff apparently influences jurors' thoughts about the compensation that is due.

Drawing on data compiled by *Jury Verdicts Weekly*, Samuel Gross and Kent Syverud (1996) painted a fairly sobering picture of the outcomes of civil jury trials in California's 58 state courts of general jurisdiction. (These cases are sobering because, in general, plaintiffs did less well by taking personal injury lawsuits before a jury than they would have by settling out of court.) However, that finding might be related to the kinds of cases that settle and the kinds that do not.

Who were the plaintiffs who brought claims in these courts, and what were they claiming? The great majority of trials (over 70%) were for personal injury of one sort or another (including vehicular negligence; nonvehicular negligence, such as slip-and-fall claims and workplace injuries; medical malpractice claims against physicians and hospitals; and products liability claims against manufacturers). In these cases the primary issue was physical injury to (or, less frequently, death of) the plaintiff.

The nonpersonal injury trials involved either some sort of commercial relationship (e.g., contract disputes, employment cases, and real estate cases) or other sorts of torts (e.g., assault, battery, false imprisonment, and fraud). In most of these cases the alleged harm was loss of money; damage to physical property; or intangible damages, such as loss of reputation or mental anguish unaccompanied by physical injury.

These cases were overwhelmingly initiated by individuals. (This holds for nearly all cases involving personal injury, for approximately 90% of cases involving other torts, and for two thirds to three quarters of commercial cases.) These data fit comfortably with those of Ostrom, Rottman, and Hanson (1992), who gathered data from 762 tort cases tried in 27 state trial courts in 1989. The plaintiff was an individual in 93% of those cases.[1]

Vidmar's (1995) comprehensive study of medical malpractice cases provides insight into the particular circumstances of injured plaintiffs that compel them to pursue their claims in jury trials. Drawing on a sample of 895 medical malpractice lawsuits that were filed in the state and federal courts in North Carolina between 1984 and 1987, Vidmar (1995) painted this picture of the injuries sustained by plaintiffs who go to trial: Not surprisingly, plaintiffs who had sustained serious injury or death (in which case the decedent's relative or estate becomes the plaintiff) were nearly twice as likely as those with only minor, temporary, or emotional injuries to pursue their claims at trial. Still, the numbers are small: Only 13% of cases that involved permanent total disability were resolved at trial, as were only 7% of cases that involved temporary disability. Permanent partial disability cases fell in the middle; 10% of these cases resulted in a trial.

Thus, most plaintiffs who find themselves inside a courtroom are individuals who claim that they have been physically injured—usually seriously—by the actions of individuals or of a corporation. It is important to bear in mind, as always, that most disputes between an injured person and the alleged wrongdoer are resolved short of trial.

THE IMPACT OF PLAINTIFF CHARACTERISTICS: EXTRALEGAL FACTORS?

In this chapter we ask how the demographic and background traits of plaintiffs affect the awards they receive. Before we do so, however, we must attend to some methodological matters. In chapter 1 we described concerns that simulation studies may highlight isolated features of a trial (e.g., the defendant's attractiveness) and may present them in a manner that underlines their importance and encourages their uncritical reception.

---

[1]The identity of the defendants in these cases was not so monochromatic. Corporations accounted for between one third (Ostrom et al., 1992) and 41% (Gross & Syverud, 1996) of the defendants, and individuals accounted for between 31% (Gross & Syverud, 1996) and 48% (Ostrom et al., 1992). In Ostrom et al.'s (1992) data set, the most common configuration of plaintiff and defendant involved a complaint filed by one individual against another.

What complicates the situation in civil cases is the fact that plaintiffs' characteristics that may be irrelevant to one of the decisions required of the jury (e.g., causation and negligence) may be quite relevant to another (e.g., compensation). It is easy to envision a situation in which the age of the plaintiff would be considered an extralegal factor with respect to the defendant's liability in a vehicular negligence case but would be quite relevant to a determination of the damages to which the plaintiff is entitled, following a liability verdict. (For example, older, more frail plaintiffs may be more seriously injured than younger, stronger plaintiffs and would therefore incur higher medical expenses. The accident may also take a higher emotional toll on older individuals. In this example, the plaintiff's age should not be determinative of liability but should be considered in the awarding of damages.) Thus, the effects of the plaintiff's identity may be quite complex and may depend on the particular decision requested of jurors. Furthermore, the plaintiff's identity may interact with other (extralegal) factors as well as with various characteristics of the jurors and of the evidence (Dane & Wrightsman, 1982).

We focus here on the impact of five plaintiff characteristics on damage award decision making: (a) race, (b) gender, (c) age, (d) locale, and (e) the number of plaintiffs.[2] Where appropriate, we explore the psychological mechanisms (e.g., stereotyping) that may explain jurors' use of these variables in their thoughts about compensation and describe how and why these extralegal considerations may really matter to jurors.

Race of Plaintiff

Mock jurors in criminal cases can be influenced by the race of the parties (Bodenhausen & Lichtenstein, 1987; Ugwuegbu, 1979), but little is known about the impact of plaintiffs' race on damage awards. Chin and Peterson (1985) of the RAND Corporation found that African American plaintiffs received lower damage awards than White plaintiffs. Vidmar (1994b) pointed out several alternatives to the hypothesis that juries discriminate against African Americans: African Americans may retain less competent attorneys; they may not be able to afford the costs of expert economists who could comment on the extent of the losses incurred; and they have lower incomes and therefore cannot substantiate requests for damages as large as those of White Americans.

We found only one simulation study that assessed the effects of race on damage awards, and its findings are somewhat confusing. Foley and Pigott (1997) varied the race of a plaintiff in a simulated civil rape case

---

[2]Note that we have not included any mention of the plaintiff's economic status, despite the fact that critics of civil juries suspect that jurors redistribute money from wealthy defendants to impoverished plaintiffs (see chapter 1). We found no support for the proposition that poorer plaintiffs receive higher damage awards than plaintiffs who are better off financially.

through the use of photographs and descriptions. At issue was the premises liability of the owner–manager of the apartment complex in which the plaintiff was raped. The two groups of mock jurors in this study (college students and jury-eligible citizens) reacted to the variation in race in decidedly different ways. College student jurors awarded higher damages to the White plaintiff than to the African American plaintiff, and jury-eligible adults did just the opposite. One might suspect that race-based stereotypes might play some role here, but the study offered little data to support that suspicion.

Gender of Plaintiff

In contrast to the lack of data related to race, a good deal is known about how a plaintiff's gender affects his or her award. What we are finding out unfortunately is not good news in terms of gender equality: Female plaintiffs are disadvantaged at several steps in the process of decision making about damages.

Descriptive analyses come from early data compiled by Jury Verdict Research Corporation and reported by Nagel and Weitzman (1971). The study tracked awards to 2,795 female and 3,976 male plaintiffs, all of whom prevailed in jury trials during the 1960s. Awards to men were 6% above the average award for the particular type of injury, medical expenses, and lost wages sustained; awards to women were 2% below average.

An interesting comparison comes from analysis of one particular kind of award examined by Nagel and Weitzman (1971): Husbands who sued for losses related to their wives' injuries collected more than wives who sued for losses related to their husbands' injuries. In other words, men collected more money both for their own injuries and, vicariously, for injuries to their spouses.

One explanation for why women apparently collect lower awards than men for similar injuries is the fact that women assume lower paying jobs,[3] are historically less educated, and have traditionally been relegated to subordinate roles in family life. Men are generally awarded greater damages because they make more money. The reported verdict data are somewhat surprising, then, in that they reveal no understanding that a wife may suffer a more significant financial loss when her husband is temporarily or permanently reduced by injury as compared with a husband who loses his wife's earning capacity.

Other archival data were amassed by the Washington State Task Force on Economic Consequences of Gender in Civil Litigation and reported by Goodman and colleagues (Goodman, Loftus, Miller, & Greene,

---

[3]Even 40 years after Nagel and Weitzman's (1971) study was published, women earn only approximately 75% of what men earn, and minority group members fare even worse (see http://www.dol.gov/dol/wb).

1991). These data consisted of jury awards in 98 wrongful-death cases tried in 20 Washington counties between 1984 and 1988. The mean, median, and range of awards were all greater in cases of male decedents than female decedents, suggesting that jurors are indeed attentive to gender.

As was true for African American plaintiffs, one cannot conclude from these archival studies that the cause of lower awards is discriminatory behavior on the part of juries. Because women have lower incomes, they are disadvantaged when it comes to showing economic loss, they may not be able to afford to hire experts, and their attorneys may be less competent than those retained by men.

To understand these findings better, and to control for the confounds noted previously, Goodman, along with two colleagues, conducted a series of experimental studies through which they were able to discern some subtle gender bias effects on damage award determinations. In the first jury analogue study, Goodman, Greene, and Loftus (1989) varied some facts (including gender) leading up to the wrongful death of the plaintiff's decedent. In all versions of a simulated jury trial, Goodman et al. (1989) described the decedent as married, self-employed, and earning $25,000 annually at the time of a fatal accident. That accident was attributed to one of three causes. Some jurors read about a products liability case in which the decedent was fatally injured when the accelerator pedal on his or her car malfunctioned. Others read about a negligence case in which a driver failed to stop for a pedestrian, killing the pedestrian–decedent. Finally, some jurors read a medical malpractice case in which the patient–decedent was injected with a substance to which he or she was known to be allergic. Goodman et al. (1989) informed mock jurors that liability had previously been determined in favor of the plaintiff and that their task was to award compensatory damages.

The results were startling: Across all three cases, survivors of female decedents were awarded 58% of what survivors of male decedents were awarded. When the decedent was male, the mean compensatory damage award was $788,000, but when the decedent was female, the award was only $458,000.

The value of experimental research on this topic is that it can move beyond simple description and facilitate understanding of the complex underpinnings of these findings. Goodman et al. (1989), for example, found that mock jurors were using very different kinds of strategies and focusing on quite different case factors as a function of the decedent's gender.

In Goodman et al.'s (1989) analysis of mock jurors' written explanations of their awards, they discerned that jurors were dramatically more likely to consider complicated exponential factors, such as salary increases, the effects of inflation, and the investment potential of an award, when the decedent was male. When the decedent was female, the strategy of choice was simply to pick a number that seemed fair, despite the fact that the male and female decedents were described as being employed in the same profession, making identical salaries, of the same age, and so on.

The decedent's gender also affected other factors that jurors considered in their judgments about compensation. For example, when the decedent was female, only 16% of mock jurors said they considered what the surviving spouse would need to live on, whereas more than 50% of mock jurors thought about this factor when the decedent was male. Mock jurors were also much more likely to consider the expected work life of a male decedent than of a female decedent.

Goodman et al.'s (1989) results provide fairly striking support for the differential treatment of men and women by juries in some tort cases. Not only were men generally awarded more (dead *and* alive), but also their gender apparently influenced jurors' very basic approaches to thinking about compensation.

They next wondered whether this disparity in awards was attributable to perceived differences in lost income for male and female decedents or to perceptions of the needs of the surviving spouses. To contextualize these concerns, they turned to the literature on gender stereotyping (Eagly & Wood, 1991; Swann, Langlois, & Gilbert, 1999).

Research on the content of gender stereotypes confirms that they are alive and well, despite the growth of the women's movement and feminism. Certain personality characteristics are associated with being male and female, and these stereotypes are held equally by men and women (Swim, 1993). People tend to regard men as more competent, intelligent, highly skilled, and valued than women (J. E. Williams & Best, 1990). Thus, jurors might tend to award more money to the estate of a deceased male than to that of a similarly situated deceased female.

Other gender stereotypes may play a role in these cases as well. For example, if jurors were influenced by the stereotype of a strong, independent male and of a weaker, dependent female, then they might award larger damages to a surviving female spouse than to a surviving male spouse.[4] Both explanations lead to the same conclusion for civil defendants: Causing the death of a male will cost more than causing the death of a female. Goodman et al. wondered if the predictions from the stereotyping literature could help them understand exactly why.

To address this question, Goodman et al. (1991) undertook a second study of the effects of gender on damage awards. This time, they provided information that had been left ambiguous in the first study (i.e., Goodman et al., 1989), namely, specific facts about the financial situation of the surviving spouse. They wondered whether jurors would still favor the man even in situations in which the female spouse was neither needy nor de-

---

[4]This hypothesis is not supported, however, by archival data collected by Nagel and Weitzman (1971).

pendent. Thus, they varied the gender of the decedent and the financial needs of the surviving male and female spouses, describing them as either clerks (high need) or judges (low need).

When jurors were asked to award damages for lost income, Goodman et al. (1991) again found a clear gap in awards for male and female victims: The mean award for lost income for a male decedent was $726,742; that for a female decedent was $576,655. They also discerned that the socioeconomic status of the surviving spouse was largely irrelevant: Judges (low need) were awarded as much as clerks (high need). The mean awards for lost income for male and female decedents as a function of the financial need of the surviving spouse are shown in Table 3.1.

As before, analysis of the strategies mock jurors used in awarding damages facilitated an understanding of their decision-making process. When the survivor was female, jurors were likely to consider the decedent's future salary increases and promotions and the impact of inflation on these figures. When the survivor was male, jurors rarely considered factors related to his late wife's earnings or earning potential. Overall, jurors were not likely to ponder the perceived needs of the surviving spouse regardless of his or her income. These findings suggest that the disparity in awards between men and women may be attributable primarily to the differences in estimated lost income of male and female decedents and that the perceived needs of the surviving spouse are much less important.

Age of Plaintiff

The age of the plaintiff should, in many circumstances, influence the size of the damage award. For a given type of injury (e.g., broken hip) an older and presumably weaker individual may be more severely impaired than someone who is younger and stronger. The older plaintiff may need more time to heal and may suffer more restrictions in activity in the process. On the other hand, lost future earnings may be greater for younger plaintiffs. Thus, the plaintiff's age may not truly constitute an extralegal factor. Still, we were interested in the effects of plaintiff age on compen-

TABLE 3.1
Lost Income Awards for Male and Female Decedents by Financial
Need of Surviving Spouse

Financial need of surviving spouse	Male decedent	Female decedent	Overall
Low need (judge)	$716,687	$591,270	$653,979
High need (clerk)	$737,467	$559,333	$653,088

Note. From "Money, Sex, and Death: Gender Bias in Wrongful Death Damage Awards," by J. Goodman, E. F. Loftus, M. Miller, and E. Greene, 1991, Law and Society Review, 25, pp. 263–285. Copyright 1991 by Law and Society Association. Adapted with permission.

satory damages. Unfortunately, we could find only one study (i.e., Goodman et al., 1989) that examined this issue.

Goodman et al. (1989) varied the age of the decedent in the wrongful-death cases described previously by informing mock jurors either that the decedent was 60 years old and had 5–10 future years of employment or that the decedent was 30 years old and had 35–40 future years of employment. It is not surprising that they found large differences in awards as a result of age: Younger decedents were awarded an average of $905,000, and older decedents were awarded an average of $376,000. They also found, predictably, that jurors were less likely to consider lost raises or promotions for older decedents than for younger decedents. Thus, jurors correctly assumed that an older victim who had fewer working years left would have less lost income than a younger victim.

What many jurors failed to consider, however, is that the widow (or widower) of an older victim would be far less likely than a younger person to remarry or to find employment. When asked to review a list of 17 factors that might have entered into their decisions and to check those that they considered, mock jurors were less likely to say they considered that the spouse might marry when the decedent was older. An older spouse presumably has fewer opportunities to attain financial security than does a younger spouse. Thus, simple calculation of the lost income of the older decedent (as performed by many mock jurors) may have underestimated the extent of the losses to be compensated. Again we see a focus on lost earning capacity rather than on the needs of the survivors.[5]

Plaintiff's Locale

Descriptive analyses of the size of jury damage awards reveal that some distinctively high plaintiffs' verdicts emanate from certain geographic locations, for example, state courts in Alabama, California, and Texas (Moller, Pace, & Carroll, 1999). This finding has led some commentators to speculate that in these locales jurors are motivated to redistribute wealth from the pockets of wealthy, usually geographically remote defendants into the hands of individual, usually local plaintiffs (Rubin, Calfree, & Grady, 1997). This wealth-redistribution hypothesis unfortunately confounds litigant identity (the corporation's deep pockets and the plaintiff's empty pockets) with geographical location (hometown or not), but it does raise intriguing questions about the role of the plaintiff's location and distance between plaintiff and defendant in damages assessments.

Hastie and colleagues examined this issue in a simulated environ-

---

[5]An alternative explanation is that jurors focused on the needs of the surviving children, who would be needier when the decedent was 30 than when he was 60. Because Goodman et al. (1989) did not ask jurors whether they considered the needs of other survivors, we cannot directly address this possibility with their data.

mental lawsuit (Hastie, Schkade, & Payne, 1999). They hypothesized that geographically local—as opposed to remote—plaintiffs would receive larger awards because jurors would more easily identify with the former. The results were mixed: Local plaintiffs were awarded more in punitive damages than remotely situated plaintiffs, but the effect was not substantial or reliable. In particular, it occurred primarily when the plaintiffs had suggested a high *ad damnum* (request for damages). We have no data on effects of plaintiff location on compensatory damages, but we suspect that in-group bias may also affect the noneconomic portion of a compensatory award. We also lack data on the effects of geographical distance between plaintiff and defendant on either punitive or compensatory damages.

Number of Plaintiffs

Is a given plaintiff more likely to be awarded damages if he or she goes after the defendant alone; if he or she is joined by other, similarly harmed plaintiffs; or if he or she represents a class of such victims? In theory, the jury should evaluate the merits of each plaintiff's claims on an absolute scale and not by comparison to other plaintiffs. Do they?

Horowitz and colleagues have looked at how the size of the plaintiff population affects jurors' judgments about damages in cases involving exposure to contaminated water and claims of repetitive-stress injuries. Their initial attempt involved either a consolidated trial or separate trials for four plaintiffs (Horowitz & Bordens, 1988). Mock jurors saw a videotaped reenactment of a tort case in which residents adjacent to a chemical plant sued the company for damages caused when effluent from the manufacturing process leached into surrounding waterways, contaminating drinking water. In the consolidated trial, the size of the nontrial plaintiff population was also varied and included either "26 others," "hundreds," or some unspecified number. Punitive awards increased significantly as a function of increasing the size of the nontrial population: Information that the trial plaintiffs represented "hundreds of others" sharply increased the size of the punitive award.

The size of the plaintiff population was not the only critical factor, however. Horowitz and Bordens (1988) also varied whether an outlier—a plaintiff whose injuries were substantially more severe than others' injuries —was included in the plaintiff group. Jurors apparently do rely on information about one plaintiff in their judgments about damages for others: The punitive awards increased sharply when a severely injured plaintiff was included in the group, suggesting that the presence of an outlier tended to inflate the awards to all plaintiffs.

It is interesting that Horowitz and Bordens's (1988) study seems to suggest that there were no effects of population size or the presence of an outlier on compensatory damages. This is not terribly surprising, as jurors were able to calculate compensable losses for various plaintiffs more precisely than punitive damages. When their judgment task is decidedly more ambiguous (i.e., to punish and deter, as punitive damages are intended to do), extralegal considerations related to characteristics of other plaintiffs apparently factor into the decision.

The next study on plaintiff population size conducted by Horowitz and his colleagues (Horowitz, ForsterLee, & Brolly, 1996) tells a somewhat different story about the impact of plaintiff number on *compensatory* damage awards, however. In Horowitz et al.'s (1996) study all jurors were to assess damages for four target plaintiffs whose injuries varied in severity. Half of the mock jurors heard testimony from plaintiffs imbedded in a trial that contained testimony and depositions from a total of eight plaintiffs; the other half heard only from the four target plaintiffs. In all cases, an immunologist had examined each plaintiff and presented evidence concerning the losses that each had suffered.

Plaintiff population size affected jurors' awards. Jurors who heard from only four plaintiffs awarded compensatory amounts that were generally consistent with each plaintiff's severity of injury. By contrast, jurors who heard from eight plaintiffs were unable to make distinctions among the four target plaintiffs when assigning compensation. Increasing the number of plaintiffs attenuated jurors' abilities to attend to each of the plaintiffs individually. As a result, their reasoning on compensatory damages assessments was affected.

These findings were further fleshed out in a more recent study (Horowitz & Bordens, 2000) that focused on awards for three plaintiffs who had mild repetitive-stress injuries and whose cases were tried either alone or with 1, 3, 5, or 9 other claimants. Compensatory damages awarded to these target plaintiffs were lowest in the 1- and 2-plaintiff conditions, reached their peak in the 4-plaintiff condition, and then decreased in the 6- and 10-plaintiff configurations. We derive two important messages from this study. First, and most obvious, is that these target plaintiffs were not remunerated in isolation; the presence of other, similarly positioned plaintiffs affected the awards they received. Second, Horowitz's work (as well as research in other venues) suggests that there is something unique about a conglomeration of four: Mock jurors award more money to plaintiffs when their cases are combined with three others than when they are tried with fewer or with more plaintiffs, and jurors are adept at analyzing the claims of four plaintiffs but no more.

CONCLUSION

Each of the various types of extralegal factors we have described (i.e., the plaintiff's age, race, gender, location, and population size) can apparently affect jurors' decisions about compensation in sometimes unpredictable and erratic ways. Having enunciated some of the ways that these factors affect jurors' decisions, we suspect that this situation contributes, at least in part, to the horizontal inequity in compensation noted by Wissler et al. (1997). However, we are quite certain that in the majority of cases these variables matter much less than evidentiary issues. We further suspect that, as in criminal cases, they may have greater impact in relatively weak cases for the plaintiff (Reskin & Visher, 1986).

Is there a remedy to jurors' occasional (or perhaps even frequent) overreliance on irrelevant considerations related to the plaintiff's identity? Jury instructions may be of some assistance, although jurors will probably respond, at some level, to these factors regardless of any instructions to the contrary. Nevertheless, instructions to ignore these extra-evidentiary considerations and to focus exclusively on the evidence would constitute a step in the right direction.

4

WHO IS THE DEFENDANT?

It is hard to avoid the conclusion that some civil defendants suffer simply by virtue of who they are. For example, consider the "plight" of the Ku Klux Klan. In 1998, a South Carolina jury deliberated just 45 minutes before finding that 3 years earlier, four former Klansmen had set fire to the Macedonia Baptist Church. The church was destroyed in the fire. In addition to holding the arsonists individually liable, the jury required the Klan itself to pay the rural Black church $37.8 million in damages, on the grounds that the organization's inflammatory rhetoric motivated the men to set the fire ("Klan must pay $37 million," 1998). As the church was not a large building, the compensatory damages amounted to only $300,000; the remaining $37.5 million was for punitive damages. Would the award have been as large if the fire had been set by unaffiliated individuals, or members of a less well-known hate group? Probably not. Was the jury's award influenced by the jurors' desire to send a message and their repugnance for the Klan's activities and philosophy? Perhaps. Should one's sense of justice be outraged by the verdict? We leave that for the reader to decide. Nonetheless, the case strongly suggests that the identity of the defendant can play a major role in jurors' damages decisions.

Jurors' sentiments about individual defendants are a major source of disagreement in criminal trials where the judge would prefer a verdict different from the one reached by the jury (which occurs in a minority of cases overall, as judges usually agree with juries' verdicts; see Kalven &

Zeisel, 1966). Kalven and Zeisel (1966) found that in the majority of cases where judges reported favoring a different verdict from that reached by juries, juries were more lenient (i.e., acquitting when judges would have convicted). In explaining the reasons for these disagreements, judges mentioned a variety of defendant characteristics capable of producing sympathy: age (i.e., youth or old age), gender, attractiveness, remorse, family responsibilities, and occupation (e.g., veterans, police officers, or clergy). Defendants who were rated as sympathetic engendered a higher disagreement rate than did unsympathetic defendants.

Would jurors also be moved by sympathy in awarding damages in civil cases? Clermont and Eisenberg (1992) found that plaintiffs were more likely to win, and recovered more in damages, when their cases were decided by a judge than when they were tried by a jury. This observation suggests that jurors find civil defendants, as well as criminal defendants, more sympathetic than do judges.[1] Such a tendency would certainly be at odds with the claims made by many tort-reform advocates (reviewed in chapter 1) that jurors are excessively proplaintiff and antidefendant, to the point where they overcompensate undeserving plaintiffs and punish blameless defendants. It is also the case that if jurors generally tend to respond to sympathy-eliciting factors, then they should demonstrate a proplaintiff bias, as plaintiffs, by virtue of their status as the allegedly injured parties, are more likely to elicit sympathy than defendants. As Feigenson (2000) pointed out, jurors may have both prodefendant and antidefendant tendencies, depending on the particular circumstances of the case. What characteristics of the defendant, then, influence jury damage awards, and in which direction?

Although a great deal has been written about the impact of defendants' appearance and demographic characteristics on criminal trial outcomes (e.g., Dane & Wrightsman, 1982; Mazzella & Feingold, 1994), little research has addressed their impact on jury damage awards (but see Hans, 2000). One notable exception is a study conducted by Zebrowitz and McDonald (1991) that investigated the relationship between litigants' appearance and the outcome of small claims court cases. These researchers looked at two aspects of individuals' appearance—baby-facedness and

---

[1] An important distinction between the methodology used by Kalven and Zeisel (1966) and that used by Clermont and Eisenberg is that the former compared jury verdicts with judges' opinions for the same cases, whereas the latter compared verdicts in cases tried by juries to verdicts in similar, yet still completely different, cases tried by judges. Thus, it is possible that the cases tried before juries and judges are in some respects fundamentally different (Vidmar, 1994b). For example, lawyers and litigants might base the decision of whether to have a bench or a jury trial on subtle case characteristics, or they might choose to present different kinds of evidence depending on who the fact-finder is. Therefore, in a sense, Clermont and Eisenberg compared apples and oranges, so their findings should be treated with a degree of caution; nonetheless, their study is one of very few attempts to compare the decisions of judges and juries, and it provides a useful point of departure to discuss the effect on jurors of various case characteristics.

attractiveness—in 506 Massachusetts small claims court cases. The researchers rated both the plaintiff and the defendant on scales measuring attractiveness (attractive–unattractive) and baby-facedness (baby-faced–mature-faced). Data on damage awards were obtained from court records after the proceedings had concluded. The results indicated that mature-faced defendants paid more in compensation than did baby-faced defendants, but only when they were opposed by baby-faced opponents. Neoteny helps, perhaps by making baby-faced litigants seem more sympathetic and needing of care.

Although few other physical or demographic features of civil defendants have been studied, there is also evidence that defendants' race may influence damage awards, with Black defendants being required to pay somewhat less than White defendants (Chin & Peterson, 1985). This effect of defendants' race may merely reflect differences among plaintiffs who sue White versus Black defendants, such as their income level (Chase, 1995).

The bulk of the research on civil defendants has tended to focus on defendants' wealth, identity (i.e., individual vs. corporation), and the nature of the case (i.e., a defendant in a malpractice vs. a personal injury or automobile accident case). In many cases these variables are confounded; for instance, individual malpractice defendants (doctors) will tend to be wealthier than individual automobile accident defendants, and corporations will, on average, have a higher net worth than individuals. Despite such potential confounds, the variables may be separated as well (i.e., there are poor doctors, just as there are wealthy nondoctors), and we therefore treat them separately in the present discussion.

As we discussed in chapter 1, according to legal doctrine, the factors that should affect damage award assessment depend on the type and function of the award. This issue is especially relevant to an investigation of how characteristics of the defendant influence jurors' damage awards. For example, the defendant's wealth is an appropriate consideration in awarding punitive damages, the purpose of which is to punish the defendant for egregious behavior, as well as to deter that defendant and others from behaving similarly in the future. Because the same dollar amount would effectively punish a millionaire defendant and a pauper defendant differentially, the goals of equivalent punishment and deterrence for the same act dictate awarding more in punitive damages against relatively wealthy defendants (Eisenberg, Goerdt, Ostrom, Rottman, & Wells, 1997; *Kemezy v. Peters*, 1996; Landes & Posner, 1987).[2] Thus, "the punishment/deterrence rationale, when implemented through monetary sanctions, suggests

_____

[2]Some commentators (e.g., Fischel & Sykes, 1996) suggest that the defendant's wealth should be considered in awarding punitive damages against individual, but not against corporate, defendants, as it is harder to pin responsibility for wrongdoing on a comparatively anonymous corporation. Consequently, innocent shareholders would bear the brunt of the cost, and there would be little deterrent effect on the behavior of the corporate entity.

fine-tuning to reflect the defendant's financial circumstances. . . . Increased award levels against wealthier defendants, therefore, do not necessarily show bias against them" (Eisenberg et al., 1997, pp. 628–629).

Whether the defendant's wealth is relevant to awarding compensatory damages is less clear. Landes and Posner (1987) argued that although the primary purpose of compensatory damages is to restore the plaintiff to his or her former state—a goal that is theoretically independent of the defendant's wealth—they also serve a secondary deterrent function (see also Leebron, 1989).[3] Thus, requiring wealthier defendants to pay more in compensation may serve a normatively appropriate deterrent purpose. However, even if one accepts this reasoning, the defendant's wealth is less directly relevant to the issue of compensatory than to punitive damages.

On the whole, then, the role of the defendant in damage award assessment raises two related questions: First, do jurors consider those characteristics of the defendant that are relevant to the awarding of different types of damages (e.g., wealth for punitive damages)? Second, do they ignore defendant characteristics that are irrelevant (e.g., wealth for compensatory damages and a variety of extralegal factors, such as defendants' gender, occupation, etc., for any type of damages)? These questions are addressed by considering separately the characteristics of civil defendants that affect compensatory and punitive damage awards.

COMPENSATORY DAMAGES

Wealth and Identity

There is a widespread perception that juries treat corporate and individual defendants differently (Hans, 1989, 1996; Peterson, 1986). This phenomenon has been termed the *deep-pocket* effect (Chin & Peterson, 1985), to reflect jurors' tendency to make defendants with deeper pockets pay more than less wealthy defendants for the same wrongful conduct. Support for the phenomenon comes mainly from archival analyses, which have found that business, professional, and government defendants tend to pay more than individual defendants who are held liable for causing similar injuries (e.g., Chin & Peterson, 1985; Ostrom, Rottman, & Goerdt, 1996; Ostrom, Rottman, & Hanson, 1992; Peterson, 1986).

The perception that a deep-pocket effect exists is so prevalent that several jurisdictions have even developed jury instructions admonishing jurors not to allow litigants' corporate status to influence their decisions (Hans, 1989). For example, the Modern Federal Jury Instructions (Sand,

---

[3]Richard Posner, a federal appellate court judge, has expressed this view in some of his judicial rulings as well (see, e.g., *Kemezy v. Peters*, 1996).

Siffert, Loughlin, Reiss, & Batterman, 1984, ¶72.01, Instruction 72–1) caution jurors in cases involving corporations as follows:

> The mere fact that one of the parties is a corporation does not mean it is entitled to any lesser consideration by you. All litigants are equal before the law, and corporations, big or small, are entitled to the same fair consideration as you would give any other individual party.

Does reality justify the perception that there is a deep-pocket effect? As we shall see, the data are sharply split on the issue.

On the one hand, several studies have indeed found that corporate defendants pay greater compensation than individual defendants in both actual (Chin & Peterson, 1985; Ostrom et al., 1996; Ostrom et al., 1992; Peterson, 1986) and simulated trials (Hans & Ermann, 1989; Wasserman & Robinson, 1980). Moreover, deep-pocket effects have been found both when individual jurors deliberate as a group (Wasserman & Robinson, 1980) and when they do not (Hans & Ermann, 1989). For example, Hans and Ermann (1989) presented mock jurors with a trial scenario in which several workers were allegedly harmed by exposure to a toxic substance. The workers then sued their employer, who was portrayed as either "Mr. Jones" (in the individual-defendant condition) or the "Jones Corporation" (in the corporate-defendant condition), arguing that the defendant was negligent in not having checked for toxic substances prior to hiring the workers.

Hans and Ermann (1989) found that the corporate defendant was held liable for a greater number of claims.[4] More important to the present discussion is that the Jones Corporation was also required to pay greater compensation than Mr. Jones, even though both entities had engaged in exactly the same conduct and the plaintiffs' injuries were held constant across the two conditions. This tendency was especially pronounced for noneconomic damages: The corporation was required to pay 5% more than the individual for hospital bills, 18% more for doctors' bills, and slightly more than twice as much for pain and suffering.

On the other hand, not all studies have found anticorporate effects. For example, Bornstein (1994) conducted a simulation study very similar to that done by Hans and Ermann (1989) but used four different personal injury cases. In each case, the defendant's status was manipulated such that the defendant was portrayed as either a large corporation or a small, in-

---

[4]Some evidence also suggests that plaintiffs are less likely to be found contributorily negligent when they sue corporate than individual defendants (Hans, 1996). It is interesting that some archival studies have failed to find anticorporate effects on liability judgments. For example, Ostrom et al. (1992) found that corporations were actually less likely to be held liable than individual defendants. As we note later in this chapter, it is possible that such effects reflect fundamental differences in cases involving corporate and individual defendants, such as the quality of counsel. Such characteristics can be controlled for in experimental studies, such as the one Hans and Ermann conducted. Nonetheless, these findings suggest that corporate defendants are not as disadvantaged at trial as some commentators tend to believe.

dependently owned company. Bornstein (1994) found that although the high-status corporate defendants were perceived as wealthier than the smaller, low-status defendants and were also more likely to be held liable (as in Hans & Ermann's study), high-status defendants who were found liable were not required to pay larger damage awards than low-status defendants in any of the four cases.

One explanation for this discrepancy is that participants might have been influenced by the jury instructions. In Bornstein's (1994) study the instructions explained the difference between compensatory and punitive damages and told participant–jurors to award compensatory damages only; Hans and Ermann (1989) appear not to have emphasized this distinction in their instructions, thereby implicitly allowing participants the opportunity both to compensate the plaintiff and to punish the defendant. Across several different case types (products liability, automobile negligence, and medical negligence), Greene, Woody, and Winter (2000) also failed to find an effect of defendants' wealth on mock jurors' compensation awards when the instructions clearly delineated compensatory from punitive damages. Moreover, simulation research has failed to find a deep-pocket effect for deliberating juries as well as individual jurors (e.g., Landsman, Diamond, Dimitropoulos, & Saks, 1998).[5]

Another reason why the deep-pocket effect appears in some studies but not others is that cases comparing defendants who differ in wealth also differ unavoidably in other respects (Hans, 1996; Vidmar, 1994b, 1995). For example, relatively wealthy defendants might be less likely to settle prior to trial, meaning that they are more likely than less wealthy defendants to find themselves in high-stakes trials with potentially large verdicts. These subtle discrepancies in case characteristics are especially hard to control for in archival analyses (Vidmar, 1994b, 1995), but they can occur in experimental research as well. For instance, a limitation of both Bornstein's (1994) and Hans and Ermann's (1989) research is that their deep-pocket manipulations confounded defendants' identity and wealth; that is, their corporate defendants differed from the individual defendants in terms of both their identity (i.e., corporate vs. individual defendant) and their perceived wealth.

Shaw and Skolnick (1996) addressed the effect on mock jurors' liability judgments of individual defendants' perceived wealth alone. Participants read a transcript summary of a civil trial involving an assault-and-battery scenario. The defendant's status (and, presumably, wealth) was manipulated by portraying him as either a well-established and respected clinical psychologist and university professor or as an average graduate student in clinical psychology. The professional relatedness of the defendant's

---

[5]Explaining the discrepancy as an effect of jury instructions suggests that the form and substance of the instructions have an impact on jury decisions. As we show in chapter 8, there is some truth to this claim (e.g., Diamond & Casper, 1992).

tortious conduct was varied as well: He allegedly assaulted the plaintiff either when the plaintiff arrived late for a therapy appointment (professionally related) or when he arrived late to repair a cable TV problem. Participants' compensation awards reflected an interaction between these two variables such that the high-status defendant was required to pay more when his conduct was professionally related but less when it was unrelated (the same pattern held for participants' liability judgments). Thus, there are some circumstances in which high status may actually be an advantage to civil defendants, which Shaw and Skolnick referred to as a *protective shield effect*.

As MacCoun (1996) pointed out, to demonstrate a true deep-pocket effect it is necessary both that verdicts (liability judgments, damage awards, or both) differ as a function of the depth of defendants' pockets and that the effect be due solely to defendants' wealth and not to some other factor correlated with wealth, such as identity. MacCoun (1996) distinguished between the deep-pocket effect, in which defendants' wealth influences verdicts, and the *defendant identity effect*, in which defendants' corporate status influences verdicts. Although wealth and identity (or status) are frequently correlated in the real world, the two effects are independent, such that jurors' verdicts may reflect either factor, neither factor, or both factors.

To assess the effects of defendants' wealth and identity separately, MacCoun (1996) conducted two experiments in which mock jurors made decisions about a number of personal injury cases. Each case involved three different defendant conditions: (a) poor individual, (b) wealthy individual, and (c) corporation (which was perceived by participants as significantly wealthier than the wealthy individual).[6] Thus, a comparison of the first two conditions allowed for a test of the deep-pocket effect, whereas a comparison of the second and third conditions allowed for a partial test of the defendant-identity effect (for a pure test, the wealthy individual and corporation would need to be perceived as equally wealthy).

In his first experiment, MacCoun (1996) found that wealthy individual defendants were less likely to be held liable than corporate defendants but that wealthy and poor individuals were held liable equally often. The same pattern was observed for compensation awards; that is, corporate defendants paid more than wealthy individuals, but wealthy individuals paid no more than poor individuals. MacCoun (1996) obtained similar findings in a second experiment, leading to the conclusion that what might appear on the surface as a deep-pocket effect was actually a defendant-identity effect. Wealthy defendants were not necessarily at a disadvantage, unless they were corporations as well.

---

[6]There are, of course, poor, financially struggling corporations, just as there are poor individuals. An ideal comparison would have therefore included a corporation that was explicitly poor as well as one presumed to be wealthy.

Two methodological limitations qualify the significance of these findings. First, MacCoun (1996) found that corporate defendants were perceived as significantly wealthier than the wealthy individual defendants. Thus, despite efforts to separate the elements of defendant identity and defendant wealth, they were still confounded, making it impossible to ascribe the difference between corporations and wealthy individuals to differences in identity alone. Second, MacCoun's (1996) preferred analysis of compensation awards included participants who found the defendant not liable; these participants were judged to have awarded the plaintiff $0 in compensation. This method of analysis blurs the very important distinction between finding the defendant not liable (and hence awarding no damages) and finding the defendant liable but awarding no damages. The former case reflects a situation in which the plaintiff failed to meet his or her burden of proof, whereas the latter case typifies a situation—not unheard of (e.g., *United States Football League v. National Football League*, 1988, the United States Football League's famous antitrust case against the National Football League)—in which this burden was met, but the jury decided that the plaintiff's injuries were not deserving of compensation and awarded only nominal damages, or none at all. Scoring a nonliable verdict as a zero compensation award does little more than report the same data twice: If participants in one condition are less likely to find the defendant liable (e.g., in the wealthy individual condition), then including nonliable verdicts in the computation of damages necessarily pulls down the average award in that condition.

A purer, and more valid, comparison would include only participants who first found the defendant liable. It is interesting that MacCoun (1996) made this comparison in his second experiment, where he found no significant differences in damage awards across defendant type as a function of either wealth or identity. This result suggests that in addition to failing to find support for a deep-pocket effect, MacCoun (1996) also obtained only qualified support for a defendant-identity effect. On the whole, then, this very intriguing study supports previous research (e.g., Bornstein, 1994) in showing quite clearly that a defendant's wealth, per se, has no effect on mock jurors' compensation awards; it also suggests that jurors make assumptions about defendants as a function of their identity (e.g., relating to their wealth) and that these assumptions might be driving their verdicts.

Jurors' Attitudes Related to Defendant Identity

To the extent that jurors treat various classes of defendants differently, these differences might reflect people's assumptions about defendants' behavior as a function of their identity. For example, Hans and Ermann (1989) found that people perceived a corporate and an individual defendant involved in an identical case quite differently (see also Fox, 1996;

TABLE 4.1
Juror Perceptions of a Civil Defendant as a Function of Individual or Corporate Wrongdoing

Item	Mr. Jones	Jones Corporation
Likelihood of insurance*	2.25	3.20
Likelihood of bankruptcy*	3.07	1.76
Fair to sue*	3.71	4.13
Fairness of claims*	2.77	3.35
Fairness of settlement offer*	2.95	2.13
Knew beforehand*	1.52	1.89
Recklessness*	2.50	3.08
Morally wrong*	2.28	2.78
Deserves punishment*	2.38	3.04
Harm to workers	3.87	3.78
Fairness of criminal charge*	2.21	2.91
Regret over incident*	3.96	3.60
Effect on reputation	3.55	3.52
Individual deterrence*	4.67	4.45
General deterrence	3.79	3.64

Note. The higher the number, the more likely, more fair, more reckless, and so on, an item was judged to be. From "Responses to Corporate Versus Individual Wrongdoing," by V. P. Hans and M. D. Ermann, 1989, *Law and Human Behavior, 13,* p. 158. Copyright 1989 by Kluwer Academic/ Plenum Publishers. Adapted with permission.
*$p < .02$.

Hans, 2000). To measure these perceptions, they asked participants a number of questions designed to assess their perceptions of the incident and the litigants. The results of this questionnaire are presented in Table 4.1. As the table shows, the corporate defendant was perceived considerably less favorably. For example, compared with Mr. Jones, the Jones Corporation was seen as more likely to be insured, more likely to have foreseen the plaintiffs' injuries, more reckless, and less likely to experience regret.

The table also shows that participants judged the corporate defendant much more harshly than the individual. Specifically, they felt that it was fairer to sue the Jones Corporation, which they perceived as more morally wrong, more deserving of punishment, and less likely to be deterred by the incident. Bornstein (1994, Experiment 2) obtained similar findings, with participants viewing corporate defendants as having less respect for consumers and a greater tendency to injure employees or consumers. In support of these results, MacCoun (1996, Experiment 2) found that differential treatment of corporations and individuals depended on whether the defendant was engaged in commercial or personal activities.

In recent years, the American public has arguably become less supportive of big business and more willing to approve sanctions against businesses in the event of corporate wrongdoing (Fox, 1996; Hans, 1989, 2000). Although Hans and Lofquist (1992) found that jurors in a number of actual cases did not appear to have blanket anticorporate defendant attitudes, they nonetheless found that juries holding stronger antibusiness attitudes tended to make larger awards. Furthermore, a substantial minority of jurors indicated that they explicitly held corporations to a higher standard than individuals, because of corporations' presumably greater expertise, ability to anticipate the consequences of their activities, and potential for causing harm (Hans, 1996). Although the majority of jurors in Hans and Lofquist's (1992) study reported that a change in the defendant's status would not have affected their decisions, research suggests that jurors' decisions are often influenced by factors that they do not acknowledge (Bornstein, 1998; Zickafoose & Bornstein, 1999).

It is important to emphasize that most of these differing perceptions either should have no bearing on any damage awards or should have greater bearing on punitive than compensatory damages. For example, the likelihood that the defendant has insurance should not affect any damage award, and expectations about the effect of awarding damages on deterring the defendant's future conduct should affect punitive but not compensatory awards. Nonetheless, participants in Bornstein's (1994) study even went so far as to agree that high-status companies should have to pay more for causing the same injury and should be held to stricter safety standards (see also Hans, 1996, 2000; Hans & Lofquist, 1992). This tendency may merely reflect a lay intuition that compensation serves a deterrent purpose (Landes & Posner, 1987), yet the participants also stated that it was more acceptable to force high-status companies to pay for harm that they clearly did *not* cause.

Thus, participants across several studies incorporated their perceptions and expectations concerning different types of defendants into their compensation awards. In so doing, they relied on a variety of assumptions. Some of these assumptions, such as the probability of causing harm, are relevant to determining defendants' liability but not to the awarding of damages; some assumptions, such as differential safety standards and deterrent effects, are relevant to punitive but not to compensatory decisions; and some assumptions, such as the likelihood of insurance or requiring clearly faultless defendants to pay more compensation if they can afford it, are not legally relevant to any decision that juries are asked to make.

Case Type

Defendant identity necessarily covaries with case type. For example, product manufacturers are considerably more likely to be involved in products liability cases than in medical malpractice cases. By the same token, although doctors may coincidentally be defendants in personal-injury or automobile litigation, their primary role as civil litigants is as malpractice defendants. A consistent finding in the literature is that malpractice defendants are relatively successful at trial compared with defendants in other types of cases (Danzon, 1985; Metzloff, 1991; Vidmar, 1995; see also chapter 2, this volume). For example, Bovbjerg, Sloan, Dor, and Hsieh (1991) found that, compared with malpractice plaintiffs' 33% success rate, products liability plaintiffs had a 44% chance of prevailing, plaintiffs suing the government had a 48% chance of prevailing, and automobile liability plaintiffs had a 64% chance of prevailing (the differences between malpractice cases and government and automobile cases were statistically significant). Substituting commercial litigation for government liability and covering different jurisdictions, Gross and Syverud (1991) obtained a very similar result: Malpractice plaintiffs won 29% of the time, as opposed to 42%, 58%, and 87% for products, automobile, and commercial liability plaintiffs, respectively. This variability may of course reflect differences across case type in factors that determine which cases go to trial, such as the relative strength of the evidence.

Despite the fact that malpractice defendants fare relatively well in terms of liability judgments, a number of commentators believe that the malpractice system is particularly susceptible to bias in the awarding of damages (e.g., Abramson, 1989–1990; Huber, 1988, 1991; Peterson, 1986; Weiler, 1991). Blame for these problems is often laid at the feet of the jury. Jurors in malpractice cases are presumed to be especially vulnerable to judgmental biases, such as deep-pocket and sympathy effects (Abramson, 1989–1990; Huber, 1988, 1991; Weiler, 1991). One reason for this claim is that nonpecuniary damages, such as pain and suffering, play a large role in malpractice cases. Because jurors receive notoriously vague guidance in determining this component of compensation (Greene & Bornstein, 2000; Wissler, Kuehn, & Saks, 2000; see chapter 1), awards for similar injuries may vary greatly (e.g., Bovbjerg et al., 1991), and there is concern that this variability becomes magnified in malpractice cases.

Supporting this concern is some evidence that the same injuries caused by malpractice and other actions are not treated equally (Danzon, 1985). For example, Bovbjerg et al. (1991) found that malpractice plaintiffs tended to receive greater compensation than plaintiffs in products, government, and automobile liability cases. This finding is troubling, because it suggests that jurors are responding to extralegal factors in awarding compensation. However, there are three reasons why this result should be interpreted with a degree of caution. First, when Bovbjerg et al. (1991) controlled for factors such as the severity of the plaintiff's injury, the compensation awarded to malpractice plaintiffs was significantly greater (in a multiple regression analysis) than only one of the three other types of liability they studied. Compensation to medical malpractice plaintiffs was greater than to automobile negligence plaintiffs but was no different compared with plaintiffs in products and government liability cases. Second, they found that the difference between malpractice and automobile cases had not increased over time, thus disputing claims of a burgeoning "crisis" occasioned by spiraling malpractice awards (e.g., Weiler, 1991; see Vidmar,

1994a, 1995, for further evidence that the crisis is more apparent than real). Third, they found that malpractice defendants were actually *less* likely to be held liable than defendants in the other types of cases, a pattern that others (e.g., Danzon, 1985; Gross & Syverud, 1991; Metzloff, 1991) have found as well. It is logical to assume that a real deep-pocket effect that works to the detriment of malpractice defendants would result in both larger and more frequent damages assessments against them—but that does not seem to be the case.

As we mentioned earlier, archival studies comparing malpractice and other types of cases are subject to criticism on the grounds that they differ in numerous ways other than the defendant's wealth (e.g., Vidmar, 1992, 1993, 1995). They might differ in the strength of cases that are selected to go to trial, the number of plaintiffs and defendants in individual cases, the nature of the relationship between the litigants, and whether comparative negligence is at issue (Vidmar, 1993). For example, although comparative negligence is a relatively common defense in automobile accident cases, it is somewhat rare (albeit increasing) in medical malpractice cases (S. W. Murphy, 1991; Vidmar, Lee, Cohen, & Stewart, 1994).

Experimental research on the deep-pocket effect has found relatively little support for the contention that malpractice defendants are singled out for special treatment (Vidmar, 1992, 1994a, 1995). For example, Vidmar (1993) found that if all of the differences between malpractice and automobile liability cases are controlled for—which cannot be done in a survey of actual cases, as in Bovbjerg et al.'s (1991) study, but can be done in an experimental simulation—then there is no difference in compensation. Specifically, Vidmar (1993) asked a sample of mock jurors to award damages for pain and suffering to a woman who had suffered a broken leg and resulting complications. Her injury had been caused either by medical negligence (i.e., she fell off the operating table during surgery to remove a benign cyst) or by automobile negligence (i.e., her vehicle was hit by another driver who swerved into oncoming traffic). A second variable involved the number and type of defendants: one individual (doctor or driver), two individuals, or a corporation (hospital or driver's employer).

Although mock jurors tended to view defendants as more negligent for the same injury when it was caused by medical negligence than by automobile negligence, there were no differences in the amount the plaintiff was awarded for pain and suffering as a function of either the type of case or the number/type of defendants. Medical defendants were required to pay an average of $93,999, whereas automobile defendants were required to pay an average of $87,783 (this difference was not statistically significant). Although case type did not matter for the one-defendant and corporate-defendant conditions, there was a difference in the amount awarded in malpractice and automobile cases when there were two defendants. However, the difference was in the direction of malpractice defendants being required to pay less. To the extent that one can generalize from simulation studies to the behavior of real juries, these findings indicate that juries' compensation awards, at least for noneconomic damages, are not greater for malpractice defendants than for other kinds of defendants (see also Vidmar, 1992; Vidmar et al., 1994).

PUNITIVE DAMAGES

As described in chapter 2, despite the publicity surrounding a small number of very large awards (e.g., *BMW of North America v. Gore*, 1996), punitive damages are actually awarded in only a small number of cases (Daniels & Martin, 1990; Eisenberg et al., 1997; Peterson, Sarma, & Shanley, 1987; Rustad, 1992). This relative scarcity of punitive damage awards is even more dramatic in areas where punitive damages have been especially controversial, such as malpractice and products liability (Daniels & Martin, 1990; Eisenberg et al., 1997; Rustad, 1998). For example, Daniels and Martin (1990) found that punitive damages were awarded in only 18 of 1,917 malpractice verdicts (less than 1% of total verdicts), comprising just 2.9% of verdicts favoring the plaintiff. Similar findings were obtained by Metzloff (1991), who examined a cohort of 895 malpractice cases filed in North Carolina during a 3-year period, 118 of which went to trial. He found that punitive damages were awarded in only 1 out of the 24 cases in which an entitlement to punitive damages was claimed.

As described previously, any deep-pocket effect—which in a strict sense refers to an effect of defendants' wealth alone (MacCoun, 1996)— with respect to punitive damages is normatively appropriate. According to the influential *Restatement (Second) of Torts* (1965), "in assessing punitive damages, the trier of fact can properly consider ... the wealth of the defendant" (§908). Wealthier defendants must pay more than less wealthy defendants to accomplish the explicit goal of deterrence (*Kemezy v. Peters*, 1996; Landes & Posner, 1987).[7] Do jurors take defendants' wealth into account when exacting punishment?

Little research has addressed the question of whether there are deep-pocket effects on punitive damage awards. In Shaw and Skolnick's (1996) study, described earlier, participants were asked to award punitive as well as compensatory damages. The same interaction between the defendant's status and the professional relatedness of his conduct was obtained, such that the high-status psychologist defendant was assessed a larger punitive

---

[7]Although it is widely accepted that the defendant's wealth is an appropriate consideration in determining the amount of punitive damages, this viewpoint is not universally accepted (see, e.g., Abraham & Jeffries, 1989). Part of the concern is that jurors might make unwarranted assumptions about the defendant's wealth. In general, the courts have not found this to be a serious enough concern either to eliminate punitive damages or to compel plaintiffs to present evidence of defendants' wealth (e.g., *Kemezy v. Peters*, 1996).

award when the assault occurred within the context of a psychotherapy session, but not when it occurred in a professionally unrelated context. Thus, status and its accompanying wealth do appear to place civil defendants at a disadvantage in the penalty phase of a trial, especially when their conduct is related to their profession (from which, at least in this case, their status derives).

However, two caveats are necessary in interpreting this finding. First, because the case involved physical (rather than financial) harm, it is not one in which punitive damages would likely be raised (Daniels & Martin, 1990), particularly in the condition where the defendant's behavior had nothing to do with his profession (i.e., assaulting the cable TV repairman).[8] Second, all participants who found the defendant liable were asked to award punitive damages without first being asked to decide whether the case was one in which punitive damages were warranted (Hastie, Schkade, & Payne, 1998). It is possible that any status effect on the *amount* of punitive damages could be explained by a greater tendency to award *any* punitive damages against a high-status defendant. As mentioned earlier, the decision to award *any* damages and the *amount* of those damages are separate, albeit related, issues (Hastie et al., 1998).

Using more realistic case scenarios, Greene et al. (2000) manipulated defendants' wealth in three different types of cases: (a) products liability, (b) automobile negligence, and (c) medical malpractice. In each case, the wealthier defendant was described as having annual profits of roughly 10–20 times those of the less wealthy defendant. For example, in the automobile negligence case, the plaintiff was struck by a tractor–trailer driven by the defendant's employee, who allegedly drove in a reckless manner. The wealthier defendant was described as employing 450 people with gross profits for the previous year of $19.7 million, and the less wealthy defendant was described as employing 4 people with gross profits of $1.1 million. Mock jurors were asked to assume that the defendant had already been found liable and to award compensatory damages, punitive damages, or both. In each case, they awarded more in punitive damages against the wealthier defendant. In the automobile negligence case, for instance, the mean punitive award was approximately $14.3 million for the wealthier defendant versus $1.5 million for the less wealthy defendant. Kahneman, Schkade, and Sunstein (1998) also manipulated defendants' wealth, by informing mock jurors that personal injury defendants had annual profits of either $10–20 million or $100–200 million. Participants similarly awarded more in punitive damages against wealthier defendants.[9]

---

[8]Aspects of the defendant's conduct that do warrant the awarding of punitive damages are covered in chapter 7.
[9]In Kahneman et al.'s (1998) study, participants were informed that compensatory damages—which did not vary depending on the defendant's wealth—had already been awarded, and that their task was just to award punitive damages (if any).

Finally, archival analyses have also found that corporate—and presumably wealthier—defendants are assessed larger punitive awards than individual defendants (Eisenberg et al., 1997; Peterson, 1986). For example, Eisenberg et al. (1997) observed that individual plaintiffs who were awarded punitive damages in lawsuits against individual defendants received an average of $279,415, but individual plaintiffs who were awarded punitive damages in lawsuits against corporate defendants received an average of $817,230.[10] Thus, jurors do appear to be responding appropriately to defendants' wealth (or at least corporate status, as a proxy for wealth) in assessing punitive damages.[11]

CONCLUSION

On the whole, jurors appear to respond to characteristics of the defendant in a legally appropriate manner. In awarding punitive damages, they take into account the single most relevant factor: the defendant's wealth. When defendants behave in a manner that warrants a judgment of liability for punitive damages, relatively wealthy defendants are punished by having to pay more than less wealthy defendants.

No characteristics of the defendant are legally relevant to determining how much to award a plaintiff in compensation. To what extent do these factors nonetheless influence jurors' compensation decisions? Contrary to the widespread perception that there is a deep-pocket effect in awarding compensation, there is little reliable evidence to indicate that wealthier defendants are required to pay more for the same injury. With regard to defendants' identity, there is likewise little evidence to support the contention that malpractice defendants have to pay more than other types of defendants. Some evidence does suggest, however, that corporate defendants do have to pay more than individual defendants for causing similar injuries. The differential treatment of corporate and individual defendants appears to be due, at least in part, to the different attitudes that people hold toward businesses as opposed to individuals.

---

[10]The median awards were $25,000 and $70,225 for individual and corporate defendants, respectively, reflecting the considerable extent to which punitive damage awards are skewed by a small number of very large awards. It is also important to point out that although corporate defendants paid more in punitive damages than individual defendants when any punitive damages were awarded, they were no more likely to be held liable for punitive damages in the first place (Eisenberg et al., 1997).

[11]Although the vast majority of studies have found an effect of defendants' wealth on jurors' punitive damage awards, there are exceptions to the rule. For example, Landsman et al. (1998) did not find an effect of defendants' wealth on the punitive damage awards of either individual or deliberating mock jurors.

5

WHO ARE THE JURORS?

For a justice system to be perceived as fair, it must treat like cases similarly and unlike cases differently. A system that delivers disparate outcomes for similar cases fails to meet the first requirement, and a system that results in comparable punishments for incomparable acts fails to meet the second (Kahneman, Schkade, & Sunstein, 1998). Whether the U.S. system of civil justice delivers on either requirement is debatable, of course. In this chapter we attempt not to settle that debate but rather to focus on whether the characteristics that jurors bring with them into the courtroom —their backgrounds, experiences, and attitudes—serve as a source of potential injustice. More specifically, we focus on the role of jurors' characteristics in influencing their decisions about damage awards.

Jurors' backgrounds and their attitudes are considered extralegal factors in that they are independent of any evidence, legal rulings, or arguments presented in the courtroom. It is only by chance, of course, that a given juror (replete with a personal biography, complex belief system, and stories to tell) will end up in the jury selection process for a medical malpractice case rather than across the hall in an antitrust lawsuit. So, in a very simple sense, because jurors are assumed to make decisions on the basis of the evidence and the law set out before them and not on the basis of these extralegal cues, their characteristics, beliefs, and biases should theoretically be irrelevant to and independent of their judgments about damages.

In a practical sense, of course, this independence is not possible and perhaps not even desirable. It is not possible because these beliefs and experiences are woven into the fabric of one's existence, and everyone who walks through the courtroom doors will have his or her personal variant. One might argue that it is undesirable to have jurors making important decisions about income redistribution and injury compensation without access to their own life experiences and convictions and those of other people. Perhaps only by comparison can judgments about injury, loss, and reparation be made. So, the argument goes, the introduction of personal experiences and constructs into a jurors' decision-making process may not necessarily be a detriment to the pursuit of justice.

If, on the other hand, these singular experiences, attainments, and attitudes are so strongly represented in a prospective juror's thought processes that they effectively trump the evidence—if they are embraced so strongly that there is no room for the particular features of the evidence to matter—then we should be concerned. A miscarriage of justice will result if truly like cases are decided differently merely because of the features of the people doing the deciding.

What do we know about the role of jurors' characteristics in guiding decisions about damages in civil cases? Actually rather little is known—certainly less than is known about their influence in criminal cases. Information about the sorts of juror characteristics that influence verdicts in civil and criminal cases comes from three sources: (a) theories based on lawyers' experiences and speculation, (b) correlational research that relates verdicts in actual or simulated cases to personal characteristics of the jurors, and (c) simulated jury research that manipulates both juror and case characteristics to determine what effect jurors' backgrounds and dispositions have on their decisions (Olczak, Kaplan, & Penrod, 1991). Although we describe some of the work related to lawyers' speculations about which kinds of jurors are preferred and the results of some correlational studies, we believe that the most useful data stem from experimental research that uses jury simulation methodology. We describe this work later, but we begin by detailing what attorneys *think* about the kinds of jurors they select and the strategies they use to find jurors more favorably inclined toward their side. We also ponder the extent to which these beliefs are based on empirical data as opposed to oversimplified stereotypes. Where possible, we focus on jurors in civil cases, as opposed to criminal cases, and on juror factors related to determining damages rather than assessing liability.

ATTORNEYS' THEORIES ABOUT JURY SELECTION

Attorneys have many notions about the kinds of jurors who will be favorably inclined toward one side or another. Although we know more about their speculations vis-à-vis criminal cases than civil cases, some folklore surrounds jury selection in civil cases as well.

Much of this information is derived from trial practice manuals written by attorneys, typically on the basis of idiosyncratic experiences in court. Some of the advice is old. Among the suggestions are these: pensioners, the unemployed, and those on relief tend to be generous in awarding damages, whereas clergy, teachers, and lawyers are less so (White, 1952); women should be avoided by plaintiffs seeking large damages as they are not used to thinking in large sums (Biskind, 1954); and Jews and the Irish favor civil plaintiffs (Harrington & Dempsey, 1969). As Fulero and Penrod (1990) noted, however, these suggestions should not be summarily dismissed as outdated. Modern trial practice guides give similar recommendations. For example, Wagner (1989) advised against suburban housewives for civil plaintiffs, suggesting that they are conservative on damages. He also posited that African Americans, Jews, Italians, Hispanics, and others who have experienced oppression would be sympathetic to civil plaintiffs.

Do attorneys actively select (or rather, deselect) jurors on the basis of these characteristics? Apparently, yes they do. They use information about jurors' gender (Tate, Hawrish, & Clark, 1974), occupation (Padawer-Singer & Barton, 1975), race (Van Dyke, 1977), and appearance (Hayden, Senna, & Siegel, 1978) to make decisions about whom to reject from the panel.

We also know this from studies conducted by Olczak et al. (1991), who examined the kind of information that attorneys use in jury selection in criminal cases and how that information is combined to judge juror bias. Olczak et al. varied 11 juror characteristics (e.g., gender, age, marital status, nationality, political views) in 32 mock juror profiles. To determine the sort of information on which lawyers typically rely, researchers asked attorneys to rate the extent to which each profiled juror would be biased toward the defense (or prosecution). Surprisingly, attorneys emphasized one or two characteristics to the exclusion of others when forming judgments of bias. Results of a separate study showed that none of the juror characteristics typically used by the attorneys actually predicted juror voting, however (Olczak et al., 1991).

In a follow-up study, Olczak et al. (1991) assessed whether attorneys rely on different kinds of information than do naïve laypersons when determining bias during jury selection. Each prospective juror was described in terms of his or her occupation, recreational interests, and attitude toward women's roles (the case ostensibly concerned rape). Attorneys and college sophomores were shown to use simple and identical patterns of reliance on these juror characteristics, suggesting that trial lawyers tend to inject lay psychology and stereotypical thinking into the jury selection process.

Why do lawyers rely on such advice, contradictory and flimsy as it seems? Fulero and Penrod (1990) offered two suggestions. First, the theories offer simplicity and intuitive appeal; jurors' characteristics are easily discerned and can inform lawyers' opinions when no other information about the juror is available. Second, lawyers get limited feedback on the efficacy of their choices. Although they may find out how a chosen juror has voted, they almost never learn how a challenged juror would have reacted to their case. As a result, opportunities to refine their oversimplified theories are practically nonexistent.

IMPACT OF JUROR CHARACTERISTICS IN MOCK JURY RESEARCH

Mock jury studies of the effects of jurors' characteristics in criminal cases have shown that jurors' demographic characteristics are related to their verdicts only some of the time, and even then the relationships are weak and inconsistent (Feild, 1978; Fulero & Penrod, 1990; Penrod, 1990). Some researchers estimate that background or demographic characteristics of jurors in criminal cases account for only 10% of the variance in verdicts (Hastie, Penrod, & Pennington, 1983), although others suggest that they may account for 30% (Moran, Cutler, & Loftus, 1990). Jurors' dispositions do not show consistent patterns on verdicts across case type (Penrod, 1990).

We know that authoritarianism is the attitudinal variable most predictive of verdicts in criminal cases (Bray & Noble, 1978; Narby, Cutler, & Moran, 1993) and that locus-of-control beliefs influence the way that criminal jurors perceive the evidence (Phares & Wilson, 1972). We also know that these variables have only modest influence in most cases. Our knowledge of the role that these and other juror-related factors play in decisions about civil damages is, by contrast, less clear.

We suspect that certain differences between criminal and civil trials (e.g., the fact that the "victim" in a tort case stands to profit materially by the outcome) might alter the effects of jurors' characteristics in those settings. Thus, juror characteristics that seem to exert somewhat weak and inconsistent effects in criminal cases may or may not matter in civil damage cases.

In the remainder of this chapter we focus on how jurors' identities —their demographics as well as their attitudes and beliefs—actually influence their judgments concerning damages. We also assess how the relationship between juror and litigant might mediate that process.

ROLE OF DEMOGRAPHIC VARIABLES IN DAMAGES CASES

Demographic or background variables, such as age, gender, and race are apparently poor predictors of verdicts in criminal cases (Mills & Bohannan,

1980; Moran & Comfort, 1986). Is demographic information any more useful for predicting damage awards in civil cases? On the basis of some early data (Strodtbeck & Hawkins, 1957, cited in Zeisel & Diamond, 1976), Hastie (1991) suggested that because the issues related to damage award allocation are "homogeneous" (a statement with which we disagree), jury awards in personal injury cases may be relatively easy to predict from juror background characteristics. As we note in the next two paragraphs, Hastie's optimistic proclamation was probably unfounded. Demographic factors typically exert a weak and inconsistent influence in civil cases, as well.

Support for that contention comes from Penrod (1990), who examined the relation between jurors' demographic and attitudinal traits on the one hand and their verdicts in a civil negligence case on the other. Participants were 367 mock jurors who listened to an audiotaped negligence case (along with three criminal cases) and determined (a) the proportion of negligence attributable to the defendant, (b) the plaintiff's contributory negligence, and (c) the total amount of damages awarded. They also answered 12 questions related to their attitudes on a range of topics (e.g., "Should negligence plaintiffs be entitled to recover for pain and suffering?" "Do large damage awards encourage people to start lawsuits?") and 14 demographic questions. Unfortunately, Penrod reported only the analyses related to predictions of the percentage of attributed negligence;[1] he found that, when regressed onto negligence judgments, the demographic and attitudinal variables were able to explain only 10% of the variance in verdict preferences. These characteristics were, at best, mediocre predictors of jurors' sentiments.

More relevant to our concerns is a study conducted by Wissler, Hart, and Saks (1999) that assessed, among other things, the relationship between jury damage awards and jurors' sociodemographic attributes. Mock jurors in two jurisdictions were asked to evaluate various injury scenarios and to provide appropriate awards. Wissler et al. (1999) examined the extent to which demographic and experience attributes of jurors predicted awards for noneconomic damages. Interestingly, the sociodemographic characteristics (age, gender, income, education, rural vs. urban location) accounted for only 2% of the variance in awards. More important predictors of awards were jurors' perceptions of the disabilities and their ratings of mental suffering and disfigurement associated with the injuries.

We now look in more detail at the data on the relationship between jurors' demographic features and their damage awards. This work is based mostly on jury simulation methodology and focuses on the impact of jurors' income, political orientations, educational attainments, and gender on awards.

---

[1]Demographic factors may be more or less closely related to damage award determinations than to attributions of negligence. Penrod's data do not address this possibility.

Economic Status

Does jurors' economic status affect their assessments of damages? One might suspect that it does insofar as people's sentiments about the value of money are related to their own financial well-being. Vidmar and Rice (1993) compared the noneconomic damages awarded by jurors and senior attorneys in response to the same medical malpractice case involving a woman who underwent surgery to have a bunion removed from her foot. During surgery a hot surgical instrument was placed on the plaintiff's knee. Because the burn did not heal, she required a skin graft and endured significant physical and emotional pain. Vidmar and Rice examined the relationship between various juror demographic characteristics and the magnitude of their awards. Jurors' income level positively but modestly ($r = .20$) related to the damages awarded for noneconomic compensation: Higher income individuals awarded more. Wissler et al. (1999) also found that jurors with higher household incomes gave larger awards than those with less income.

Hastie, Schkade, and Payne (1998) showed that individual differences in jurors' income are related, if only weakly, to damage award judgments, but in the opposite direction from Vidmar and Rice's (1993) study. Hastie et al. (1998) investigated civil jury decisions concerning a defendant's liability for punitive damages in tort cases. One hundred twenty-one 6-member juries read summaries of previously decided cases and assessed liability for punitive damages. (The main objective of the study was to determine whether jurors could distinguish between negligent conduct and conduct that showed "reckless disregard.") Most juries determined that punitive damages were warranted although appellate and trial judges had concluded otherwise. Also, although other demographic variables were inconsequential, jurors' income was weakly related to their decisions ($r = -.10$): Higher income individuals were more likely to decide that the defendants were not liable for punitive damages.

Why is there a discrepancy between Hastie et al.'s (1998) finding and that of Vidmar and Rice (1993)? Recall that Hastie et al. (1998) measured the relationship between jurors' income and *liability for* punitive awards, whereas Vidmar and Rice assessed the relation between income and the *magnitude of awards* for noneconomic damages. One possibility is that there are fundamental differences in the ways that jurors think about noneconomic and punitive damages assessments; a second explanation is that the decision about whether to award damages is different from the decision about how much to award. Jurors at different levels of personal wealth apparently reason differently about these issues.

The results of an early study concluded that jurors' judgments regarding damages can be predicted on the basis of their income levels. Strodtbeck and Hawkins (1957, cited in Zeisel & Diamond, 1976) had attorneys make judgments about juror verdict preferences in personal injury cases. Both plaintiff and defense attorneys accurately predicted the awards of prospective jurors on the basis of jurors' income and occupation. (This study differs from the others, of course, because it assessed whether attorneys are good judges of prospective jurors' judgments and not whether the absolute level of a juror's income influences his or her preferred award.) Finally, some studies have found no relationship between income level and size of the award (e.g., Bornstein & Rajki, 1994; Vidmar, 1993). Taken together, these studies suggest that there is probably little systematic relationship between civil jurors' income or economic status and the magnitude of their damage awards.

Political Orientation

We could find only one study that assessed the role of political beliefs in damage award decision making. Hastie, Schkade, and Payne (1999) showed a videotaped environmental damage lawsuit to mock jurors who were asked to assign a punitive damage award. The researchers determined that Republican mock jurors gave somewhat lower punitive awards than mock jurors who had more liberal political beliefs, although political orientation was not a statistically significant predictor of jurors' verdicts. It stands to reason that individuals with conservative political beliefs would align themselves with the defendant in this case: a large corporation. In general, we suspect that the effects of jurors' political beliefs on the process of damages determinations is highly case specific.

Education

Jurors' educational attainments also have no consistent effect on the magnitude of assessed damages. In one simulation study, Vidmar (1993) varied two factors central to the deep-pockets hypothesis: (a) the cause of an accident in which a young woman suffered a broken leg (either medical negligence or an automobile accident) and (b) the number and type of defendants (either one defendant, two defendants, or a corporation). Jurors were asked to award damages for pain and suffering. Vidmar (1993) found that jurors who were better educated tended to give smaller awards ($r = -.20$).

However, in Vidmar and Rice's (1993) study, described earlier, better educated jurors tended to give larger awards ($r = .28$). This finding is supported by work done by Goodman, Loftus, and Greene (1990) that showed that the amount awarded in damages increases as jurors' education level increases.

To complicate matters further, another study (Bornstein & Rajki, 1994) showed that jurors' education levels have no effect on the amounts of compensatory damages they award. (This study varied the source of a plaintiff's ovarian cancer in a products liability case; it was attributed either to an ink used in her calligraphy work, to birth control pills, or to a chemical from a nearby dump that had leached into the local water supply.) The impact of education on assessments of damages may also be case specific; however, no discernible relationship between education level and damages level is apparent from these studies.

Gender

Of the demographic variables that have been studied in this context, the issue of jurors' gender has drawn the most attention. Again, the findings are not consistent. Some studies (e.g., Goodman, Loftus, Miller, & Greene, 1991; Hastie et al., 1999; Nagel & Weitzman, 1972; Snyder, 1970; Wissler et al., 1999) suggest that women give lower awards. For example, Hastie et al. (1999) investigated the manner in which civil jurors assess punitive damages in an environmental lawsuit. They told mock jurors that the defendant had already been found liable for compensatory damages and asked them to award punitive damages. The awards from men were significantly higher than the awards from women.

Snyder (1970) examined the magnitude of damages awarded by actual juries in personal injury cases that came to trial in South Carolina in 1966 and 1968. Because women were not permitted to serve on juries in 1966, Snyder was able to compare awards from all-male juries of 1966 and mixed-gender juries of 1968. Although the data are somewhat difficult to interpret, because the average amount sought by plaintiffs in 1966 was less than the amount requested in 1968, still the results are dramatic: Male-only juries awarded approximately 52% of the damages requested by plaintiffs, whereas mixed-gender juries awarded only 20% of the amount requested.[2]

A study conducted by Kahneman et al. (1998) gives the opposite result, however. Mock jurors read of set of vignettes of personal injury cases in which the plaintiff sued a firm for compensatory and punitive damages. The wealth of the defendant and the degree of harm suffered by the plaintiff were varied across 10 cases (involving an employee who suffered anemia due to benzene exposure on the job, a motorcycle driver who was injured when his brakes failed, a circus patron who was shot in the arm by a drunken security guard, a disabled man who was injured when a wheelchair lift malfunctioned, and so on). In all cases, jurors were informed that the plaintiffs had been awarded $200,000 in compensatory damages and that their task was to assess punitive damages. Despite the fact that men and women rated the defendant's behavior as equally outrageous, female jurors assessed higher punitive damages than did male jurors.

---

[2]It is unclear whether these data derive from all cases tried to juries or only those cases in which the plaintiff prevailed on liability.

Several other studies that have examined the effects of jurors' gender suggest that it might not matter at all (e.g., Bornstein & Rajki, 1994; Greene, Goodman, & Loftus, 1991; Vidmar, 1993; Vidmar & Rice, 1993). For example, Fishfader and colleagues (Fishfader, Howells, Katz, & Teresi, 1996) assessed whether video re-creations of an accident scene would affect jurors' decisions about liability and damages. They found that although jurors who saw videotaped re-enactments of a drowning scene experienced greater emotional reactions than those who read transcripts, there were no significant differences in awards as a function of gender (or as a function of reported emotional distress).

In light of these findings on jurors' background characteristics, we now reassess Hastie's (1991) suggestion that demographic factors may be reliable determinants of jury damage awards (at least in personal injury cases). Apparently this is not the case. If they matter at all, individual demographic differences exert a small and inconsistent influence on award values and probably account for a tiny fraction of the variance in assessed damages. Even then, the effect is likely to be case specific. Jurors' decisions about compensation—like their judgments of a criminal defendant's guilt—apparently cross gender, political, and economic lines.

Perhaps the most compelling recent demonstration of the noninfluence of demographic factors comes from a large-scale jury simulation study that measured individual differences among mock jurors who watched a taped products liability trial (Diamond, Saks, & Landsman, 1998). The researchers assessed the ability of a variety of individual-difference variables (e.g., age, gender, race, politics, education, income, prior jury service) to predict awards for economic losses as well as for pain and suffering. The considerable variation in awards could not be explained by any of these demographic predictors. The strongest predictors of jurors' damage awards were characteristics of the case rather than attributes of the particular jurors who decided that case.

Should this lack of predictability be cause for concern? Saks (1998) said it is not, and we agree. Like Saks, we deem the lack of variation in awards attributable to juror characteristics a good thing, because it means that jurors are making damage awards on the basis of attributes of the case and not on the basis of their personal idiosyncrasies.

We turn now to another question: Does similarity between the juror and the litigant have any effect on decisions about damages?

ROLE OF JUROR–LITIGANT SIMILARITY

Many jury observers have maintained that the effects of jurors' characteristics cannot be understood in isolation and that features of other actors in the courtroom drama—primarily the litigants themselves—must also be considered (Hans, 1992; Hans & Vidmar, 1986). For example, some data suggest that jurors favor plaintiffs of their own gender (Stephan, 1974, 1975). Nagel and Weitzman's (1972) study of data from jury verdict reporters showed that disparities in treatment of male and female litigants may be related to the gender of the decision maker: The awards from male-dominated juries were 12% above average for the type of injury, medical expenses, and lost wages when the plaintiff was male and 17% below average when the plaintiff was female. The pattern is nearly reversed for female-dominated juries: Their awards were only 3% above average when the plaintiff was male but 17% above average when the plaintiff was female.

Social psychologists have a ready explanation for this finding. As noted by Norbert Kerr and his colleagues in the context of criminal cases (Kerr, Hymes, Anderson, & Weathers, 1995), a well-liked defendant will receive more lenient treatment from jurors than one who is disliked; this is called the *liking–leniency effect* (Davis, Bray, & Holt, 1977). Another well-grounded tenet of social psychology is that people like those who are similar to themselves; this is called the *liking–similarity effect* (Byrne, Clore, & Smeaton, 1986). A coupling of these principles leads to the hypothesis that the more similar the juror and the defendant, the more lenient the juror is likely to be. This is the *similarity–leniency* hypothesis, which, in the context of civil damages cases, may result in more lucrative awards to plaintiffs who are similar to the jurors. Indeed, plaintiffs' attorneys often attempt to select jurors who are similar in some ways to their clients.

But one should not make assumptions quite so fast. There may be serious flaws in the similarity–leniency hypothesis, particularly as applied to civil damage cases, because similarity can sometimes lead to harsher, rather than more lenient, treatment (Kerr et al., 1995). Why?

People tend to view similar others more positively than those who are different because such favorability maintains or even raises one's own sense of self-esteem. We feel better about ourselves if we are like people whom we view positively. However, because we tend to view similar others (our in-group) positively, we also tend to derogate unlikable or deviant in-group members who pose a threat to the positive image of our in-group. Marques and Yzerbyt (1988) termed this negative view of in-group members the *black sheep effect*: Positively valued in-group members are viewed more favorably than out-group members, but negatively valued in-group members are viewed less favorably than out-group members.

In a case involving civil damages, jurors may derogate a plaintiff who is ostensibly like them, because that plaintiff may threaten jurors' positive views of themselves. For example, older jurors may be unwilling to seriously consider an elderly plaintiff's request for damages in an automobile negligence case if there are hints that the injuries were related to the plaintiff's own conduct behind the wheel. Older jurors may not be willing to acknowledge concerns about their own driving abilities.

Another body of research supports the notion that similarity between juror and litigant can lead to harsher, rather than more lenient, treatment. People use similarly situated individuals as a primary source of social comparison, but when one senses that such similarity to others carries negative implications about oneself, one may attempt to dissociate oneself from those persons (Taylor & Mettee, 1971). This process also may involve derogating those individuals or evaluating them in a negative way.

Thus, several lines of social psychological theorizing lead to the conclusion that the relationship between juror and litigant may indeed matter. Although we have little data to corroborate the notion that similarity between plaintiff and juror influences damages decisions, the idea that similarity between plaintiff and juror begets largess in damage determinations (or the converse: that similarity between defendant and juror will result in diminished awards) is overly simplistic.

ROLE OF ATTITUDINAL FACTORS

If demographic factors have an inconsistent relationship to jury awards, and if the extent to which juror–litigant similarity matters is unclear, then one must ask whether other factors might be better predictors of jury awards. Some studies have concluded that an individual's attitudes, beliefs, and personality characteristics may account for a small but significant amount of the variance in criminal jury verdicts (Bray & Noble, 1978; Narby et al., 1993; Phares & Wilson, 1972). Indeed, jury simulation research has indicated that certain personality attributes of mock jurors, such as authoritarianism, belief in a just world, and locus of control, may be related to criminal jury verdicts. What role do these factors play in civil damage cases?

Perceptions and attitudes about the so-called *litigation crisis* affect judgments regarding damages. Hans and Lofquist (1994) explored the influence of beliefs about the tort litigation system on jurors' judgments in cases involving business and corporate defendants. They interviewed 269 jurors who had served on 36 cases and asked questions related to the legitimacy of civil lawsuits, the size of damage awards, and other litigation-related questions (collectively referred to as *litigation crisis attitudes*). They also asked jurors to answer a number of attitudinal scales (e.g., regarding authoritarianism, belief in a just world, political efficacy) to assess the relationship between these well-studied attitudinal variables and the less well-known beliefs about civil litigation.

According to these jurors, the civil justice system is in trouble. Approximately four fifths of them agreed that "There are far too many frivolous lawsuits today" and that "People are too quick to sue, rather than trying to solve disputes in some other way." More people agreed than disagreed that jury damage awards are too high.

Authoritarianism was not related to these concerns about a litigation crisis, however, leading Hans and Lofquist (1994) to suggest that civil and criminal litigants must be evaluated differently by authoritarian persons. Several contextual differences may explain this finding. Parties to a civil lawsuit are not as strongly associated with deviance as criminal defendants, and most civil cases do not involve the government and its considerable powers of authority.

Concerns about a litigation crisis *were* related to beliefs in a just world: Jurors who believed in a just and predictable world in which people get what they deserve tended to discount concerns about a litigation crisis and expressed less worry about the number of seemingly illegitimate lawsuits. Jurors who endorsed the idea of a just world tended to express more faith in the existing tort litigation system.

As Hans and Lofquist (1994) pointed out, the correlations between litigation crisis attitudes and other variables were quite modest, and these scores were unrelated to education or income, suggesting that concerns about the legitimacy of the civil litigation system are apparent in all sectors of society. According to these authors, belief that the litigation system is in crisis is a shared cultural truism: "Concern about others seeking compensation for minor, contrived, or self-inflicted injuries and getting something for nothing appears to be a collectively shared feature of our individualistic culture rather than the province of any particular social group" (Hans & Lofquist, 1994, p. 193).

Hans and Lofquist (1992) also had a subset of jurors (141 who served in 1 of 18 tort cases) answer questions about their attitudes toward business and corporate responsibility. Despite their insistence on product safety and the high expectations they hold of corporations, jurors were more favorably inclined toward business defendants than toward plaintiffs. They were generally skeptical of the profit motives of individual plaintiffs and expressed the desire to hold down large jury awards. In a study that assessed whether jurors exhibit judgmental biases in their attributional analyses of civil disputants, Lupfer, Cohen, Bernard, and Smalley (1985) also found evidence of an antiplaintiff bias.

What role do litigation crisis attitudes play in the deliberation room? Are damages assessments derived from these belief systems? The answer apparently, and not surprisingly, is yes. Hans and Lofquist (1992) computed the mean attitudinal scale judgment for each jury separately and then correlated these mean judgments with the final jury award. They found that these litigation crisis attitudes were negatively correlated with the verdicts rendered by jurors in the cases they heard ($r = -.54$): The more strongly jurors perceived a litigation crisis, the lower the jury award. The authors concluded that concerns about a litigation crisis can affect decisions in civil cases by shaping views of the legitimacy of injured plaintiffs and of the society-wide consequences of large jury awards.

Although the data are not entirely consistent,[3] several studies converge on the notion that attitudes about the civil litigation system affect the magnitude of damage awards. Hastie et al. (1999) found that mock jurors who endorsed the statements "Lawyers ask much more in damages than is warranted" and "There are too many lawsuits in this country" gave lower punitive damage awards. Astolfo (1991) found that residents of Miami, Florida, who favored tort reform also recommended lower compensatory damages than did residents who were less favorable toward tort reform. Goodman et al. (1990) found that attitudes toward monetary damages and their effects on insurance rates were more reliable predictors of jury awards than were demographic factors.

Greene et al. (1991) reached a similar conclusion about the role of attitudinal factors. They evaluated the relationship between jurors' beliefs about tort reform and their decisions in a mock personal injury lawsuit. Greene et al. (1991) wondered whether jurors who believed in the existence of a litigation explosion would attempt to contain costs by awarding less to the plaintiffs who appeared in cases before them.

Mock jurors read the facts of one of several types of wrongful-death cases in which the plaintiff had previously proven the defendant's liability. They decided on a compensatory damage award and answered several questions related to their beliefs about the tort litigation system.[4] Greene et al. (1991) recoded and combined jurors' responses to these attitudinal statements so that responses generally favoring tort reform had lower numbers. They found a positive correlation ($r = .20$) between jurors' attitude scores and their damage awards: Jurors who favored tort reforms gave lower awards.

Greene et al. (1991) also found a significant correlation between jurors' estimates of the number of plaintiffs who receive large awards and their own damage awards in the mock wrongful-death case. The greater the presumed frequency of plaintiffs who receive million-dollar damage awards (in actuality, a rare event), the larger the damage award in the mock trial. In other words, rather than attempting to counteract the trend toward large verdicts by issuing a relatively small award, jurors' decisions were apparently influenced by their beliefs about the incidence of large

---

[3]For example, Vidmar (1993) found that the extent to which mock jurors endorsed beliefs such as "Too many people file lawsuits in hopes of making a fast buck" and "Medical doctors are sued too often" was unrelated to the size of their award.

[4]Some examples include "No one deserves more than a million dollars in damages"; "There are too many lawsuits"; "The insurance industry is not experiencing a crisis because of large jury awards"; and "I would use the amount the lawyers suggest as a starting point, then add more to arrive at a reasonable amount."

awards. Jurors who believed that million-dollar awards were common tended to award more, not less.

ROLE OF PRIOR EXPECTATIONS

The schemas one holds about accidents, lawsuits, and compensation affect one's processing of information related to those issues (Finkel, 1995; A. J. Hart, Evans, Wissler, Feehan, & Saks, 1997). More specifically, in translating their perceptions of injuries into monetary values, people rely —at least to some extent—on their prior knowledge and beliefs. Why? In part this is because the law provides so little guidance to jurors about how damages decisions—particularly for noneconomic injuries—are to be assessed. In the absence of clear guidelines, people fall back on their personal experiences and belief systems to help them determine appropriate compensation for pain, suffering, and lost enjoyment of life.

People's theories and expectations about the cause, or likely cause, of an injury can also affect their perceptions of the injuries and of the monies necessary to compensate someone who sustained that harm. For example, in products liability cases, jurors' verdicts may be affected by intuitions about what types of substances or events (collectively referred to as *sources*) are likely to cause certain kinds of injury. People might naively assume, in the absence of scientific evidence, that cancer is less likely to be caused by an ingested substance, such as medication, than by an environmental contaminant, such as toxic waste. Kraus, Malmfors, and Slovic (1992) found that people tend to share intuitions about what sources pose the greatest risk of causing various diseases. Given those naïve assumptions, and the general effect of prior expectations of jurors' judgments, it follows that jurors will rely on their intuitions where the cause of an injury and compensation for that injury are at issue.

Bornstein and Rajki (1994) asked whether mock jurors' judgments about compensation would be influenced by their intuitions about what types of sources cause a certain kind of injury. We describe this work in detail in chapter 6, but the findings are generally that mock jurors' naïve intuitions about the likely cause of cancer may play a role in their compensation judgments. Jurors awarded money when the alleged source of an illness corresponded to their notions about what typically causes that disease.

Some interesting work has assessed the role that jurors' schemas play in damages determinations. Allan Hart and his colleagues (Hart et al., 1997) asked whether people have schemas for various injury-causing situations and for the injuries that are likely to result from these situations. They also wondered whether these schemas affect jurors' awards for noneconomic damages. That work, which we also detail in chapter 6, showed that people apparently do have well-defined schemas or expectations about what typically happens in various accident situations. Furthermore, mock jurors awarded larger and more variable noneconomic damages for accidents that resulted in atypical, rather than typical, injuries. Thus, noneconomic damages for pain and suffering and loss of enjoyment of life are apparently affected by people's prior expectations and in particular by whether the circumstances of the injury match the schema that people hold for injury-causing situations.

CONCLUSION

What role do jurors' personal characteristics—their backgrounds, experiences, and beliefs—play in their decisions about damage awards? Although few studies have set out to address this issue directly, several have attempted to quantify personal information about jurors and correlate this information with the resultant jury (or juror) awards. From these studies, we have learned that demographic characteristics such as gender, educational attainments, and economic status are apparently not strongly related to jurors' judgments about compensation. As in criminal cases, jurors' demographic characteristics seem not to matter, or at least do not matter much. This finding challenges the notion espoused by trial lawyers that certain kinds of jurors (e.g., women or people of color) will be more or less responsive to their arguments.

The similarity between juror and litigant may influence damage award decisions, but this relationship is not straightforward and has not been well researched. As we have suggested, jurors may be more sympathetic toward litigants who are like them, but only if their sense of self-esteem and positive self-regard are not threatened by their resemblance to that litigant. If it is, then jurors may be less sympathetic to someone they perceive to be similar to themselves. The litigant will have fallen from grace. We await empirical data to test these theories.

Although trial lawyers often try to find jurors who match their clients on certain theoretically desirable traits, still it is virtually impossible to predict whether a particular juror's sense of self-esteem will be threatened or enhanced by exposure to this person and whether the resulting damage award will be augmented or reduced as a result. Certainly, any attempt to find and seat jurors who are like the parties to the lawsuit oversimplifies the juror–litigant relationship.

So far we have shown that neither the background characteristics of jurors nor their similarity to the litigants are particularly good predictors of their assessments of damage awards. Are their attitudes more closely related to these decisions? Yes and no. Those clusters of attitudes that best predict decisions about guilt and innocence in criminal cases (e.g., locus of control, authoritarianism) seem to matter little when the context is a civil case and the required decisions are whether the plaintiff should be awarded damages and in what amount.

What does seem to matter, however, are jurors' more specific beliefs about the system of tort litigation. So, for example, jurors' attitudes about others' propensity to sue, their beliefs about the frequency of large damage awards, and their desires for tort reform do apparently correlate with their judgments on damages. This finding fits nicely with Fishbein and Ajzen's (1975) theory of reasoned action which, stated simply, suggests that a person's behavior (in this case, concerning the decision to award damages and the amount) can be predicted from his or her intention which is, in turn, a function of attitudes toward the behavior. Specific attitudes predict specific behaviors. Specific attitudes about the tort litigation system correlate with the magnitude of damage awards.

Why might this be so? To the extent that a particular attitude involves a person's self-interest, people are more likely to act on it (Sivacek & Crano, 1982). This finding explains why people who have concerns about the litigiousness of U.S. society (and, in particular, about the likelihood that they would be sued and about their escalating insurance rates) will be likely to act on those beliefs by holding down awards in cases they decide. In general, beliefs and cognitions that have implications for one's life predict behaviors better than beliefs that are not personally relevant (e.g., Morrison, 1989).

It is interesting that many beliefs about the tort litigation system are undoubtedly misguided. As we noted in chapter 1, Bailis and MacCoun's (1996) content analysis of coverage of civil litigation issues by the popular media showed that, compared with objective data, the media overrepresented the relative frequency of certain controversial forms of litigation, the proportion of disputes resolved at trial (rather than by settlement), plaintiffs' win rates, and the size of the typical jury award. It is ironic, then, that to the extent that jurors rely on these sources to provide information about the tort litigation system, their own judgments concerning damages will be based on misinformation and mistaken impressions.

The relationship between attitudes on issues related to damage awards and jurors' and juries' actual decisions concerning award amounts needs further clarification. This process might examine, for example, which specific (perhaps erroneous) beliefs are most likely to be related to the decisions concerning damages and in which situations jurors' belief systems are likely to moderate their judgments on damages. With this knowledge, we will have come several steps closer to understanding how a person's unique set of beliefs, priorities, and objectives influence his or her thoughts about who gets how much and why.

II

THE EVIDENCE:
HOW INJURY SEVERITY AND
LITIGANTS' CONDUCT
INFLUENCE DAMAGE
AWARD DECISIONS

INTRODUCTION

THE EVIDENCE:
HOW INJURY SEVERITY AND
LITIGANTS' CONDUCT
INFLUENCE DAMAGE
AWARD DECISIONS

In the preceding three chapters we examined the influence on damage awards of extralegal factors, namely, characteristics of the plaintiff, the defendant, and the juror. In a world free of decisional bias—a normative utopia, perhaps—none of these factors would matter in terms of damage awards. Jurors would arrive at the courthouse as blank slates, waiting to be filled with evidence, and neither the identity of the plaintiff nor the identity of the defendant would dent their resolve to deliver justice in a neutral, unbiased fashion. However, jurors are human and, as we know, humans are non-normative (D. E. Bell, Raiffa, & Tversky, 1988; Tversky & Kahneman, 1974), so it is of little surprise that the identities of the players in these courtroom dramas *do* matter, if only a little.

In truth, though (as we discussed in the previous section), they matter less than the evidence itself. In the next two chapters we take a look at how the evidence that comes out during trial affects jurors' decisions about awards. We look in detail at the effects of two broad categories of evidence relevant to damage awards: (a) evidence concerning the severity and nature of the plaintiff's injuries (chapter 6)—arguably the single most important determinant of jury damage awards—and (b) evidence concerning the conduct of the litigants (chapter 7).

In terms of the injury, we consider how jurors use evidence of injury severity when assessing total compensation, pain and suffering awards, and punitive damages. We also contemplate whether there are ways to quantify the inherently unquantifiable; that is, whether jurors' decisions concerning damages for pain and suffering could be guided by various structural features incorporated into the trial. We also consider how the nature of the injury—its cause and timing—affects judgments of damages.

In terms of the litigants' conduct, we describe the twin influences of plaintiff and defendant misconduct on compensatory and punitive awards, respectively. In many negligence cases, the defendant is not the only one presumptively at fault; the plaintiff may also have played a role in causing the misfortune at hand. (This is a very common occurrence in automobile negligence cases, for example.) So it is appropriate to ask what use jurors make of evidence regarding the plaintiff's behavior as well as that of the defendant.

A theme that pervades these discussions is the half-empty versus half-full metaphor. To hint at our findings, there is a great deal of evidence that the glass is half-full: that jurors generally attend to and are influenced by evidence on which they *should* rely in making these decisions. The most obvious example is their reliance on evidence regarding the severity of the plaintiff's injury. Across a wide array of case types and varying methodologies, jurors have been shown to heed the evidence of injury severity; it is the single best predictor of compensatory damage awards. There is more good news: Jurors consider evidence of the plaintiff's disability and mental suffering when assigning damages for pain and suffering; injuries that do not result in long-lasting suffering or disability lead to lower awards. With respect to the litigants' conduct, highly reprehensible conduct on the part of defendants apparently influences jurors' judgments of punitive damages but not compensatory damages. Also, as seems reasonable, expressions of remorse on the part of a defendant can apparently reduce the size of the award assessed against him or her.

However, the glass is also half-empty in the sense that, on occasion, jurors attend to, and use, evidence in ways not intended. We have learned, for example, that the damages awarded to partially negligent plaintiffs are probably not as large as they should be, because jurors award less when the plaintiff is more blameworthy, even though the judge typically instructs them to assess the full damages proven by the evidence.

Another example of this misuse of evidence concerns the possibility that jurors misapply evidence of the defendant's conduct in assessing compensatory damages. (The defendant's behavior is, of course, highly relevant to liability decisions and to the awarding of punitive damages, but not to the amount of compensatory damages.) Another finding is that jurors who hear about the defendant's errant ways may give higher awards because this evidence makes the plaintiff's injuries seem worse.

Thus, jurors' use of evidence in their decisions regarding damages, although often correct or at least defensible, may nonetheless veer from legal dictates on occasion. Again, one can ask why. We speculate that some of the apparent missteps may actually be intentional, as jurors attempt to deliver their own personal variants on justice when they assess the size of damage awards. Indeed, jurors may have multiple, complementary motives for awarding damages: giving each party what it deserves, doing what seems fair even if that means ignoring the legal rules, and using the evidence for broader purposes than it was intended. On other occasions, of course, jurors may simply get it wrong. In the next two chapters we discuss these possibilities and some more general findings regarding jurors' use of evidence in judgments of damage awards.

6

SEVERITY AND NATURE OF
THE INJURY

A necessary feature of all tort cases is that someone has, at least allegedly, been injured.[1] Thus, an important variable in the constellation of factors that may vary across these cases is the extent of the plaintiff's injury. Two acts may be identical in every way except for their consequences. Imagine, for instance, unrelated incidents in which two cars run separate red lights and hit two other cars. Both "offending" cars could have the same speed, point of impact, driver's mental state, and use of seat belts, but the occupants of the cars that are hit—subsequently the plaintiffs— might suffer vastly different consequences. One might have merely superficial cuts and bruises, whereas the other could be paralyzed or killed.

Injury severity is of special interest in the trial context because it is often normatively relevant to some judgments that jurors are asked to make but not to others. Specifically, it is directly relevant to the amount of compensatory damages, as a plaintiff who has been hurt worse requires more in the way of compensation; but it is not relevant to determining punitive damages, which should be influenced instead by the reprehensibility of the defendant's conduct (Cather, Greene, & Durham, 1996). Conversely, punitive—but not compensatory—damages should be affected by

---

[1]As we noted in chapter 1, one may also make a tort claim for property damage, but we limit our discussion to personal injury claims, including physical and emotional damage.

whether the defendant deliberately or maliciously rammed into the plaintiff's car. Likewise, injury severity is not normatively relevant to the defendant's liability for the act itself. Factual matters under dispute that speak to liability, such as the color of the traffic light or whether the plaintiff's car was sticking too far out into the intersection, are independent of what happened to the plaintiff after the car was hit. (We consider jurors' fusing of liability evidence and damages evidence in detail in chapter 7.)

Psychological research on attribution of responsibility has addressed the issue of the severity of an action's consequences (Burger, 1981; Robbennolt, 2000). For example, Walster (1966) asked participants to rate a young man's responsibility for an automobile accident in which his unoccupied car rolled down a hill. The accident's consequences varied in severity, ranging from minor damage to the car to badly injuring a bystander. Participants attributed greater responsibility for the accident to the car's owner as the accident's consequences became more severe. This tendency for worse outcomes to elicit greater attributions of responsibility has been replicated across a wide variety of experimental situations (Burger, 1981; Feigenson, 2000; Robbennolt, 2000).

On the basis of these findings, one might predict that a civil defendant is more likely to be found liable when factors that increase attributions of responsibility, such as relatively severe outcomes, are present. However, the applicability of these findings to personal injury trials is limited (Robbennolt, 2000). Although the accident situations described in the attribution literature (e.g., Walster, 1966) are similar to those one might find in a legal personal injury context, they are typically not presented within a simulated trial framework. Study participants make responsibility attributions by assigning numerical ratings, but they are not instructed on how those ratings might correspond to a definition of legal liability and be used in reaching a verdict. The general sense of "responsibility" and its legal usage are clearly related (Fincham & Jaspars, 1980), but they are not the same (see H. L. A. Hart & Honore, 1985; Robbennolt, 2000). Most important is that participants in attribution studies typically do not award damages, which are a central concern in civil trials. Thus, it is difficult to extrapolate from findings on the general phenomenon of responsibility attribution to a trial situation involving specific criteria for jurors' verdicts.

Consistent with the attribution literature, several researchers have found that injury severity inappropriately affects mock jurors' liability judgments as well (e.g., Bornstein, 1998; Feigenson, Park, & Salovey, 1997, 2001; Greene, Johns, & Bowman, 1999; Robbennolt, 2000). This extralegal effect of severity on liability judgments appears to be mediated by participants' feelings toward the parties involved in the case. Compared with plaintiffs with relatively mild injuries, plaintiffs who are hurt worse arouse greater feelings of sympathy and sadness in jurors; whereas defendants who allegedly cause more severe injuries are less sympathetic and arouse more anxiety and anger (Bornstein, 1998; Feigenson et al., 1997). It is interesting that such feelings do not mediate the effect of severity on compensation, which operates more directly.

In this chapter we address two aspects of the injury that might affect jurors' damage awards: (a) the severity of the injury and (b) the nature of the injury itself.

INJURY SEVERITY

Because the severity of the plaintiff's injury should legitimately affect some of jurors' judgments (e.g., the amount of money awarded as compensation) but not others (e.g., the amount of money extracted from the defendant as punishment), we divide this section according to judgments about compensatory and punitive damages. We ask how and why the severity of the injury influences these judgments. Because compensation awards for noneconomic damages are especially controversial (e.g., Baldus, MacQueen, & Woodworth, 1995; Calfee & Rubin, 1992; Priest, 1987), we examine the effect of severity both for total compensation and for the separate, noneconomic component of compensation.

Total Compensation

The main goal of tort law is compensation for the injury, so jurors who award more money to more severely injured plaintiffs—once liability has been established—are behaving in a normative, legally appropriate manner. A number of archival studies have found that jurors do behave equitably in this respect: More severely injured plaintiffs receive greater compensation than less severely injured plaintiffs, across the tort system as a whole (Bovbjerg, Sloan, Dor, & Hsieh, 1991; Chin & Peterson, 1985; Rodriguez & Bogett, 1989) and within subdomains, such as products liability (Bordens & Horowitz, 1998; Rodgers, 1991; Viscusi, 1986, 1988), personal injury (Bovbjerg, Sloan, & Blumstein, 1989), and medical malpractice (Bovbjerg et al., 1991; Danzon, 1985; Sloan & Hsieh, 1990; Taragin, Willet, Wilczek, Trout, & Carson, 1992; Vidmar, 1995; Vidmar, Gross, & Rose, 1998).

Injury severity has been found to correlate positively with total compensation awards in simulation studies as well (e.g., Darden, DeConinck, Babin, & Griffin, 1991; Feigenson et al., 1997, 2001; ForsterLee, Horowitz, Athaide-Victor, & Brown, 2000; Horowitz, ForsterLee, & Brolly, 1996). Like the archival studies, these experiments have found an effect of severity across a wide range of case types, including home and workplace accidents (Feigenson et al., 2001), train and automobile accidents (Feigenson et al., 1997; Greene, Johns, & Smith, 2001), medical malpractice (Feigenson et al., 1997), toxic torts (ForsterLee et al., 2000; Horowitz et al., 1996), and products liability (Bornstein, 1998; Darden et al., 1991). There is some evidence that the effect of severity may depend somewhat on case type (Cather et al., 1996), the manner of presenting expert testimony (ForsterLee et al., 2000), and the timing of the judge's substantive instructions (Bourgeois, Horowitz, ForsterLee, & Grahe, 1995). However, if one considers all of these studies, both archival and experimental, as a whole, one observes that the severity of plaintiffs' injury is by far the single best predictor of plaintiffs' compensation award (Robbennolt, 2000).

For example, Bovbjerg et al. (1991) analyzed jury verdicts from 1980 to 1985 in five jurisdictions. They included several different types of cases: malpractice, products liability, suits against governments, and automotive liability. For each case, the plaintiff's injury was rated on a 6-point severity scale that ranged from minor injury to death. In general, more severe injuries received larger awards, regardless of case type. Thus, there is *vertical* equity in compensation awards, in the sense that as injuries go up in severity, awards increase accordingly. It is interesting, however, that plaintiffs with the most severe injuries—death—received less compensation than the most severely injured plaintiffs who survived their injuries (e.g., paralysis). This trend for compensation to increase with severity, but to dip at death, has been replicated elsewhere (Bovbjerg et al., 1989; Sloan & Hsieh, 1990; Sloan & van Wert, 1991; Vidmar et al., 1998).

As death is arguably the most extreme consequence of tortious activity, why should it be compensated less than milder injuries that the plaintiff survives? The answer likely has to do with the specific components of compensation awards. As we described in chapter 1, compensation is typically divided into economic and noneconomic damages. The former category includes costs such as medical expenses and lost wage earnings, whereas the latter category—frequently referred to as *pain and suffering* (which we discuss in greater detail later in this chapter)—includes costs that are harder to quantify, such as loss of enjoyment of life, mental anguish, disability, and disfigurement. Some of these specific costs may be greater if the plaintiff dies as the result of severe injuries than if the plaintiff survives, whereas other costs may be lower.

Consider the following hypothetical case: Joe Plaintiff is sitting in his car, stopped at a red light; Stuart Defendant negligently runs the light and crashes into Plaintiff's car. Plaintiff sues Defendant to recover damages for his injuries, and Defendant is found liable. Now consider two alternative scenarios: Plaintiff either dies in the accident or survives but remains a quadriplegic. In the latter situation, he is permanently disabled and unable to return to work. What are Plaintiff's economic and noneconomic losses? Table 6.1 offers a hypothetical comparison.

Plaintiff's medical costs are clearly greater if he survives; depending on his age at the time of the accident, the complications and expenses

TABLE 6.1
Hypothetical Costs for Death vs. Quadriplegia

Type of damages	Deceased Plaintiff A	Quadriplegic Plaintiff B	Who deserves more compensation, and how much more?
Economic			
Medical costs	Lifesaving, funeral expenses	Lifesaving, lifelong maintenance	B, a lot
Future earnings	Will have none	Will have little if any	A, slightly
Noneconomic			
Disability	Total, permanent	Severe but not total	A, a lot
Lost enjoyment	Total, permanent but without awareness	Severe but not total, and with awareness	B, slightly
Mental anguish	Extreme but short	Extreme, prolonged	B, a lot
Disfigurement	Extreme but short	Extreme, prolonged	B, a lot

pursuant to quadriplegia can easily run to millions of dollars. The deceased plaintiff deserves compensation for any lifesaving medical efforts and funeral expenses, but these costs will be significantly less than for the surviving plaintiff. Future earnings are a bit trickier: The deceased plaintiff will have none, and his spouse is therefore entitled to full compensation, although most courts require first deducting the decedent's own future consumption had he survived (Bovbjerg et al., 1989).[2] The surviving plaintiff is disabled and unable to return to work, but he may eventually find some occupation at which he can earn some, albeit reduced, income. So the deceased plaintiff deserves slightly more compensation for lost future earnings.

Table 6.1 also addresses several components of noneconomic damages. Disability appears to be greater for the deceased plaintiff than for the survivor, as the survivor can almost always still do some things, whereas the decedent can do nothing. Similarly, the survivor can still derive some enjoyment from life, whereas the decedent cannot. However, one could argue conversely that some fates are worse than death and that many elements of pain and suffering—such as lost enjoyment, disfigurement, and mental anguish—would be greater for the survivor than for the decedent. The surviving plaintiff, who is reminded daily of his injuries and lost capacities, might plausibly endure much greater, and longer lasting, psychological suffering than the deceased plaintiff, who, although dead, suffers no more and is therefore unaware of his lost enjoyment of life. For this reason, lost enjoyment of life in fatalities is usually limited to the plaintiff's conscious pain and suffering prior to death, whereas the enjoyment lost from not living longer is not compensable (Bovbjerg et al., 1989; Coyle, 2001).[3] Thus, if death reduces a life to zero, then devastating injuries short of death, such as those producing brain damage, might be said to reduce a life to a value of "zero minus one" (Charfoos & Christensen, 1986).

A case can therefore be made for why survivors of severe injury deserve greater compensation, in various aspects of both economic and noneconomic damages, than do fatalities. This speculation is consistent with research findings that fatalities do, on average, receive less compensation (Sloan & Hsieh, 1990; Sloan & van Wert, 1991). This "death dip" occurs both for total awards and their noneconomic component alone (Bovbjerg et al., 1989).

---

[2]In cases where the plaintiff has died as a result of the alleged wrongdoing, the decedent is represented by his or her estate. Damages to the estate are typically limited to costs incurred between the accident and death, funeral expenses, and so on. Lost future earnings are recoverable by the decedent's dependents (spouse and children) as part of a separate wrongful-death claim. In the present analysis we treat both claims together, as they represent the totality of compensatory damages that the defendant may be required to pay as a consequence of his or her actions.
[3]By the same logic, surviving plaintiffs who are unaware of their pain, suffering, or lost capacities—by virtue of being in a coma, for instance—are usually barred from recovering damages for these aspects of their injury (Coyle, 2001; see, e.g., McDougald v. Garber, 1989).

Despite the research that shows that jurors behave equitably in the sense of awarding more for greater injuries, Frank Sloan and his colleagues (Sloan & Hsieh, 1990; Sloan & van Wert, 1991) have found that jury awards may not be fair in the sense of adequately meeting the actual and projected costs of plaintiffs' injuries. In fact, this research has found that, except for cases involving relatively minor injuries, compensation tends to lag behind the past and anticipated future costs incurred by plaintiffs (see also Graddy, 1997; Viscusi, 1986). For example, Sloan and van Wert (1991) found that malpractice plaintiffs with birth-related injuries received, on average, only 57% of incurred costs, whereas plaintiffs with emergency room injuries received 80% of their costs on average. Consistent with the research described earlier on awards to deceased plaintiffs, Sloan and van Wert (1991) also found that the discrepancy between the amount of compensation received and actual monetary losses was greatest for plaintiffs who died as a result of their injuries. The finding that plaintiffs receive less compensation than is merited by the extent of their injuries is strong evidence against the claim that jury damage awards are spiraling out of control.

Damage awards have also been criticized on the grounds that, although considerable vertical equity exists, *horizontal equity*—that is, consistency within injuries of a particular severity level—is much less than one might desire (Bovbjerg et al., 1989; Broder, 1994; Leebron, 1989). For example, Bovbjerg et al. (1989) found that awards for the most serious nonfatal injuries ranged from $147,000 to $18.1 million.[4] They acknowledged that individual circumstances might legitimately contribute to this variability, especially with respect to economic losses: A finger amputation would result in more lost future income for a professional pianist than for a factory worker. Some of this variability can doubtless also be attributed to the imprecision inherent in rather crudely classifying complex, disparate injuries in terms of their overall severity, but some of it is likely due simply to unpredictability within and across jurisdictions. A number of problems can arise from such horizontal inequity, such as perceptions of unfairness on the part of litigants, erosion of confidence in the civil justice system, and inefficiency of tort law's deterrent function (Bovbjerg et al., 1989).

Compensation for Noneconomic Damages (Pain and Suffering)

Pain and emotional injury almost inevitably accompany serious physical injuries. The recovery of damages for psychological injuries has a long and well-established history (O'Connell & Bailey, 1972); the first award for pain and suffering appears to date from the late 1700s (Bovbjerg et al.,

---

[4]Only 16 cases fell into this severity category, so the variability in a larger sample might be less than it appears here.

1989). Although there is some debate about whether to compensate plaintiffs at all for pain and suffering (Calfee & Rubin, 1992), some degree of compensation for psychological injury is now almost universal. As we noted in chapter 1, jurors receive precious little guidance in determining the exact amount of damages (Bovbjerg et al., 1989; Greene & Bornstein, 2000; Leebron, 1989); their freedom to do essentially whatever they want in setting an amount is especially apparent in the case of damages for pain and suffering, for which the criteria are poorly specified by even this low standard (Dobbs, 1973; Wissler, Kuehn, & Saks, 2000). Some jury instructions admit to the law's inability to help jurors in this respect, by confessing simply that "there are no objective guidelines by which you can measure the money equivalent of [pain and suffering]; the only real measuring stick, if it can be so described, is your collective enlightened conscience" (Douthwaite, 1988, §6–17). This imprecision is also reflected in the variety of terms used to describe this type of damages, which are also referred to as *noneconomic* or *nonpecuniary* losses, to indicate that they are harms other than the loss of wealth (Calfee & Rubin, 1992). Thus, "pain and suffering is generally recognized by the courts as being a legitimate component of compensation, but one for which we have no accepted procedure of measurement" (Viscusi, 1988, p. 204).

Although documentation is typically required in estimating past economic losses, it is difficult to estimate future economic losses,[5] and there is no universally agreed-on formula for doing so (Charfoos & Christensen, 1986; Diamond, Saks, & Landsman, 1998; O'Shea v. Riverway Towing Co., 1982). Nonetheless, a variety of means do exist for calculating the amount of economic loss, which can be presented as expert testimony (Diamond & Casper, 1992; Greene, Downey, & Goodman-Delahunty, 1999). It is harder still to estimate past and future noneconomic losses, because of their very nature. "An inescapable reality of the pain and suffering conundrum is that tort law requires the monetization of a 'product' for which there is no market and therefore no market price" (Chase, 1995, p. 765; see also Dobbs, 1973). Thus, it is quite logical to expect pain and suffering awards to be highly variable, inasmuch as these types of damages are more difficult to quantify, and rarely are quantified, compared with economic damages (Diamond et al., 1998; Viscusi, 1988; see chapter 8, this volume).

Some legal commentators view this lack of specificity as a positive attribute that allows juries to tailor their judgments to their subjective, at times emotional, response to the case, leading Bovbjerg et al. (1989) to conclude that "for intangible losses as for overall damages, conventional wisdom seems almost to revel in the imprecision of valuation" (p. 913). However, critics of the civil jury have also laid much of the blame for the

---

[5]The speculative nature of future damages once led many courts to deny their recovery, but they are now generally allowed (Bovbjerg et al., 1989).

perceived tort crisis on jurors' awards for noneconomic damages (e.g., Baldus et al., 1995; Geistfeld, 1995; Huber, 1988, 1991; Priest, 1987; Weiler, 1991), and some legal commentators have advocated the abolition or sharp curtailing of plaintiffs' ability to recover noneconomic damages (Jaffe, 1953; Morris, 1959; Plant, 1958).[6]

The major criticisms proffered are that pain and suffering awards are excessive; capricious; and only loosely, if at all, tied to plaintiffs' actual pain and suffering. Moreover, some observers have noted substantial variation in pain and suffering awards for similar kinds of injury (Bordens & Horowitz, 1998; Broder, 1994; Diamond et al., 1998; Leebron, 1989; Saks, Hollinger, Wissler, Evans, & Hart, 1997; Viscusi, 1988); in fact, the noneconomic component of juries' awards varies even more widely than their total awards (Bovbjerg et al., 1989; Diamond et al., 1998). For example, Diamond et al. (1998) found that the standard deviation of mock jurors' pain and suffering award was 313% of the mean award, whereas the standard deviation of their economic damages award was only 138% of the mean award, even though the mean pain and suffering award was actually lower ($278,000 vs. $400,000 for economic damages). In perhaps the most compelling example, Broder (1994) found that plaintiffs who had died in the same event, in exactly the same manner (the Korean Air Lines disaster), received pain and suffering damages ranging from 0 to $1.4 million. However, other commentators, such as Vidmar (1993, 1995), have argued persuasively that the claims of jury excess in compensating pain and suffering are exaggerated and unsubstantiated by the empirical evidence. In this section we address several related questions: What constitutes "pain and suffering"? Are the terms *pain and suffering* and *noneconomic damages* synonymous? How do jurors place a dollar value on something as intangible as pain and suffering? What help is available to jurors in performing this difficult task?

Criteria

What constitutes pain and suffering? According to the *Restatement (Second) of Torts* (1965, § 905), "Compensatory damages that may be awarded without proof of pecuniary loss include compensation (a) for bodily harm, and (b) for emotional distress." It defines *bodily harm* as "any impairment of the physical condition of the body, including illness or physical pain" (Comment *b*), whereas terms used to elaborate "emotional distress" include "disagreeable emotions," "humiliation," "fear and anxiety," and "loss of companionship or freedom" (Comments *c–g*). In other words, the *Restatement (Second) of Torts* essentially equates nonpecuniary harm with pain and suffering.

---

[6]This argument has been revisited more recently in the debate over caps on noneconomic damages, discussed more fully in chapter 9 (for a review, see Geistfeld, 1995).

However, the components of noneconomic loss vary widely by jurisdiction (Bovbjerg et al., 1989) to such an extent that it is not entirely accurate to use the terms *noneconomic damages* and *pain and suffering* synonymously, as do many commentators (and as we do ourselves, for the sake of simplicity). In some jurisdictions the terms *are* synonymous, referring to all nonpecuniary losses. In other locales, however, pain and suffering is but one element of noneconomic damages, while other, separate categories exist as well, such as loss of enjoyment of life, shortened life expectancy, injury to professional standing or reputation, and loss of health (Bovbjerg et al., 1989; Dobbs, 1973; Goodman-Delahunty & Foote, 1995; "Loss of enjoyment of life," 1981). These additional categories permit the distinction between the occurrence of new, negative harms resulting from an injury (e.g., pain, distress) and the loss of previously enjoyed positive capacities (e.g., lost enjoyment of life; Bovbjerg et al., 1989; Coyle, 2001; "Loss of enjoyment of life," 1981; Poser, Bornstein, & McGorty, in press).

For example, awarding damages for lost enjoyment of life (also referred to as *hedonic damages*) "compensates the victim for the limitations on the person's life created by the injury" (*Thompson v. National Railroad Passenger Corporation*, 1980, p. 824). The effect of an injury on a person's lifestyle is strongly correlated with perceptions of the injury's severity and noneconomic damage awards (Andrews, Meyer, & Berlá, 1996; Vidmar & Rice, 1993; Wissler, Evans, Hart, Morry, & Saks, 1997). Although lost enjoyment of life seems like a rather nebulous concept, it can in fact be measured somewhat reliably, at least in relative terms (i.e., in comparing different injuries to one another; see Andrews et al., 1996; Terman, 1995). This element of damages is currently recognized in nearly every jurisdiction,[7] but even when such damages are allowed there is still debate about whether they should be integrated into pain and suffering or considered as an independent element of damages (Coyle, 2001; Dobbs, 1973; "Loss of enjoyment of life," 1981; *McDougald v. Garber*, 1989; Poser et al., in press; Terman, 1995). Whether lost enjoyment of life is included as part of pain and suffering or itemized as a separate element of damages can have an effect on jurors' total award for noneconomic damages (Poser et al., in press).

Pain and suffering is defined differently in different contexts: jury instructions, case law, and statutory law. These definitions use a wide range of terminology and refer to various kinds of suffering (Dobbs, 1973). For example, the Civil Rights Act of 1991 allows recovery in employment discrimination cases for "emotional pain, suffering, inconvenience, mental anguish, loss of enjoyment of life, and other nonpecuniary losses."[8] The case law is similarly broad. In one representative case, the California Su-

---

[7]See, for example, *Sherrod v. Berry* (1985) and *Huff v. Tracy* (1976). Hedonic damages have also been recognized as legitimate by the U.S. Supreme Court (*Molzof v. U.S.*, 1992).
[8]See 42 U.S.C.A. 1981a(b)(3) (West, 1994).

preme Court, in *Capelouto v. Kaiser Foundation Hospitals* (1972, p. 859), defined pain and suffering as "a convenient label under which a plaintiff may recover not only for physical pain but for fright, nervousness, grief, anxiety, worry, mortification, shock, humiliation, indignity, embarrassment, apprehension, terror or ordeal."[9]

Unfortunately, research has not examined how jurors interpret such a laundry list of negative states and whether different definitions of pain and suffering would influence their verdicts. For instance, are "nervousness," "anxiety," and "worry" independent aspects of an injury, overlapping categories, or wholly synonymous? Wissler et al. (1997, Experiment 1) provided a partial answer to this question. They found that mock jurors' perceptions of different injuries loaded onto four discrete factors: (a) mental suffering, (b) physical pain, (c) visibility of the injury, and (d) disability. Perception of the plaintiff's overall suffering was highly correlated with perception of the plaintiff's disability, disfigurement, and the effect of the injury on the plaintiff's life ($rs = .54–.83$), but perception of the plaintiff's overall pain was much more modestly correlated with these same dimensions ($rs = .26–.37$). Thus, it seems to make sense to characterize pain and suffering as two separate components of noneconomic damages, but these components, by themselves, do not seem to cover the entire spectrum of such damages (neither, as we discuss later in this section, were they the sole predictors of mock jurors' ultimate verdicts).

The issue of the criteria used to define pain and suffering is an important one, as research in the criminal domain has shown that the manner in which important legal concepts are defined—such as "reasonable doubt"—can have profound effects on mock jurors' verdicts in cases containing identical evidence (Horowitz & Kirkpatrick, 1996). Moreover, "whatever the categories of non-economic damages allowed in a given jurisdiction, the law provides no objective benchmarks for valuing them" (Bovbjerg et al., 1989, p. 912).

An important factor in considering damages for emotional injuries is whether they are accompanied by physical injuries. All American jurisdictions appear to allow recovery for pain and suffering that result from physical injury (Perrin & Sales, 1993). Most jurisdictions also allow recovery of damages for the infliction of emotional distress, even in the absence of any physical injury. This is almost always true if the plaintiff can show that the infliction was intentional; however, only a minority of states allow recovery for the negligent infliction of emotional distress, and when they do they typically require an additional showing of physical injury (Melton, Petrila, Slobogin, & Poythress, 1997; Perrin & Sales, 1993; see, e.g., *Twyman v. Twyman*, 1993). Physical injury is also usually required in order to

---

[9]Elsewhere, the same court has characterized mental suffering as again including nervousness, grief, anxiety, worry, shock, humiliation, or indignity but omitted mortification, embarrassment, apprehension, terror, or ordeal (*Crisci v. Security Insurance Co.*, 1967).

recover damages for psychological injury that results from witnessing injury to a third party (i.e., "bystander recovery"; see P. A. Bell, 1984; Leibson, 1976–1977; *Restatement (Second) of Torts*, 1965, § 436A).

What makes an injury severe? In assessing degree of injury, most studies have relied on ratings made by the insurance industry (e.g., Bovbjerg et al., 1989, 1991; Danzon, 1985; Taragin et al., 1992; Viscusi, 1986) or holistic judgments made by mock jurors (e.g., Bornstein, 1998; Saks et al., 1997) that generally fail to define the specific features of an injury that make it severe. Wissler et al. (1997; see also Wissler et al., 1999) gathered empirical data to address the question of what elements of an injury contribute to perceptions of varying severity. In their first experiment, they asked mock jurors to award damages for pain and suffering for five personal injury cases that varied widely in terms of how severe the plaintiff's injury was: a fractured neck resulting in quadriplegia; a broken leg requiring several operations to repair; facial cuts that left a permanent scar; serious permanent brain damage; and second- and third-degree burns requiring skin grafts and leaving permanent scars. Participants evaluated each injury (using a 10-point scale) on nine dimensions: (a) visibility of the injury, (b) amount and (c) duration of physical pain, (d) amount and (e) duration of mental suffering, (f) severity of disability, (g) severity of disfigurement, (h) overall injury severity, and (i) effect on the plaintiff's everyday life.

It is not surprising that quadriplegia and brain damage, the most severe injuries, received the highest ratings on all dimensions and led to the highest pain and suffering awards. This finding is consistent with the typical finding (discussed previously) that greater severity leads to higher total compensation (see also Bordens & Horowitz, 1998; Robbennolt & Studebaker, 1999). Of greater interest is the degree to which the different dimensions contributed to perceptions of overall severity. Wissler et al. (1997) found that the seven specific dimensions (excluding the effect on everyday life) accounted for an impressive 75% of the variance in ratings of overall severity, although some dimensions played a larger role than others. Regression analyses showed that the extent of the plaintiff's disability contributed most strongly to perceptions of overall severity, followed by the amount and duration of mental suffering. The remaining dimensions (visibility, amount and duration of pain, and disfigurement) were relatively weak contributors to perceptions of overall severity and pain and suffering awards. This result is consistent with other research showing that the manner in which an injury is depicted (e.g., a color vs. a black-and-white photograph) does not affect damage awards (Fishfader, Howells, Katz, & Teresi, 1996; Whalen & Blanchard, 1982), as such manipulations are related to the injury's visibility but are unlikely to affect perceptions of the plaintiff's disability or mental suffering.

Wissler et al. (1997) replicated these basic findings in a second experiment containing a larger and more diverse set of injuries in 25 different cases. Again, disability made the greatest contribution to perceptions of overall severity and pain and suffering awards, followed by mental suffering. These results provide some insight into the case characteristics on which jurors rely in evaluating an injury's severity, with the extent of the plaintiff's disability and the amount and duration of the plaintiff's mental suffering—more than the plaintiff's physical pain or disfigurement—being the largest determinants of perceived severity.[10] Hence, the greater the plaintiff's disability and mental suffering, the larger the plaintiff's pain and suffering award. It follows, then, that injuries that are very painful but that do not produce long-lasting suffering or disability—such as some acute fractures or burns—should lead to relatively low compensation awards.

Quantifying the Unquantifiable

The judge's instructions to the jury can have a profound effect on the jury's pain and suffering awards. For example, McCaffery, Kahneman, and Spitzer (1995) asked mock jurors to choose an "appropriate amount of compensation" for pain and suffering in cases where liability had already been established. Some participants were then given a "making-whole" instruction, in which they were told:

> To determine the appropriate compensation, imagine that you are the plaintiff. You have already suffered the described injury. What amount of money is needed to make you "whole" again—that is, as fortunate as if nothing (i.e., neither the injury nor the payment) had happened? (p. 1356)

Other participants were given a "selling-price" instruction, in which they were told:

> To determine the appropriate compensation, imagine that you are the plaintiff. Before any injury has taken place, the defendant offers you a sum of money to suffer the described injury exactly as it is later experienced. What amount of money would you demand to willingly accept the injury? (p. 1356)

In two experiments, participants (both law students and a diverse adult sample) awarded significantly more compensation if they adopted the selling-price than the making-whole perspective. For example, the median awards in one experiment were $775,000 and $245,000, respectively. McCaffery et al. (1995) explained this result in terms of a *framing effect*, whereby the different instructions induced participants to adopt different frames of reference. Greater compensation is required to move from a healthy, or *ex ante* reference point than from an injured, *ex post* reference

---

[10]Perceptions of disfigurement can, however, be a significant predictor of nonpecuniary damage awards in cases where disfigurement is specifically listed as a separate element of damages (Vidmar & Rice, 1993).

point. Although conventional legal practice consistently takes a making-whole perspective in instructing jurors during the damages phase,[11] these results nonetheless suggest that judges need to be very careful in implementing specific procedures to guide jurors in making their pain and suffering awards.

Given that documentation is not applicable to noneconomic losses, as it often is for economic losses, how can litigants—and, subsequently, jurors—attempt to quantify damages that seem to be inherently unquantifiable? Little research has sought to identify the processes by which jurors make pain and suffering awards. Special verdict forms (see chapter 8) are one way of helping jurors quantify noneconomic damages; lay and expert testimony is another way. Plaintiffs may support a claim of pain and suffering through lay testimony—from the plaintiff, friends and family, or others (e.g., clergy)—who have had the opportunity to observe the plaintiff both before and after the injury and can report any changes. Alternatively, or in addition, plaintiffs can offer expert testimony from medical or mental health professionals about the injury's noneconomic effects, such as lost enjoyment of life, the character and duration of the pain, or the plaintiff's mental state (Coyle, 2001; Goodman-Delahunty & Foote, 1995; Werchick, 1965). Defendants may, of course, dispute the same claim by relying on their own experts. In cases where emotional distress is the primary, or even sole, cause of action, expert testimony about the extent and effects of the alleged injury is quite common (Perrin & Sales, 1993).

Goodman-Delahunty and Foote (1995) identified several reasons why experts are helpful at justifying noneconomic injuries. First, plaintiffs may lack insight into their own injuries, especially if they developed slowly over time, as is often true in employment discrimination claims. Second, many plaintiffs have little basis on which to compare their experience to that of others, whereas experts possess a larger knowledge base that allows them to make comparative judgments. Third, plaintiffs may downplay the extent of their psychological injuries in order not to appear (to themselves or others) emotionally fragile and vulnerable, which could have significant social and professional costs. Although experts rarely testify in order to support a precise figure for nonpecuniary damages, their testimony can aid jurors by making the intangible elements of psychological harm (e.g., its nature, duration, and relative severity) more salient. Previous research indicates that expert testimony about the monetary value of plaintiffs' injuries influences jurors' verdicts for economic damages (Raitz, Greene, Goodman, & Loftus, 1990; but see Greene, Downey, & Goodman-Delahunty, 1999). This suggests that expert testimony that specifically seeks to quantify

---

[11] As McCaffery et al. acknowledged, selling-price instructions by judges (or arguments by attorneys) are in fact explicitly disallowed because of their potentially prejudicial impact (see, e.g., *Danner v. Mid-State Paving Co.*, 1965; *Dunlap v. Lee*, 1962). Nonetheless, there are plausible arguments for implementing such a system (Geistfeld, 1995).

pain and suffering would likewise affect noneconomic damage awards (we cover this topic at greater length in chapter 8).

Guidance in quantifying pain and suffering damages can also come from the attorneys, who are allowed, in many jurisdictions, to argue that jurors adopt a particular method of quantifying pain and suffering. The most common of these methods, attributed to the attorney Melvin Belli (e.g., Belli, 1982, §64.3), is the *per diem method* (see also Dobbs, 1973; Werchick, 1965). According to this approach, jurors are encouraged to multiply some unit of time (e.g., a day) by a dollar amount that seems to correspond to the plaintiff's injury. For example, a burn victim's suffering might be estimated to be worth $5/day; a plaintiff with a life expectancy of 30 more years would therefore warrant $54,570 for future suffering ($5/day × 365 days/year × 30 years). Using this algorithm, relatively low rates, as in the $5/day example, can translate into quite substantial total awards.[12] Because attorneys' arguments are obviously meant to benefit one party or another, they may be viewed with some suspicion. Although research has found that the content of attorneys' arguments can be persuasive in influencing jurors' verdicts (Diamond, Casper, Heiert, & Marshall, 1996; Linz & Penrod, 1984), a mere recommendation by attorneys of a specific dollar figure may not have much of an effect (Greene, Downey, & Goodman-Delahunty, 1999).[13]

Neither expert testimony nor oral argument would necessarily reduce the considerable variability in jurors' noneconomic damage awards. "Efforts to reduce variability across juries for pain and suffering awards may ... require providing the jury with a set of reference points against which to assess potential damage awards" (Diamond et al., 1998, p. 318), such as presenting jurors with an award matrix containing a recommended (or mandatory) range of awards for different injuries as a function of injury severity and the plaintiff's age (Bovbjerg et al., 1989; Chase, 1995). The matrix would inform jurors of the range of pain and suffering awards made by other juries in the same jurisdiction during a contemporaneous time period (Chase, 1995; we cover in detail studies implementing such reforms in chapter 9).

In summary, jurors could receive guidance on quantifying the unquantifiable from several sources: from judges, in the form of special ver-

---

[12]The propriety of the per diem approach is quite controversial because of concerns that it would be prejudicial by leading jurors to treat it as evidence rather than argument. Dobbs (1973, p. 546) concluded that "Apparently the real basis of most decisions [to bar per diem arguments] is simply a distrust of the jury and a feeling that the jury will be too easily impressed by the apparent certitude of the mathematical calculations." Consequently, the per diem approach is usually subject to a cautionary instruction by the judge when it is allowed (e.g., *Vanskike v. ACF Industries, Inc.*, 1981) and sometimes is prohibited altogether (e.g., *Botta v. Bruner*, 1958; for a review of the relevant case law, see Belli, 1982).

[13]Greene, Downey, and Goodman-Delahunty (1999) found no effect of attorney damage award recommendations for economic damages. They acknowledged that an effect might be found for noneconomic damages, an area in which jurors have less guidance and fewer benchmarks.

dicts or schedules for valuing pain and suffering in different types of cases; from attorneys, in the form of oral arguments about how to place a dollar value on pain and suffering; or from lay and expert witnesses, in the form of testimony about the nature, effects, and monetary value of plaintiffs' pain and suffering. Because recommendations from attorneys, who overtly represent one of the parties, or witnesses, who are called to testify by one of the parties, are likely to be viewed as partisan and self-serving, judicial guidance would probably be most effective at reducing variability in pain and suffering awards and providing the fairest compensation. Research is needed that compares these different approaches.

Punitive Damages

Punitive damages are designed to punish and deter the defendant rather than to compensate the plaintiff. Hence, any effect of injury severity on punitive awards would appear to violate legal doctrine. In fact, though, several commentators (e.g., Landes & Posner, 1987) have argued that punitive damages should also reflect injury severity, as it is more important to deter actions that result in relatively severe injury than those that result in negligible injury.[14] Nonetheless, even these commentators agree that injury severity is less directly relevant to punitive than to compensatory damages. Thus, severity should normatively exert less, if any, effect on punitive than on compensatory damages.

Archival studies of punitive damage awards have typically not addressed the effect on awards of variables such as severity, focusing instead on chronological trends (e.g., Daniels & Martin, 1990; Peterson, Sarma, & Shanley, 1987; Rustad, 1992). An examination of such variables is difficult to undertake because of the relative infrequency with which punitive damages are awarded (Daniels & Martin, 1990; Eisenberg, Goerdt, Ostrom, Rottman, & Wells, 1997; Rustad, 1992, 1998). In one of the most comprehensive analyses of punitive damages to date, Rustad (1992) identified 260 nonasbestos products liability cases (355 including asbestos cases) involving punitive damage awards from 1965 to 1990. These cases showed that the majority of cases in which punitive damages were awarded involved serious injury to the plaintiffs, with 60% involving death or permanent total disability (see Table 6.2). Interestingly, the relationship between the degree of severity and the size of the award increased monotonically throughout the range of severity and did not dip when the plaintiff died, as is the case with compensatory damages (see also Eisenberg et al., 1997; U.S. General Accounting Office, 1989).

These results seem to imply that in awarding punitive damages, jurors consider a factor—injury severity—that is normatively irrelevant to that

---

[14]See also TXO Production Corp. v. Alliance Resources Corp. (1993).

TABLE 6.2
Percentage of Nonasbestos Cases in Which Punitive Damages Were Awarded, as a Function of Injury Severity

Severity of injury	%
Temporary partial disability	4
Permanent partial disability	29
Temporary total disability	7
Permanent total disability	33
Death	27
Total	**100**

Note. From "In Defense of Punitive Damages in Products Liability: Testing Tort Anecdotes With Empirical Data," by M. Rustad, 1992, *Iowa Law Review, 78*, p. 63. Copyright 1992 by Iowa Law Review. Adapted with permission.

particular decision. The problem with drawing such a conclusion is that in archival studies it is difficult to disambiguate the contribution of various confounding factors. It is quite possible that products liability defendants behaved more recklessly in cases resulting in more severe injury, in which case higher punitive damages *should* be assessed against them. All things being equal, more reckless behavior on the part of product manufacturers will, on average, result in more severe injuries to consumers. Archival studies are unfortunately unable to hold all other variables equal, which is why simulation research plays such a vital role in understanding jury behavior (Bornstein, 1999; Diamond, 1997; Vidmar, 1994b).

Only a few simulation studies have explored what factors influence mock jurors' punitive damage awards, and even fewer have directly addressed the effect of variations in injury severity. Bornstein (1998, Experiment 2) created a situation comparable to the awarding of punitive damages, in which some participants determined liability and the amount of damages to be paid by the defendant as punishment. The situation differed from what is customary in civil suits in that these damages were not to be paid to the plaintiff; furthermore, participants did not award compensatory damages to the plaintiff. Thus, participants in this condition were not in a position to award any money to the plaintiff but could still punish the defendant. Damage awards in this condition were significantly greater when the plaintiff was more severely hurt, suggesting that participant–jurors were influenced by the variable of injury severity even when it was not relevant —that is, in punishing the defendant.

Because the situation developed by Bornstein (1998) differed from legal custom in at least one important respect—that is, whether the plaintiff receives any award paid by the defendant in punitive damages—it is necessary to treat these results with a certain degree of caution. This caution is especially warranted inasmuch as other researchers, using a simulation task that adheres more closely to actual practice in American courtrooms, have obtained conflicting results.

For example, Cather et al. (1996) asked mock jurors to award compensatory and punitive damages in three different cases: (a) personal injury, (b) products liability, and (c) insurance bad faith. Each case varied the severity of the plaintiff's injury as well as the reprehensibility of the defendant's conduct (which we discuss in chapter 7). For example, in the products liability case, a boy's injury while operating a lawnmower resulted in either hand lacerations requiring stitches or lacerations and the amputation of one arm above the elbow. Across all cases, although severely injured plaintiffs were awarded roughly twice as much in punitive damages as mildly injured plaintiffs, this difference was not statistically significant.

There are two explanations for Cather et al.'s (1996) failure to find an effect of injury severity on punitive damage awards. First, in light of the high variability in awards (Diamond et al., 1998; Robbennolt & Studebaker, 1999; Saks et al., 1997), the experiment might have had insufficient power to detect a difference. Cather et al. had 80 participants make judgments in three different cases. By way of comparison, Kahneman, Schkade, and Sunstein (1998) had 899 participants make judgments in four different cases. Kahneman et al. found that defendants did have to pay more in punitive damages when the plaintiff was severely, as opposed to moderately, injured. The effect of injury severity was especially pronounced when the defendant was relatively wealthy. Thus, the combination of small sample size and high response variability may have prevented Cather et al. from detecting a statistically significant difference in punitive damage awards across different levels of injury severity.

Second, as proposed by Cather et al., jurors might be capable of adhering to legal instructions about what factors to consider and to ignore in awarding different types of damages, but only in some types of cases. Consider the following study, involving a medical defendant (also used in Bornstein's [1998] study). Robbennolt and Studebaker (1999, Experiment 2) presented participants with a simulated trial in which the plaintiff contracted either Hepatitis B (low severity) or HIV (high severity) from a blood transfusion. The plaintiff argued that officers of the company responsible for testing the blood for such viruses had encouraged sloppy testing procedures and that punitive, as well as compensatory (limited to pain and suffering), damages were therefore warranted. More severely injured plaintiffs (i.e., those with HIV) were awarded significantly more money in both types of damages than were less severely injured plaintiffs (i.e., those with Hepatitis B). Thus, injury severity had an effect on punitive damages, even though these damages are intended primarily to punish the defendant. Although punitive damages are relatively uncommon in cases involving medical defendants (Eisenberg et al., 1997; Rustad, 1998), there is also some evidence that jurors treat this class of defendants differently from defendants in other types of cases (see chapter 4). The psycholegal literature is rife with examples of experimental findings that vary across different case types.

NATURE OF THE INJURY

As Wissler et al. (1997) and others (e.g., Bornstein, 1998; Robbennolt, 2000) have documented, an injury's severity is one of its most—if not *the* most—salient characteristic. Nonetheless, injuries vary in other respects as well, and these characteristics may also affect jurors' damage awards. Features of the injury that we subsume under the rubric of "nature of the injury" and discuss in this section include such factors as: (a) the cause of the injury and (b) the timing of the injury.[15]

Cause of the Injury

One of the fundamental characteristics of an injury is the manner in which it was caused. Indeed, causality is central to the question of the defendant's liability for the plaintiff's injury (H. L. A. Hart & Honore, 1985). Although issues of causality may also have a legitimate impact on punitive damages, by virtue of punitive damages' deterrent function, they are normatively irrelevant to the matter of compensation (Baron & Ritov, 1993). As we noted earlier, because the primary goal of compensation is to restore the plaintiff, as much as possible, to his or her pre-injury condition, compensatory awards should be the same for a particular injury regardless of how the injury occurred. One useful distinction in categorizing how different types of injuries occur is in terms of *omission* versus *commission*. An injury may occur because some actor/agent acted in a manner that produced an injury to someone else (i.e., a commission), or it may occur because the actor/agent failed to act, and the failure to act produced an injury (i.e., an omission).

Baron and Ritov (1993) addressed participants' compensation judgments in a series of experiments that varied whether the plaintiff's injury was caused by an act (commission) or an omission on the part of the defendant. In one case, for example, a pharmaceutical company discovered a vaccine to prevent a potentially lethal type of flu, but the vaccine had potentially lethal side effects (although fewer children would die from the vaccine than from the flu). In one version (commission), the company

---

[15]One could also consider who caused the injury to be a characteristic of the injury itself. We discussed the role of defendant characteristics separately in chapter 4. In addition, the physical versus psychological aspect of the injury could be construed as part of the nature of the injury. We discussed this distinction in this chapter, in the section on noneconomic damages. We also note that the distinction, although readily made, is in fact quite fuzzy, in light of the psychological contribution to physical pain and the physical ramifications of mental suffering (P. A. Bell, 1984).

manufactured the product, and the parents of a child who died from taking the vaccine sued the company; in another version (omission), the company decided not to make the product, and the parents of a child who died from the flu sued the company. Participants were less likely to award compensation when the injury was caused by an omission than when it was caused by a commission, even though the injury was the same and the compensation came from the same source. This finding is consistent with other research showing that people tend to find harm produced by a commission morally more blameworthy than if the same harm had been produced by an omission (Spranca, Minsk, & Baron, 1991).[16]

One reason people might award greater compensation for injuries caused by acts than by failures to act is that their intuitions lead them to believe that injuries are more likely to result from actions. People have well-organized, systematic beliefs about what sorts of events are likely to cause what sorts of injuries (Feigenson, 2000; A. J. Hart, Evans, Wissler, Feehan, & Saks, 1997, Experiment 1). For example, A. J. Hart et al. (1997) asked participants to describe the most typical features of four different injury-producing situations: (a) a car accident, (b) a slip-and-fall case, (c) use of a defective product, and (d) medical malpractice. They found that participants had fairly consistent schemas about the types of injuries that most typically result in each situation.

In a second experiment, A. J. Hart et al. (1997) presented mock jurors with two of the situations (car accident and slip and fall) in a trial context. They varied the plaintiff's injury so that it was described either as a broken arm or whiplash. Thus, the plaintiff's injury was either typical (a broken arm in the slip-and-fall case or whiplash in the car accident) or atypical (whiplash in the slip-and-fall case or a broken arm in the car accident). Participants' pain and suffering awards were both larger and more variable when the plaintiff's injury was atypical for a certain type of situation than when it was typical. In other words, compensation for the same injury varied depending on the manner in which it was caused. Interestingly, this effect occurred despite participants' awareness that the typical and atypical injuries themselves were essentially the same in terms of their severity (with one notable exception, which we describe later in this section). What is most interesting about this result is that the manner of causation does not reflect a simple effect of the identity of the defendant; rather, it reflects the importance of the relationship between the type of harm (i.e.,

---

[16]Baron and Ritov's (1993) participants assessed whether *any* compensation or punishment was appropriate, but they did not apparently make a separate judgment of the amount of damages. Their main finding comports well with the basic principle of tort law that harm caused by nonfeasance is less deserving of recovery than harm caused by misfeasance (Epstein, 2000). Their study did not specifically address the question of whether mock jurors would award more for harm caused by a commission than for harm caused by an omission, once liability had already been established.

the alleged effect) and who the defendant is (i.e., the potential cause), as manifested in mock jurors' prior beliefs about causality.

Bornstein and Rajki (1994) conducted a similar study, in which the plaintiff was a woman with ovarian cancer who alleged that her illness had been caused by her birth control pill, toxic calligraphy ink, or chemical waste that had leaked into her neighborhood's water supply. Participants in a separate study reported believing that, of the three potential causes, ovarian cancer was most likely to result from chemical waste, next most likely from birth control pills, and least likely from calligraphy ink. Although mock jurors' liability judgments reflected these intuitions—that is, they were most likely to find the defendant liable in the chemical waste (or "typical cause") version of the case—their compensation awards did not differ across the three variations of the case (participants in A. J. Hart et al.'s [1997] study did not make liability judgments). The discrepancy in damage award findings between this experiment and the one conducted by A. J. Hart et al. (1997) can be explained by the fact that mock jurors in Bornstein and Rajki's experiment awarded total compensation, whereas those in Hart et al.'s (1997) experiment awarded damages for pain and suffering only. As we discussed earlier, there is some evidence that pain and suffering awards are unique (e.g., Diamond et al., 1998; Saks et al., 1997; Wissler et al., 1997). In the present context injury typicality may affect noneconomic but not economic damages. In combination, these studies offer the intriguing possibility that more typical injuries for a particular situation will increase the probability of finding the defendant liable while decreasing the amount that the defendant is required to pay in noneconomic (but not economic) compensation.

This effect of typicality on compensation is consistent with research on *counterfactual thinking*, "the propensity of individuals to imagine alternative scenarios that undo negative events" (C. W. Williams, Lees-Haley, & Price, 1996, p. 2102; see Roese, 1997, for a review). It is easier to imagine such an alternative scenario when the cause of the negative event was atypical or somehow exceptional than when it was typical or routine. For example, if a diner becomes sick after eating at a restaurant that she has never been to before, there is a tendency to think that "if she had only gone to her usual restaurant, she would not have become sick"; on the other hand, if she becomes sick at her usual restaurant, an alternative scenario is harder to imagine (Macrae, 1992). The easier it is to imagine the alternative outcome, the greater the sympathy that observers have for the victim (Macrae & Milne, 1992; Miller & McFarland, 1986; C. W. Williams et al., 1996).[17]

A number of studies of counterfactual thinking have addressed par-

---

[17]Robbennolt and Sobus (1997), whose study we discuss later in this section, did not find an effect of an event's mental mutability on participants' sympathy for the victim.

ticipants' judgments about compensation and financial penalties in both atypical and typical circumstances. Although most of these studies are not jury simulations in the sense of explicitly asking participants to take on the role of jurors in a simulated trial context, they are similar in that participants typically read about accident cases and answer questions assessing the behavior of the parties involved and concerning how much compensation the victim is entitled to or how much of a fine the perpetrator should have to pay. Consistent with the findings of A. J. Hart et al. (1997), victims of atypical or unexpected injuries (e.g., developing food poisoning at a restaurant one does not usually patronize) are awarded greater compensation than those with injuries resulting from more typical or routine events (Macrae, 1992; Macrae & Milne, 1992; Miller & McFarland, 1986; Ritov & Baron, 1994). In addition, perpetrators who cause atypical injuries are deemed more negligent (Macrae, 1992) and are required to pay larger financial penalties than those who cause more typical injuries (Macrae, 1992; Macrae & Milne, 1992; Ritov & Baron, 1994; C. W. Williams et al., 1996).

Robbennolt and Sobus (1997) addressed the effect of counterfactual thinking within a jury simulation paradigm. They presented mock jurors with a trial for a civil rights action in which the plaintiffs were two young men whose automobile was stopped and searched because it matched a drug courier profile. Relying on the profile, the police officer in the case determined that he had probable cause and emptied the car of its occupants in order to search the vehicle. As a result of their forcible removal from the vehicle, both plaintiffs were injured (one was cut, and the other fractured his wrist). The plaintiffs filed a civil rights action, seeking both compensatory and punitive damages. The description of the case varied the police officer's history in regard to using the drug courier profile: He was described as being either very successful (i.e., finding drugs in 3 of 4 searches) or very unsuccessful (i.e., finding drugs in 1 of 10 searches) in searches based on the profile. The purpose of this manipulation was to induce more counterfactual reasoning in the unsuccessful condition—that is, because successful searches were unusual, it should be easier for participants to imagine how the officer could have acted otherwise.[18]

The officer's relative degree of success in using the profile affected both compensatory and punitive awards. More damages of both types were awarded when the profile was typically ineffective than when it was typically effective. These effects appear to be due, at least in part, to a greater tendency to find the defendant liable (i.e., to award *any* damages) when

---

[18]In such cases, the outcome of the search is legally irrelevant and should not be considered in awarding damages. Robbennolt and Sobus also manipulated the outcome of the search in order to test this assumption; as the outcome of the search is related to issues of the defendant's conduct, this component of the study is taken up in chapter 7, in which we address this "hindsight" effect in greater detail.

the profiling practice was ineffective. This finding suggests that jurors' determination of whether a defendant's conduct caused a plaintiff's injury is strongly affected by their ability to imagine how the defendant might have acted otherwise (see also Wiener et al., 1994). Indeed, such an analysis is an important tool in answering the crucial legal question of *cause-in-fact* (i.e., whether the plaintiff's injury would have occurred but for the defendant's conduct).

The effect of typicality on negligence and punitive judgments has a logical legal basis: The easier it is to imagine how the defendant could have acted otherwise, the stronger the apparent causal connection between the defendant's actions and the plaintiff's injury. The stronger the causal connection, the more negligent and blameworthy (and hence deserving of punishment) the defendant will appear. The effect of typicality on the amount of compensatory damages, on the other hand—once liability has been established—has no legal basis; rather, it suggests that counterfactual thinking influences mock jurors' perceptions of the litigants, particularly with respect to the perceived severity of the plaintiff's injury. For example, both A. J. Hart et al. (1997) and Ritov and Baron (1994) found that victims/plaintiffs injured by atypical or unexpected events were perceived as suffering more than those who were injured in a more typical fashion. The finding that plaintiffs with atypical injuries receive greater compensation than those with more typical injuries from the same causal event can therefore be explained in terms of atypical injuries making it easier for mock jurors to imagine how the event's outcome might have been otherwise, leading them to perceive the plaintiff's injury as worse, even though the plaintiff's injuries are objectively identical. This interpretation is consistent with the general tendency of counterfactual thinking to have affective consequences (Roese, 1997).

Timing of the Injury

The studies we just discussed concerned jurors' judgments when the same injuries were caused by events having different characteristics. Other research suggests that damage awards might even vary when identical injuries are allegedly caused by exactly the same events. Johnson and Drobny (1987, Study 2) presented mock jurors with two trial scenarios in which the plaintiff's injury and actions, and the defendant's identity and actions, were held constant but that varied the timing between the alleged cause of the injury and its effect. For example, in one scenario a mechanic (the defendant) repaired the emergency brake on the plaintiff's car. The brake subsequently failed when the plaintiff left the car in neutral, leading it to roll down a hill and smash into the plaintiff's house. The car owner sued the mechanic, claiming that the brake had been repaired improperly. In one version of the scenario the delay between the brake repair and the accident was several days; in an alternative version it was 5 years. Participants found the defendant more negligent, and more liable, when the delay was short than when it was long, which doubtless reflects the proper legal inference that causation is more strongly established when the delay between cause and alleged effect is relatively short (H. L. A. Hart & Honore, 1985). However, the defendant in the short-delay condition was also required to pay greater compensation; once negligence has been determined, compensation for the same injury should legally be the same regardless of the timing of the injury.

In a follow-up study, Johnson and Drobny (1987, Study 3) showed that defendants were also found more liable and required to pay greater compensation when the delay between an injury and its alleged cause was atypically brief than when it was atypically long. In other words, if some medication usually produces an undesirable side effect in 6 months (i.e., on the occasions when that side effect appears), mock jurors will respond more favorably to a plaintiff who developed the side effect in 1 month than to one who developed it 1 year after taking the medication. A limitation of Johnson and Drobny's findings is that, in awarding damages, participants were asked to estimate the proportion of damages that the defendant should pay, ranging from 1 (none) to 9 (all). Thus, a rating of 1 was tantamount to a judgment finding the defendant not liable, meaning that the liability and compensation variables were conflated. Because of this procedural artifact the results speak most directly to the factors that influence mock jurors' liability judgments, and it is unclear whether defendants who have already been held liable would be assessed variable damage awards based on the temporal contiguity between cause and effect. Nonetheless, the results are intriguing and suggest that jurors might perceive the same injury (i.e., the side effect) to warrant differential compensation, not as a function of characteristics of the defendant or injury-causing event, per se, but of the temporal relationship between the defendant's actions and the alleged injury.

CONCLUSION

The most consistent finding in research on how jurors respond to variations in the nature and severity of the plaintiff's injury is that they award greater compensation, in both total and noneconomic damages, to more severely injured plaintiffs. In doing so, they are sensitive to injury characteristics that are especially indicative of greater severity, such as disability and suffering; this sensitivity is particularly true when jurors award only noneconomic damages. Although there is some evidence that jurors inappropriately award greater punitive damages to more severely injured plaintiffs as well, this tendency appears to be limited to cases involving medical defendants. Moreover, despite claims that damage awards are frequently excessive, some research suggests that if jurors are erring at all, it is in the direction of awarding too little compensation to meet plaintiffs' actual and projected expenses. Thus, in the important respect of vertical equity, jurors do a reasonably good job of adhering to legal dictates. Nonetheless, jurors' compensation awards are highly variable, especially for non-economic damages, producing considerable horizontal inequity. This variability can be reduced somewhat by procedural changes designed to give jurors more guidance in quantifying the unquantifiable, such as by providing them with data on representative awards in similar cases.

Although jurors adhere fairly closely to the law when it comes to injury severity, the manner in which jurors reason about the causes of different types of injuries can have a non-normative effect on their damage awards. In particular, their intuitions about what is normal or typical in various situations influence their awards. Injuries that stand out as being atypical—such as getting whiplash from a fall—appear to induce jurors to think about "what might have been." These situations evoke greater sympathy in jurors, which, as in the case of relatively severe injuries, leads them to award more in compensation.

7

THE LITIGANTS' CONDUCT

In previous chapters we addressed the effect on damages of qualities of the litigants, such as their gender and wealth, as well as characteristics of the plaintiff's injury and how it was caused. In this final chapter on how features of the evidence influence jurors' verdicts we consider the nature of the plaintiff's and the defendant's conduct. The issue of the plaintiff's conduct is relevant to jurors' decisions because if the plaintiff's actions contributed to his or her injuries, then jurors must reduce their compensation accordingly, or even disallow recovery altogether. The issue of the defendant's conduct is relevant because aspects of the defendant's behavior, such as wantonness, recklessness, or reprehensibility, should be considered in some decisions (e.g., the awarding of punitive damages) but not in others (e.g., the awarding of compensatory damages). As we have noted, these distinctions are quite subtle, and the expectations of jurors' cognitive abilities are high. Are jurors up to the task?

THE PLAINTIFF'S CONDUCT

In some cases the plaintiff's own actions contributed to his or her injury. Such *contributory negligence* is defined as

> conduct on the part of the plaintiff which falls below the standard to which he should conform for his own protection, and which is a legally

contributing cause cooperating with the negligence of the defendant in bringing about the plaintiff's harm. (*Restatement [Second] of Torts*, 1965, § 463)

Under the common-law rule of contributory negligence, "when a plaintiff's negligence contributes to the happening of an accident, he cannot recover damages from a defendant who negligently injures him" (Schwartz, 1994, 1999 Cum. Suppl., p. 5). This standard has received criticism for a number of reasons (e.g., Prosser, 1953; Schwartz, 1994), primarily its failure to allocate responsibility in proportion to fault. For example, in overturning its contributory negligence doctrine, the California Supreme Court stated that

the basic objection to the doctrine—grounded in the primal concept that in a system in which liability is based on fault, the extent of fault should govern the extent of liability—remains irresistible to reason and all intelligent notions of fairness. (*Li v. Yellow Cab Co. of California*, 1975)

As a result, the federal government and most states have enacted statutes changing the standard to one of comparative negligence, according to which negligent plaintiffs in some cases may still recover a portion of their damages.[1] Currently, all but four states (Alabama, Maryland, North Carolina, and Virginia, as well as the District of Columbia) use a comparative negligence rule (Schwartz, 1994).

Under comparative negligence, jurors assign percentages of fault attributable to the plaintiff(s) and the defendant(s), and the plaintiff's damages are reduced proportionally (see, generally, *Restatement [Third] of Torts: Apportionment of Liability*, 2000, §§ 7–8 and accompanying comments). For example, if a plaintiff in an automobile accident is found 30% responsible for the accident, and the jury determines that his injuries warrant $100,000 in compensation, then he would receive only $70,000.[2]

Archival studies suggest that changing from a contributory to a comparative negligence standard has resulted in more verdicts in favor of the plaintiff—because it is easier to demonstrate the defendant's partial fault than complete fault—but also smaller average awards when the plaintiff does recover damages, because compensation is reduced according to the

---

[1] Legislative adoption of comparative negligence dates back as far as the late 1800s and early 1900s, but most of the legislative changes have occurred since the late 1960s (Epstein, 2000; Prosser, 1953; Schwartz, 1994). A few states have adopted comparative negligence by judicial holding rather than by legislative statute.

[2] There are two main types of comparative negligence: (a) modified and (b) pure. Under the more common, modified form (used in 35 states), the plaintiff may recover damages only if his or her negligence is less than (in some states, less than or equal to) 50%. In yet another variant of the modified form, the *slight–gross* system (e.g., South Dakota), a negligent plaintiff may recover only if his or her negligence is *slight* and the defendant's is *gross* in comparison (Prosser, 1953; Schwartz, 1994). Under the pure form (used in 11 states and the Commonwealth of Puerto Rico), a plaintiff may recover damages regardless of his or her degree of negligence, as long as it is less than total. Several jurisdictions with the modified form apply pure comparative negligence in limited cases (Schwartz, 1994).

plaintiff's degree of fault (Hammitt, Carroll, & Relles, 1985; Shanley, 1985). For example, Shanley (1985) compared jury verdicts in automobile accidents[3] in San Francisco County for the period 1970–1974 (under contributory negligence) to those for the period 1975–1980 (after comparative negligence went into effect in California). Plaintiffs were significantly more likely to win under comparative than contributory negligence, regardless of the plaintiff's actual degree of negligence. The difference in plaintiff win rates under contributory and comparative negligence regimes increased as the plaintiff's degree of negligence increased. This trend makes sense, because relatively negligent plaintiffs may still recover under comparative negligence—especially under the pure form used in California—but are legally barred from recovery under contributory negligence.

Reduced damages to the plaintiff because of his or her conduct are, of course, the intent of the comparative negligence rule in the first place. However, comparative negligence may have a more insidious effect in that the *gross* damage awards to partially negligent plaintiffs—that is, before their reduction—may be less than those for comparably injured, non-negligent plaintiffs. In other words, jurors may first discount their award to reflect the plaintiff's wrongdoing, and the judge then further reduces the award to reflect the jury's decision about the proportionate fault of the two parties. This so-called *double discounting* results in plaintiffs with similar injuries who receive disparate outcomes, creating what we referred to earlier as *horizontal inequity*. Indeed, archival studies indicate that plaintiffs who are found comparatively negligent receive smaller gross damage awards than comparably injured non-negligent plaintiffs (Hammitt et al., 1985; Shanley, 1985; Shanley & Peterson, 1983). For example, Shanley (1985) found that plaintiffs whose special verdicts stated they had been found 25% negligent actually had their awards reduced by 39%; plaintiffs who were 50% negligent had their awards reduced by 66%, and so on. Overall, "winning" plaintiffs received, on average, about one-fifth less in gross awards in the comparative negligence than in the contributory negligence era.[4]

The law in most jurisdictions intends that juries will not discount their gross damage award as a function of the plaintiff's blameworthiness but rather that the judge will perform that job. A typical instruction on awarding damages in a (modified) comparative negligence jurisdiction reads as follows:

> If you find the plaintiff was damaged and that the plaintiff's damages were caused by both the negligence of the plaintiff and the defendant, then you must determine to what extent the negligent conduct of each contributed to the damages of the plaintiff, expressed as a percentage

---

[3]Automobile litigation was selected because it comprises roughly half of all civil litigation, and it frequently involves issues of comparative negligence (Shanley, 1985).
[4]There is some evidence that this pattern is more true for automobile litigation than for other types of cases involving comparative negligence issues (Shanley & Peterson, 1983).

of 100 percent. . . . If the plaintiff is allowed to recover [i.e., if the plaintiff's negligence was less than the defendant's], the total damages you award will be reduced by the Court by the percentage of the plaintiff's negligence. (*Colorado Jury Instructions 3d: Civil*, 1989)

These instructions are fairly explicit in that they establish both that negligent plaintiffs may still recover damages and that any damage award will subsequently be reduced by the court. In some states, as in Colorado, jurors simply make a gross award, and the judge subsequently does the math; in other states, jurors are required to do the math themselves. For example, jurors in California (where pure comparative negligence applies) are instructed:

First: You will determine the total amount of [all economic and non-economic] damages to which the plaintiff would be entitled under the court's instructions if plaintiff had not been contributorily negligent.

Second: You will determine what proportion or percentage is attributable to the plaintiff of the total combined [negligence] [fault] [wrongful conduct] of the plaintiff and of the defendant[s] . . . whose fault contributed to the injury.

Third: You will then reduce [both] the total amount of plaintiff's [economic] damages [and plaintiff's noneconomic damages] by the proportion or percentage of negligence attributable to the plaintiff.

Sixth: The resulting amount[s], after making such reduction, will be the amount[s] of your verdict[s]. (*California Jury Instructions: Civil, Book of Approved Jury Instructions*)

Jurors' knowledge of a pending reduction in the gross award could have countervailing effects. On the one hand, knowing that the plaintiff is partially at fault could produce a smaller gross award through double discounting, as we described previously. On the other hand, knowing that a negligent plaintiff will have his or her award reduced could lead jurors to increase the gross award in order to offset any anticipated reduction, especially if this manner of apportioning fault offends their sense of justice, or if they wish the plaintiff to receive a larger damage award than this scheme allows (Finkel, 1995).

What do we know about how evidence of the plaintiff's conduct affects jurors' thoughts about compensation? Little jury simulation work has manipulated the plaintiff's conduct. Thomas and Parpal (1987) found an indirect relationship between the degree of the plaintiff's fault and the amount of the damage award, such that more blameworthy plaintiffs received less compensation, but the reductions in the amounts of the awards were not directly proportional to the level of negligence actually assigned by participants to the plaintiffs.

Feigenson, Park, and Salovey (1997) also manipulated plaintiffs' blameworthiness, in order to ask whether jurors' judgments track legally relevant inputs or whether, instead, jurors conflate elements of fault and damages into a single compensation judgment. Participants in this study read summaries of four cases that varied the plaintiff's blameworthiness and the severity of the outcome (a home accident where a gas leak caused a house to explode, a workplace accident involving a railway worker, a pedestrian–automobile accident, and medical malpractice involving allegedly negligent anesthetization). They apportioned fault between the plaintiff and defendant and assessed both gross and discounted damages.

The results suggest that mock jurors did not compartmentalize their decisions as neatly as the jury instructions mandate; rather, they based their determinations of damages (and responsibility) on legally irrelevant criteria. In particular, they awarded less in gross damages when the victim/plaintiff was more legally blameworthy. This finding amounts to double discounting, in that the jurors discounted the award when informed of the plaintiff's role in the accident, and the judge would have further discounted the award by multiplying the resulting damage award by the percentage of fault attributed to the plaintiff. Moreover, this discounting effect was steeper the more severely injured the plaintiff was.

Why do jurors diverge from the legally prescribed decision-making process? Feigenson et al. (1997) wondered whether jurors simply misunderstood their instructions regarding comparative negligence. Although the researchers could not discard this possibility altogether, they essentially ruled out misunderstanding as the true culprit. The mock jurors in this study were highly educated college and law school students who should have been able to comply with a simple instruction to reduce the gross award by the percentage of fault attributed to the plaintiff.

A second possibility is that mock jurors actively resisted following the judge's instructions and used an alternative decision-making strategy instead—one that fit with their conceptions of justice and common sense (Finkel, 1995; Sommer, Horowitz, & Bourgeois, 2001) and that Feigenson (2000) described as subserving jurors' goal of "total justice." This explanation is supported by research indicating that jurors often discuss plaintiff fault during deliberation and are not at all sympathetic toward plaintiffs whose actions contributed in some way to their own injuries (Hans, 1996). If this interpretation of the double-discounting effect is valid, then it suggests that there will be limits as to how much jury decision making can be improved by enhancing the comprehensibility and clarity of instructions on damages. It suggests further that efforts to increase compliance with the law will have to account for jurors' use of these alternative, personally derived decision-making approaches.

A limitation of both Thomas and Parpal's (1987) and Feigenson et al.'s (1997) studies is that they manipulated the level of plaintiff negligence indirectly (i.e., through descriptions of the plaintiff's behavior) and had participants determine liability prior to awarding damages. This methodology does not allow for the comparison of awards across specific, predetermined levels of plaintiff negligence.

Zickafoose and Bornstein (1999) explicitly manipulated the level of the plaintiff's negligence, allowing for direct comparisons across various levels of plaintiff conduct. Mock jurors in this study (undergraduates and citizens called for jury duty) were asked to award damages in a medical malpractice case in which liability had already been determined. They were informed that in a previous trial the defendant had been found liable for negligence; in addition, the plaintiff had been determined to be 0%, 20%, or 40% at fault. The jury instructions informed participants that "the plaintiff may be responsible for his own injuries" but that they were to determine the gross amount of damages (limited to compensation) on the basis of the nature and severity of his injuries and without regard to his own degree of negligence. Finally, they were told that this amount would be reduced by the judge according to the plaintiff's level of negligence.

Participants awarded significantly higher damages in the 0% fault condition (M = $54,103) than in the other two conditions combined (M = $38,273). Moreover, awards in the 20% and 40% fault conditions did not differ from one another. In response to a question about how they determined the amount awarded, 14% of participants said that they explicitly reduced their award because of the plaintiff's negligence. It is interesting that they did not do this consistently: Although they awarded more to faultless plaintiffs, they nonetheless made comparable awards to plaintiffs found 20% negligent and plaintiffs found 40% negligent. Apparently, the absolute level of the plaintiff's responsibility has less effect on the likelihood of double discounting than does the fact that he or she was partially responsible at all.

These findings support the notion that jurors might simply find it impossible to ignore evidence of plaintiffs' liability—despite their best intentions—once they have been exposed to it. We elaborate on this possibility later in the chapter. Alternatively, jurors might nullify the law by explicitly reducing assessed damages by the degree of the plaintiff's negligence, despite instructions to the contrary. Nullification in the case of double discounting works to negligent plaintiffs' detriment; however, nullification can also work to negligent plaintiffs' advantage, depending on the law. For example, Sommer et al. (2001) found that mock jurors who were instructed to apply a contributory (as opposed to a comparative) negligence standard were more likely to ignore the law and distort the facts so that blameworthy plaintiffs were still able to recover.

What can be done to prevent jurors from unfairly discounting damages to negligent plaintiffs? In *Li v. Yellow Cab Co. of California* (1975) the court, recognizing that "the assigning of a specific percentage factor to the amount of negligence attributable to a particular party, while in theory a matter of little difficulty, can become a matter of perplexity in the face of hard facts" (p. 1240), recommended the use of special verdicts. "Special verdicts have an important role to play in administering a comparative negligence system, given that the plaintiff's final award is dependent upon both the extent of his damages and the degree of his negligence" (Epstein, 2000, pp. 373–374). Nineteen states provide for the use of special verdicts in their comparative negligence statutes (Schwartz, 1994). In some states these guidelines merely require the jury to itemize the percentage of negligence, gross award, and reduced award, whereas in other states the jury must also separate the gross (and, subsequently, the reduced) award into its economic and noneconomic components (Schwartz, 1994). In addition to providing jurors with greater guidance, an advantage of special verdicts is that they reveal a jury's thought processes, allowing for more thorough appellate review (Baldus, MacQueen, & Woodworth, 1995; Epstein, 2000; Greene & Bornstein, 2000; for a review of special verdicts in general, see chapter 8, this volume).

Zickafoose and Bornstein (1999) conducted a second experiment to assess the efficacy of special verdicts in comparative negligence cases. Using the same case as in their first experiment, where the plaintiff was 0%, 20%, or 40% negligent, they asked participants to itemize compensation for two types of economic damages (lost earnings and medical expenses) and two types of noneconomic damages (bodily harm[5] and pain and suffering). Because, as we have noted, noneconomic damage awards tend to be more variable, and because jurors receive less guidance in determining this element of compensation, Zickafoose and Bornstein predicted that the likelihood of double discounting would be greater for noneconomic damages than for economic damages (see also Hammitt et al., 1985).

The findings partially supported this hypothesis. Regardless of plaintiffs' degree of negligence, they received the same gross compensation for economic damages (Zickafoose & Bornstein, 1999). That's the good news. However, the bad news is that discounting of the gross award occurred for one of the two components of noneconomic damages (bodily harm, but not pain and suffering). The conclusion that can be drawn from these results is that double discounting is most likely to occur when jurors in comparative negligence cases are simply asked to award total compensation. Double discounting is also likely to occur when jurors are asked to itemize the components of compensation using special verdicts, but it is limited to noneconomic damages (specifically, bodily harm). Overall, then, we find support for the contention of the *Li v. Yellow Cab Co. of California* (1975) court and others (see chapter 8) that special verdict forms reduce undesirable variability in verdicts and promote closer adherence to the law.

---

[5]This element of noneconomic damages referred to consequences of the injury such as lost physical function, disfigurement, and so on.

THE DEFENDANT'S CONDUCT

Although the plaintiff's conduct is relevant to decisions about the amount of compensatory damages, the defendant's conduct, in theory, is not. This is because the defendant's conduct is legally irrelevant to the extent to which the plaintiff should be compensated. The nature of the plaintiff's injuries, and not the nature of the defendant's behavior, drives that decision. In contrast, the defendant's conduct is extremely relevant to the issue of punitive damages—both whether to award them at all and, if so, the amount.

In the *Restatement (Second) of Torts* (1965) the following position is adopted on punitive damages:

§908. Punitive Damages

(1) Punitive damages are damages, other than compensatory or nominal damages, awarded against a person to punish him for his outrageous conduct and to deter him and others like him from similar conduct in the future.

(2) Punitive damages may be awarded for conduct that is outrageous, because of the defendant's evil motive or his reckless indifference to the rights of others. In assessing punitive damages, the trier of fact can properly consider the character of the defendant's act, the nature and extent of the harm to the plaintiff that the defendant caused or intended to cause and the wealth of the defendant.[6]

Although the common law has explicitly authorized punitive damages for hundreds of years (Owen, 1994), the awarding of punitive damages, as we noted in chapter 2, is relatively rare (Daniels & Martin, 1990; Eisenberg, Goerdt, Ostrom, Rottman, & Wells, 1997; Koenig & Rustad, 1993; Rustad, 1992, 1998), despite a number of well-publicized claims to the contrary (see Koenig & Rustad, 1993, for a review). According to Rustad (1992, p. 37), "Punitive damages awards are a teaspoon-sized drop in an ocean of civil litigation." In addition, as we described in chapter 2, the frequency of punitive damage awards varies considerably across case type, occurring most frequently in intentional torts, employment-related torts, fraud, and slander/libel (where they are awarded in up to one quarter or one third of all verdicts) and less often in malpractice and products liability cases (Eisenberg et al., 1997; Rustad, 1998). Nonetheless, in cases where they are considered justified, punitive damages are generally regarded as an effective deterrent (e.g., Landes & Posner, 1987; Polinsky & Shavell, 1998).[7]

---

[6]We discussed the effect of defendants' wealth on punitive damage awards at length in chapter 4. The focus here is on the effect of defendants' allegedly outrageous conduct.

[7]Polinsky and Shavell (1998) argued that the defendant's conduct should be a factor in assessing punitive damages only for individual, but not for corporate, defendants, as punitive damages are likely to subserve the goals of deterrence and punishment in the former case but

In allowing punitive damages the courts have applied roughly the same criteria as those embodied in the guidelines of the *Restatement (Second) of Torts* (1965), deeming them appropriate when the defendant's behavior was reckless, reprehensible, willful, wanton, or malicious (Owen, 1994). The question then arises whether these aspects of the defendant's conduct affect the awarding of punitive damages, as they should, and whether they affect the awarding of compensatory damages, as they should not.[8]

Edie Greene and her colleagues have conducted a series of experiments addressing the extent to which mock jurors appropriately use evidence relating to the defendant's conduct. In the first of these studies, Cather, Greene, and Durham (1996) presented mock jurors with summaries of three different tort cases: (a) personal injury, (b) products liability, and (c) insurance bad faith. Each case varied the severity of the plaintiff's injury and the reprehensibility of the defendant's conduct. For example, the plaintiff in the products liability case was a 12-year-old boy who was injured while operating a lawnmower. He was described as either having lacerations on both hands requiring stitches (mild injury) or, in addition, having one arm amputated above the elbow (severe injury). In the low-reprehensibility condition the defendant manufacturer was described as having conducted considerable safety research in developing the lawnmower and as having been previously notified of only a few similar accidents. In the high-reprehensibility condition the defendant had conducted less safety research and been notified of many similar accidents.

Participants received instructions on the determinants of both compensatory and punitive damages, and they were told to assume that the defendant had already been found liable. As the law prescribes, reprehensible conduct by the defendant affected the amount of punitive damages awarded but not the amount of compensatory damages. This finding suggests that mock jurors were properly influenced by evidence of the defendant's conduct: It affected judgments that it should affect (i.e., punitive damages) without affecting judgments that it should not affect (i.e., compensatory damages).

In a follow-up study, Greene, Woody, and Winter (2000) again included a defendant-reprehensibility condition but used a somewhat different constellation of cases: products liability, automobile negligence, and

---

not the latter (see also Elliott, 1989). Some commentators have also argued that punitive damages, at least in certain types of cases, may actually result in overdeterrence and provide plaintiffs with an unjustified windfall (e.g., Breslo, 1992; D. D. Ellis, 1989; Polinsky & Shavell, 1998).

[8]The defendant's conduct is also, of course, central to the determination of liability. Jurors are properly sensitive to variations in the defendant's conduct in deciding whether to hold the defendant liable for that conduct (e.g., Anderson & MacCoun, 1999; Greene, Johns, & Smith, 2001), although they might not pay as much attention to this legally relevant factor as the instructions on punitive damages seem to require (Hastie, Schkade, & Payne, 1998).

medical malpractice. In the malpractice case, for instance, the plaintiff was described as the wife of an elderly man who died from complications resulting from infected bedsores. The defendant nursing home had either done nothing about a foul odor in the decedent's room (mild reprehensibility) or, in addition, had a documented history of leaving unattended patients in their beds for extended periods, had a poor patient-to-staff ratio, and received financial incentives for keeping down its costs (high reprehensibility). Echoing results of Cather et al.'s (1996) study, the defendant's conduct did not affect mock jurors' compensation awards in this case or in the automobile negligence case, although it did in the products liability case. On the other hand, reprehensibility affected punitive damage awards in two of the three cases (products liability and automobile negligence), as the law dictates. These effects were the same whether participants received all of the evidence before making their judgments (i.e., about both the plaintiff's injury and the defendant's conduct) or received evidence relevant to compensation prior to making that judgment, followed by evidence relevant to punitive damages (we discuss such bifurcation manipulations further in chapter 9). Thus, jurors appear able, for the most part, to keep the goals of different types of damage awards straight, although the extent to which they are able to do so varies across different types of cases. Other researchers (e.g., Anderson & MacCoun, 1999, Experiment 2) have likewise found that reprehensible conduct by the defendant does not affect mock jurors' compensation awards.[9]

In a third study, Greene, Johns, and Smith (2001) addressed whether reprehensible conduct by the defendant would influence mock jurors' compensation verdicts when they did not have the option of awarding punitive damages. Using a more realistic mock trial,[10] they asked participants to determine negligence in an automobile negligence case and any compensation award to which the plaintiff was entitled. They manipulated evidence about the defendant's conduct by describing mildly careless conduct, very careless conduct, or by providing no conduct information. In the mildly careless conduct condition the defendant truck driver was traveling near the speed limit with one lane change prior to the accident. In the very careless conduct condition he was traveling approximately 10 mph over the speed limit, had changed lanes twice just prior to the accident, and had taken a Breathalyzer test that revealed alcohol consumption but not legal intoxication. The severity of the plaintiff's injury was also manipulated (fractured skull and concussion vs. the same injuries plus a bro-

---

[9]Anderson and MacCoun (1999) did, however, obtain the somewhat curious finding that although defendants who had behaved reprehensibly were more likely to pay *any* punitive damages than defendants who had not behaved reprehensibly, the *amount* of punitive damages did not differ between the two groups.

[10]Greene et al. (2001) used an audiotaped mock trial, along with photographs and demonstrative evidence, as opposed to the brief written summaries used by Cather et al. (1996) and Greene et al. (2000).

ken leg and bruised ribs). Participants were asked to judge whether the defendant was negligent and, if so, to award compensation (but not any punitive damages).

Individuals and deliberating juries both awarded greater compensation when they had some evidence of the defendant's conduct than when they did not. It is interesting that this was true whether that evidence indicated that the defendant had been mildly or very careless. However, these effects of the defendant's conduct characterized compensation awards only when the plaintiff's injury was relatively less severe. With more severe injuries, there was no effect of the defendant's conduct on compensation awards. Thus, mock jurors fused their evaluation of the defendant's conduct (i.e., judging negligence) with their evaluation of the plaintiff's injury (i.e., awarding compensation). Further evidence of this fusion comes from the finding that participants who heard evidence of the defendant's conduct perceived the plaintiff as having been harmed to a greater extent than participants who had not received any information about the defendant's conduct, even though actual evidence of the plaintiff's injury was held constant. Again, this effect of defendant conduct was true for mild but not for severe injuries. Thus, evidence of the defendant's carelessness—even if it was not especially egregious—serves to make the same injury seem worse. In other words, evidence of the defendant's liability colors perceptions of the plaintiff's injury, so that more negligent defendants appear to be responsible for greater harm than less negligent defendants, even for the same injury. Consequently, more negligent defendants may be required to pay more in compensation than they should, especially for relatively mild injuries.[11]

These somewhat conflicting results make it difficult to characterize the effect of defendant reprehensibility on mock jurors' verdicts. The glass is half full in the sense that jurors' compensation awards are often unaffected by evidence about the defendant's conduct, while the size of their punitive damage awards usually is affected by such evidence. On the other hand, the glass is half empty in the sense that their compensation awards sometimes are affected by defendant reprehensibility (e.g., Greene et al., 2001; Greene et al., 2000), while the size of their punitive damage awards sometimes is not (e.g., Anderson & MacCoun, 1999; Greene et al., 2000). It is likely that these discrepancies reflect variations in trial type and complexity (Feigenson, 2000) as well as normally occurring variation. More

---

[11]Although Greene et al. (2001) found that any evidence of the defendant's conduct increased compensation awards, it is important to note that their mildly careless condition was still indicative of some degree of defendant negligence. It is probably not the case that evidence of exculpatory conduct by the defendant would also increase compensation. Explicit evidence that the defendant had acted in a non-negligent fashion (e.g., by adhering to all traffic regulations and exercising an unusually high degree of caution) would presumably reduce compensation, although in such cases the defendant would of course be unlikely to be held liable in the first place.

important is that the findings suggest that claims either that the jury system operates in perfect accord with legal guidelines or (more commonly) that it is woefully inadequate are overly simplistic.

Information about the defendant's reckless conduct might not have to be presented at trial in order for it to exert an effect. Bornstein, Whisenhunt, Nemeth, and Dunaway (2002, Experiment 2) conducted a study in which mock jurors read a summary of a personal-injury case where a woman diagnosed with ovarian cancer had filed suit against a chemical company, alleging that some of the company's chemicals had seeped into her water supply and caused her injury. Before reading the trial summary, all participants read pretrial publicity about the case. One group read a publicity story with neutral content, and a second group read a story indicating that the defendant had acted in a wanton manner (e.g., "Greenpeace, an environmental watchdog organization, reported that the chemical company was polluting the environment and trying to cover up these allegations"). Both groups received general jury instructions telling them to determine the facts solely on the basis of the evidence presented in the case.

Pretrial publicity had a significant effect on participants' compensation awards, with participants who were exposed to adverse publicity about the defendant awarding more money (M = $591,768, Mdn = $500,000) than participants in the control condition (M = $381,373, Mdn = $350,000). Thus, jurors' compensation awards can be influenced by evidence of the defendant's conduct that is not even presented as formal evidence at trial. A second manipulation involved giving some participants additional judicial instructions that specifically directed them to disregard any pretrial publicity to which they may have been exposed. The effect of the pretrial publicity was not reduced by specifically instructing participants to ignore it.

All of the research described so far has addressed the defendant's conduct in allegedly causing the plaintiff's injury. Although we have paid little attention to the litigants' conduct during trial, their conduct at this stage can also affect jurors' damage awards. For example, Bornstein, Rung, and Miller (2002) conducted a study in which mock jurors received one of three case scenarios in which a physician had been found liable for malpractice. During the damages phase of the trial the researchers manipulated the physician's level of remorse. In the *no-remorse* condition the physician did not indicate remorse. In the *remorse* condition he expressed his sorrow "for the unfortunate death" of the plaintiff's husband without admitting wrongdoing. In the *remorse–responsibility* condition the physician "expressed extreme remorse for his obvious negligence and for the unfortunate result in which [the patient] died." Participants awarded compensation and rated their perceptions of both the plaintiff and the defendant on several dimensions.

The defendant was understandably perceived as significantly less remorseful in the no-remorse condition than in both the remorse and the remorse–responsibility conditions. Of greater interest is that defendant remorse also had an effect on compensation awards, with the defendant who expressed remorse (without admitting responsibility) being required to pay less than in the other two conditions. Participants' perception of the plaintiff and defendant (other than the defendant's remorsefulness) did not vary significantly across conditions. Thus, an expression of remorse at the damages phase can apparently benefit defendants, but not if the apology includes an admission of responsibility.

BLAMEWORTHY CONDUCT BY PLAINTIFF AND DEFENDANT

If the plaintiff's and the defendant's conduct can each individually affect jurors' judgments, what happens when both litigants behave in an especially blameworthy or reprehensible manner? Would their faulty behaviors cancel each other out? Some indirect support for this proposition comes from Rustad's (1992) analysis of 355 products liability cases in which some personal injury resulted and punitive damages were awarded. The plaintiff was contributorily or comparatively negligent in only 7% of these cases. There are two possible interpretations of this surprisingly low figure: First, negligent plaintiffs do not seek to recover punitive damages in the first place (i.e., a case selection effect); second, negligent plaintiffs who do seek punitive damages usually do not get them, perhaps because their own negligence makes the defendant's conduct seem less egregious and therefore less deserving of punishment.

Feigenson, Park, and Salovey (2001) recently conducted an attempt to investigate these issues. They presented mock jurors with two accident cases that varied the severity of the plaintiff's injury, the plaintiff's blameworthiness, and the defendant's blameworthiness. For example, in one case the defendant gas company had, at an insurance company's request, begun replacing propane tank valves. They either had replaced (low blameworthiness) or had not yet replaced (high blameworthiness) the valve in the plaintiff's home. After detecting a gas leak in his home, the plaintiff went outside, either running away from the house (low blameworthiness) or turning to go back toward the house (high blameworthiness). At that point, the house exploded, causing the plaintiff to suffer either a black eye and facial bruises (low severity) or a spinal injury and paraplegia (high severity). Participants rated their emotional reactions to each case (i.e., anxiety, fear, anger, sympathy, sadness, and disgust). They then apportioned fault between the plaintiff and the defendant and determined both gross and adjusted compensation (i.e., reduced proportionately by any fault they had assigned to the plaintiff). Participants did not award punitive damages.

Both parties' blameworthiness affected how they were perceived in terms of their apparent fault, an effect that was mediated by participants' anger toward the parties (Feigenson et al., 2001). In other words, participants were angered by the litigants' blameworthy conduct, and this anger led them to attribute greater fault to the blameworthy parties. The only variable that affected gross awards was the severity of the plaintiff's injury.[12] Of particular note is that there was no direct evidence of double discounting due to the plaintiff's negligence, although there was some evidence that participants who perceived the defendant as having acted in a more blameworthy fashion awarded more damages, whereas those who perceived the plaintiff as having acted in a more blameworthy fashion awarded less damages. Participants who felt sadder for the plaintiff awarded greater damages, although the effect of sadness on compensation was subsumed by the effect of injury severity. Thus, although jurors' emotional reactions may influence some of the judgments they are asked to make, such as determining liability or apportioning fault (see also Bornstein, 1998; Whalen & Blanchard, 1982), as we discussed in chapter 6, injury severity is still the main driving force in determining compensation.

Although Feigenson et al. (2001) manipulated both litigants' blameworthiness, the defendant's conduct fell well short of aggravated fault (recall that participants were not asked to consider punitive damages). It is logical to suppose that when the defendant's conduct is wanton or reckless, juries would view the plaintiff's behavior as comparatively less negligent (i.e., there is only so much fault to go around). In addition, punitive damages may be available to plaintiffs in these circumstances. Although few courts have analyzed the intersection between comparative negligence and punitive damages (Schwartz, 1994), the general rule has been to not let comparative negligence on the part of the plaintiff bar recovery for punitive damages against reckless defendants (e.g., *Danculovich v. Brown*, 1979), as long as the plaintiff him- or herself did not act with reckless disregard for his or her own safety (*Kozar v. Chesapeake & Ohio Railway Co.*, 1970). Of course, juries might be disinclined to award punitive damages to plaintiffs who were themselves negligent.

It is interesting that "the majority of cases that have addressed the issue . . . hold that punitive damages will not be reduced even though the plaintiff's own fault contributed to the accident" (Schwartz, 1994, p. 424, footnote omitted).[13] This ruling creates a situation in which juries are re-

---

[12]There was also a significant interaction between plaintiff and defendant blameworthiness. This interaction is difficult to interpret, as it shows that gross damage awards were lower when defendant blame was high and plaintiff blame was low than in the other conditions. If gross compensation were to differ at all depending on the legally irrelevant factors of plaintiff and defendant blameworthiness, one would expect it to be highest in this condition, which should (and in fact did) elicit the strongest emotional responses favoring the plaintiff and against the defendant.
[13]One way around this apparent inconsistency, adopted by some courts (e.g., Colorado,

quired to apportion fault in order to reduce one type of damages (compensatory) but not another (punitive). In light of the research described earlier in this chapter (e.g., Hammitt et al., 1985; Zickafoose & Bornstein, 1999) showing that jurors have a tendency to overdiscount compensatory damages, it seems highly unlikely that they would be able to resist discounting punitive damages because of a plaintiff's negligence.

EXPLANATIONS AND SOLUTIONS

Jurors' tendency to let information about the litigants' conduct influence their compensation awards—what we refer to as the *fusion* of judgments—may reflect a common cognitive heuristic known as the *hindsight bias* (Fischhoff, 1975; Hawkins & Hastie, 1990; Rachlinski, 1998). According to the hindsight bias, people are unable to disregard outcome information that they already possess in estimating the judgments that they would have made a priori. In the civil jury context this means that jurors' notions of how foreseeable, justifiable, and negligent a defendant's actions were will depend on the outcome of those actions (Casper, Benedict, & Perry, 1989; Hastie, Schkade, & Payne, 1999; Kagehiro, Taylor, Laufer, & Harland, 1991; Kamin & Rachlinski, 1995; LaBine & LaBine, 1996; Wexler & Schopp, 1989). For example, Kamin and Rachlinski (1995) found that mock jurors who knew the outcome (flood damage) of a civil defendant's possible negligence were more likely to view the defendant's failure to take precautions to prevent that outcome as negligent, compared to mock jurors who evaluated the same behavior without knowledge of the outcome.[14] Similarly, mock jurors view a possibly unconstitutional police search as more likely to turn up the sought-after object (e.g., a suspect or illegal drugs)—and hence as more justified, by virtue of its greater foreseeability—if they know that it actually did uncover the object than if they do not know the outcome of the search (Casper et al., 1989; Kagehiro et al., 1991).

Most research on jurors' susceptibility to the hindsight bias has concentrated on how outcome information influences jurors' evaluation of the evidence and subsequent liability judgments. However, some research has addressed the effect of hindsight on damage awards as well. For example, mock jurors award plaintiff/victims of successful illegal searches less com-

---

Oklahoma), is effectively to reduce punitive damage awards in such cases by capping the amount of punitive damages that may be awarded to partially negligent plaintiffs (Schwartz, 1994). For the effect of caps in general, see chapter 9.

[14]Kamin and Rachlinksi (1995) used a case modeled on *Petition of Kinsman Transit Co.* (1964), in which a barge moored in a river broke loose and ran into a drawbridge, and the resulting dam caused flooding (for purposes of the study, the barge was changed to debris). Plaintiffs (whose property was flooded) claimed that the city–defendant was negligent in not employing a drawbridge operator during the winter, when the bridge was not in use, as the operator could have raised the bridge if the river threatened to flood.

pensation than plaintiff/victims of unsuccessful searches, even when injuries in the two cases are identical (Casper et al., 1989; Robbennolt & Sobus, 1997). Plaintiffs also receive less in punitive damages when hindsight information indicates greater culpability on their part (Casper et al., 1989), even though the defendant's conduct is identical regardless of whether outcome information is available.[15]

What accounts for these effects? According to Feigenson (2000, chapter 4), jurors in tort cases seek "total justice" in a number of interrelated senses. For example, they tend to view their task as one of squaring accounts between the litigants. This goal requires restoring order—typically by taking from the defendant and giving to the plaintiff—even if doing so conflicts with legal prescriptions. In addition, jurors tend to use all of the information that is relevant to their decision, even if they are expected to compartmentalize their judgments, using certain evidence for some judgments and different evidence for other judgments. It is in this sense that jurors' susceptibility to the hindsight effect and inability to disregard certain pieces of information come into play. This "holistic" approach to jury decision making often leads jurors to make global judgments about who did what to whom, who should pay for it, and how much, rather than separating judgments about liability and damages, or about different types of damages, into discrete steps as the law requires. As a result, jurors have a tendency to fuse discrete judgments into a jumbled, interrelated whole.

Such cognitive shortcuts are common, and to be expected, in situations where decisionmakers are forced to consider a great deal of complex information concerning events with which they have little or no expertise. Jurors' civil decision making is clearly such a situation, so it is unsurprising that they rely on cognitive heuristics in making their decisions (Arkes, 1989; Saks & Kidd, 1980). In this context, it is worth noting that some heuristics, such as the hindsight bias, only increase in magnitude the less familiar decisionmakers are with the task (Hawkins & Hastie, 1990).

What can be done in light of these findings? An obvious option would be to make jury instructions more explicit, to minimize any potential confusion on jurors' part about what evidence is appropriate to which judgments. However, clarification of jury instructions is unlikely to be very effective, as it essentially asks jurors to ignore certain information that they already have before them. Instructing decisionmakers to ignore information that they already have has been found not to reduce bias in everyday

---

[15]In referring to the hindsight effect as demonstrating "bias," the thrust of our argument is that it is a bad thing; that is, it biases decisionmakers toward making suboptimal decisions, leading them to consider information in making a type of decision from which that information should be excluded. There are limited senses in which information provided in hindsight can actually be helpful, as in the public policy objective of managing risk (Lempert, 1999). However, risk management is typically not under the jury's purview.

(Fischhoff, 1982) or legal contexts (Greene & Dodge, 1995; Kamin & Rachlinski, 1995; Kassin & Sommers, 1997).[16]

Another solution to the apparent fusion of conduct- and injury-related information in awarding compensation is to bifurcate trials, so that jurors who award compensation are not privy to details about the litigants' conduct (e.g., D. D. Ellis, 1989; Greene et al., 2000). There is some evidence that bifurcation does lead to more equitable verdicts, although there are also drawbacks to its implementation, as we discuss in chapter 9.

CONCLUSION

How well can juries make the subtle distinctions that the law expects them to make? What the empirical findings broadly suggest is that jurors' judgments on one set of issues—such as the amount deserved in gross compensation—might be influenced by their knowledge of other information, such as the plaintiff's negligence or the defendant's reckless conduct, that is ostensibly unrelated but that they cannot ignore. In terms of determining compensation, the law expects juries to determine fair compensation in light of the severity and nature of the plaintiff's injuries and not in light of either the plaintiff's conduct (which might legitimately influence the apportionment of compensatory damages and, depending on the comparative negligence standard in force, the defendant's liability) or the defendant's conduct (which might legitimately influence the awarding of punitive damages and the defendant's liability). The research findings we described in this chapter suggest that it is unreasonable to expect jurors who have heard conduct evidence regarding either the plaintiff or the defendant to ignore that information when attempting to award just compensation.

Nonetheless, the jury usually does manage to get it right. Most of the time, evidence of the defendant's outrageous conduct appropriately influences punitive but not compensatory damage awards, and most of the time, evidence of the plaintiff's negligence appropriately influences whether he or she receives any compensation at all. Also, although partially negligent plaintiffs do have their gross awards doubly discounted, the primary determinant of compensation is, as it should be, injury severity. Thus, our review of the literature leads us to conclude that, at least in this realm, the civil jury system is not in need of a major overhaul. We are not so sanguine as to argue that jury behavior regarding damages has no room for improvement, however, and we consider a number of possible reforms in chapter 9, after first describing the strategies that jurors use in making sense of the evidence to arrive at a verdict.

---

[16]For a useful review of potential techniques to correct for hindsight bias in the civil jury context, see Wexler and Schopp (1989).

III

DECISION PROCESSES AND
REFORMS: HOW JURORS
REASON ABOUT DAMAGES
AND HOW DAMAGE
AWARD DECISIONS MIGHT
BE IMPROVED

INTRODUCTION

DECISION PROCESSES AND REFORMS: HOW JURORS REASON ABOUT DAMAGES AND HOW DAMAGE AWARD DECISIONS MIGHT BE IMPROVED

Our survey of the influences on jury damage awards culminates in chapter 8, in which we detail the decision-making processes jurors use to assess damages, including how they deal with complex information, what they do when blindfolded to the consequences of their decisions (and how removal of the blindfold changes their reasoning), and how they discuss damages during deliberation. More than 40 years ago, the original observers of the civil jury—members of the University of Chicago Jury Project— proposed a variety of means by which jurors transform their perceptions of injury and conduct into monetary values (e.g., Broeder, 1959; Kalven, 1958). Now, decades later and with the backing of years of accumulated data (something these early writers lacked), we can determine whether the early theories are still valid.

As suspected long ago, jurors use a variety of decisional schemes to arrive at their damage awards. They sometimes assimilate their awards to monetary figures provided by the litigants during the trial, they sometimes evaluate separate components of a plaintiff's complaint and compute a single sum only after making these componential calculations, and they sometimes search for a figure that reflects their general sentiments about the case and the parties involved. The particular circumstances of the case and of the jurors will dictate when each of these decision-making strategies is likely to be used. In general, jurors do a sizable amount of calculating and adjusting to arrive at a number that is, at least in their minds, fair and just. These data suggest that the analogy of damage awards to a lottery system is almost always incorrect.

However, as we have stated repeatedly, the assessment of damages is not a straightforward process, and jurors who are assigned this task are not infallible thinkers. Those two conditions combine to create, on occasion, less than optimal decisions. So we must ask whether the process can be improved and whether the system can be tweaked (or perhaps even re-vamped in some fundamental ways) to enhance the likelihood of fair, pre-dictable, and reasoned judgments regarding damages.

This is our focus in chapter 9. In particular, we describe significant work that has been conducted (and, in some cases, is still under way) on reforming the jury system in civil damages cases. We look at the effects of capping damage awards; the possibility of circumscribing jurors' decisions by offering them a range of awards from previous, comparable cases; the effects of bifurcating, or separating their decisions into smaller, more dis-crete judgments; the effects of providing clearer instructions; and the ways that jurors gauge damages when awards are shared between the plaintiff and the government. Finally, we consider the possibility of eliminating jurors completely and instead relying on judges to make damages assess-ments.

Ten years ago, we would have had very little to say about jury reforms regarding damage awards. Today, we know that some attempts at reform are better than others, that some revisions in the system have moved jurors closer to the normative ideal, and that other reforms have had the opposite effect. Ten years from now (and with additional accumulated knowledge), we will have an even better understanding of the ways that jurors put values on priceless objects and subjective states of mind. We will also know more about how to make jurors' decisions more rational. It is our profound hope that the legal system will welcome the notion of reform so that the decisions required of jurors and the ways in which their tasks are structured will better coincide with how people reason and make decisions.

8

HOW JURORS REASON
ABOUT DAMAGES

In this chapter we focus on the processes and strategies that jurors use to reason about damages. Psychologists have identified several components of the cognitive process involved in assessing damage awards. First, as we described in chapter 6, jurors must judge the extent and severity of the plaintiff's losses. (Also, as we noted in chapter 7, they sometimes also take note of elements of the plaintiff's and defendant's conduct that preceded and followed from the injury-causing incidents.) Next, they must attempt to translate those losses into a dollar value that will return the plaintiff to a status quo *ante*. In this chapter we take a detailed look at the second step in the process: the translation of losses into monetary awards; specifically, how do jurors transform their perceptions of the plaintiff's losses into monetary terms?

We begin by examining the strategies that jurors use to map their assessments of injuries onto a dollar award scale. On the basis of Kalven's (1958) theorizing, Edie Greene (1989) described two competing models that attempt to capture this decision-making process: (a) anchoring and adjustment, a componential approach in which individual components of the loss are calculated and then summed, and (b) a more holistic reasoning approach in which jurors derive some approximation of a reasonable award without explicit computation.

In the second half of this chapter we explore the influence of various trial-related features on award decision making. In particular, we examine the effects of evidence complexity, the opportunity to deliberate, and "blindfolds" that effectively keep jurors in the dark about information relevant to their decisions about damages. In so doing, we consider the possibility that certain structural and procedural elements of the trial can impair jurors' decision-making processes.

ANCHORING AND ADJUSTMENT

Cognitive psychologists suggest that anchors provide a basis for simplifying judgments that involve uncertainty and that people often rely on a salient numerical reference point, or *anchor*, when making quantitative judgments (Tversky & Kahneman, 1974). Although new information may lead to adjustments away from the anchor, the resulting response will still have been influenced by the location of the anchor on a numerical scale. When people reason in this way, they are using the so-called *anchoring and adjustment heuristic* (Tversky & Kahneman, 1974). Anchors are likely to carry weight in decisions about damages because people may lack confidence in their own ability to assign dollar values to various injuries. When people are not confident of their judgments, they are more susceptible to being influenced by an anchor (Jacowitz & Kahneman, 1995).

When judgments are made in the context of an anchor, both *assimilation* and *contrast* effects can occur. If the anchor falls within a range of response alternatives that a decisionmaker deems acceptable, then *assimilation* occurs, and the response is drawn toward the anchor. If, on the other hand, the anchor falls outside of the range of acceptable responses, then an individual's response would be displaced from the anchor (a *contrast* effect). We use the example of caps, or limits on damage awards, to illustrate assimilation and contrast effects.

Suppose that a juror deems reasonable a damage award in the range of $100,000–$200,000. Further suppose that a cap is located at the upper end of a range of acceptable responses (e.g., $200,000). In this situation, damage awards would, on average, be assimilated toward the anchor and would be larger than awards made in the absence of a cap (a result opposite the intention of tort reform advocates, who perceive the cap as a way to reduce damage awards).[1] If, on the other hand, the cap is equivalent to an

[1]This example assumes, of course, that jurors are aware of the level of the cap. In some jurisdictions (e.g., Colorado), jurors are explicitly instructed that their punitive damage award cannot exceed their compensatory award. In other jurisdictions (e.g., Florida), jurors are not told about limits imposed on their awards. We suspect that even if jurors are not directly instructed that damages are capped at a certain level, they may nonetheless have this expectation from information available in the media, conversations with others, or from general knowledge of tort reform legislation. Kang (1999) argued against disclosing to jurors that their awards will be capped, reasoning that such a disclosure would lead juries to distort their damages assessments without regard to the evidence.

amount that the juror deems objectionable (e.g., an exorbitantly high number, say $2 million), then the cap would have the opposite effect, causing jurors to reduce their awards (Hinsz & Indahl, 1995).

Because of a common practice in litigating civil cases, it is likely that jurors deciding those cases would invoke the anchoring and adjustment heuristic when setting monetary awards. A standard practice in these cases is for the plaintiff's attorney to supply a number stating the amount of damages sought by his or her client (the *ad damnum*) and, on occasion, for the defense attorney to counter with a second recommended figure.[2] Thus, most jurors are provided with at least one, and sometimes two, monetary figures that have the potential to influence the resulting award. If the anchor seems even remotely acceptable, individuals may adjust their judgment toward this initial value.

As an example, consider the *ad damnum* offered in the wrongful death and survivorship claim brought in New Jersey by Mary Beth DeHanes, whose husband died as a result of a tear in the lining of his aorta. The defendant, Dr. Michael Rothman, had failed to properly diagnose the condition in the emergency room of the Raritan Bay Medical Center. At the time of his death, Joseph DeHanes was a 38-year-old machine operator earning more than $55,000 per year. An economist testified that if the deceased had lived and worked until age 65, he would have had 26 more years of earning potential. The plaintiff's lawyer argued that with salary raises, inflation, and other reasonable adjustments, Mr. DeHanes's total earnings would have been $2,042,246. He offered this amount as the *ad damnum*. The jury eventually awarded Mrs. DeHanes $1.5 million in lost wages (*DeHanes v. Rothman*, 1999).

Dale Broeder (1959), writing about the University of Chicago Jury Project in the 1950s, suggested that the *ad damnum* does "yeoman service as a kind of damage jumping-off place for the jurors" (p. 756). Marti and Wissler (2000) described a number of processes by which jurors' award decisions might be affected by attorney recommendations. For example, an anchor might affect judgments by serving as a standard for comparison or as a "candidate for the judgment" (p. 92), by altering perceptions of the injury or of the range of acceptable values, or by activating information that affects the interpretation of both the anchor and the injuries. They further posited that an award recommendation would be an especially powerful anchor because it is highly relevant to the jurors' task of setting damages and because jurors have little knowledge or experience of assigning damages and, therefore, lack confidence in their intuitive judgments.

What evidence exists to support this hypothesized anchoring and adjustment effect? Broeder (1959) was the first to document the influence of

---

[2]This is not a universal practice, however. *Ad damnums* are permitted in some jurisdictions, forbidden in others, and required in still others. Such inconsistency in procedures could lead, of course, to significant inequity in resulting awards (Saks, 1997).

the *ad damnum* on jurors' awards. He interviewed jurors in 11 personal injury cases and found that in 6 of the 7 cases in which the plaintiff prevailed, damages were determined, at least partially, with reference to the *ad damnum*. Broeder described the case in which the *ad damnum* had its most significant impact: The plaintiff was seeking $2,400 for loss of the use of his tractor, among other things. The influence of the *ad damnum* was demonstrated by the fact that jurors apparently began their deliberations with a protracted discussion of the appropriateness of this amount. They eventually agreed to award half of that requested figure.

The first experimental demonstration that the *ad damnum* would function as an anchor came from a study conducted by Zuehl (1982). Sixty-nine mock juries watched a personal injury trial in which the *ad damnum* was systematically varied while the facts of the case were held constant. Different groups of jurors were given suggested amounts of $10,000, $75,000, $150,000, or "substantial compensation." (Jurors in the actual case had awarded $65,000.) Data showed that half of the damage awards precisely matched the dollar figure requested; however, acceptance of the requested figure decreased as the amount increased. Thus, the average awards from jurors with explicit monetary requests were $18,000, $62,800, and $101,400, respectively.

These findings, and others that show similar effects of the anchor (e.g., Chapman & Bornstein, 1996; Greene, Downey, & Goodman-Delahunty, 1999; Malouff & Schutte, 1989; Marti & Wissler, 2000; Raitz, Greene, Goodman, & Loftus, 1990), suggest that "the more you ask for, the more you get." In a particularly compelling demonstration of this effect, Hinsz and Indahl (1995) showed mock jurors a re-enactment of a civil trial in which the defendant was being sued for wrongful death by the parents of two children killed in an automobile accident. In one condition the plaintiff's lawyer requested $2 million, and in a second condition requested $20 million. Jurors were asked to fairly and reasonably compensate the plaintiffs for the losses they had sustained. The mean award from the $2 million *ad damnum* condition was $1,052,917, and the mean from the $20 million condition was a whopping $9,061,538!

Chapman and Bornstein (1996) also included an extremely high request, for $1 billion, in the trial of a personal injury lawsuit in which the plaintiff claimed that her birth control pills had led to her ovarian cancer. Although the plaintiff who requested the extremely high award was perceived as more selfish, less honorable, and less generous than plaintiffs who had asked for less, still jurors tended to use the *ad damnum* as an anchor and adjust their awards from this starting point. They awarded significantly more to that plaintiff than to the plaintiff who requested (only) $5 million. Hastie and colleagues (Hastie, Schkade, & Payne, 1999) showed dramatic effects of the plaintiff's request for punitive damages on resulting awards.

Plaintiffs' lawyers undoubtedly exploit these situations. In fact, some trial manuals explicitly advise plaintiffs' attorneys to exaggerate the amount of the *ad damnum* (DeMay, 1977).

One wonders if there is an upper limit to the amount that jurors will award, based on the *ad damnum*. In other words, will jurors' awards boomerang if the request is simply out of line with reality, resulting in a contrast effect? We saw no evidence of this phenomenon in Chapman and Bornstein's (1996) study, despite the fact that the request for a $1 billion award was accompanied by a statement that the amount was much more than the average amount requested by plaintiffs in comparable cases.

One intimation of a boomerang effect comes from an experimental study conducted by Malouff and Schutte (1989) but is limited to a particular combination of circumstances: when attorneys for a female Hispanic plaintiff requested $800,000 as compensation for temporomandibular joint and shoulder injuries, their client was awarded less than when they requested a lower amount. A second example of the boomerang effect was provided by Marti and Wissler (2000). Mock jurors read the case summary of a personal injury lawsuit in which a longshoreman was injured by the actions of the defendant shipping company and in which the level of plaintiff *ad damnum* requests and defense rebuttals were systematically varied. The $25 million plaintiff's request resulted in significantly lower awards than did the $15 million request, and the $0 defense rebuttal produced awards that were significantly higher than when a $100,000 rebuttal was offered. In general, though, the results of these studies support others in showing a strong anchoring effect: The amount requested had a significant effect on the amount awarded.

What happens when the defense offers its own, more modest proposal for compensation? Several years ago, Edie Greene and her colleagues began to investigate the effects of a defense counteranchor on mock jurors' damage awards (Greene, Downey, & Goodman-Delahunty, 1999; Raitz et al., 1990). In many cases (especially those in which the defendant's liability has already been established and the main issue is the assignment of damages), the defense team will challenge the plaintiff's request and suggest that a lower amount should be awarded instead. For example, when Anna Lloyd sued American Airlines for physical and emotional injuries that resulted from a plane crash in Little Rock, Arkansas, she asked for $15 million, whereas lawyers for the airline argued that $330,000 was sufficient ("Woman gets $6.5 million," 2001).

In jury analogue studies it has been hypothesized that, assuming no differences in the credibility of the parties, mock jurors exposed to both the anchor (*ad damnum*) and counteranchor (defendant's suggested award) would view the suggested amounts as constituting a range and set a figure that falls between the two extremes. (The jury in Anna Lloyd's case awarded her $6.5 million.) One study (Raitz et al., 1990) involved an employment discrimination lawsuit. In one condition, neither side offered a compensatory damage award recommendation. In a second condition, the plaintiff's expert economist testified that, on the basis of his calculations, the plaintiff should be awarded $719,000 for lost wages. In this condition the defense attorney countered with a figure of $321,000. The third experimental condition involved a "battle of experts" in which the same suggested amounts were calculated by opposing experts.

Mock jurors gave higher damage awards in the plaintiff–expert condition than in the counterexpert condition, suggesting that the defense was effective in reducing the award but only when it offered the testimony of an expert economist (Raitz et al., 1990). The words of the defense attorney were apparently less persuasive. In addition, little support was found for the notion that jurors would simply "split the difference"; rather, they tended to favor one expert or the other. In the counterexpert condition 21% of jurors gave awards that exactly matched the plaintiff's figure, and 20% awarded the defendant's recommendation, providing further support for the effect of the anchor on jurors' awards. In studies addressing similar issues, Marti and Wissler (2000) found that the defendant's rebuttal amount served as a counteranchor and reduced the amount awarded in damages in personal injury cases, and L. Ellis (2002) found that jurors' awards were anchored by the defense recommendation in a premises-liability trial: An extremely low recommendation reduced damage awards.

The studies we have reviewed to this point all involve data from individual, nondeliberating jurors. Perhaps the hypothesized compromise awards are less apt to occur in these studies than in more realistic circumstances in which jurors must reach consensus by deliberating as a group. That possibility was put to a test by Greene, Downey, and Goodman-Delahunty (1999), who used the same employment discrimination lawsuit to replicate Raitz et al.'s (1990) study and to evaluate the effects of anchors on jury (as opposed to juror) awards. The authors suspected that juries would be less likely than individual jurors to assimilate their awards to the amounts suggested by the parties because, during deliberations, jurors could rely on the assembled wisdom of their colleagues, rather than on their personal abilities, to gauge the appropriateness of the requested amounts. In addition, jury awards might represent compromises among differing juror preferences.

There were two findings of note. First, only 3 of the 22 juries awarded exactly the amount requested by the plaintiff (all were in the condition in which the plaintiff's economist testified to this amount and was not challenged by a counterexpert), and no jury returned a verdict equal to the defendant's request (Greene, Downey, & Goodman-Delahunty, 1999). Second, and more relevant to the juror–jury comparison, the mean jury award in the counterexperts condition ($529,000) was midway between the extremes suggested by the opposing experts ($719,000 and $321,000). So what effect does a counteranchor have on *juries'* sentiments regarding compensation? Apparently, jury awards may be reduced when the defense presents a counteranchor, at least when that amount is offered by an expert.

Why do these attorney requests function as anchors toward which awards are assimilated? Marti and Wissler (2000) argued that award recommendations alter jurors' beliefs about what constitutes acceptable awards. In essence, award recommendations offer a concrete, arguably objective norm that influences award determinations.

By contrast, another trial procedure that apparently functions as an anchor—the imposition of a cap, or limit on damage awards—is considerably more arbitrary and may have little relevance to the facts of the case (Robbennolt & Studebaker, 1999; we describe capping schemes in more detail in chapter 9). Nonetheless, caps can also serve as anchors that influence the resulting jury decisions regarding compensation. Hinsz and Indahl (1995) found that even though the injuries remained constant across three conditions of their study, awards varied as a function of the cap. So, for example, in the absence of a cap the median award in their double wrongful-death case was $37,500. When the cap was set at $2 million, the median award rose to $775,000, and when the cap rose to $20 million, the median award rose even more—to $1 million.

A study conducted by Saks, Hollinger, Wissler, Evans, and Hart (1997) has relevance here, also. They examined the effects of several types of jury guidance procedures, including caps, on the amounts awarded for pain and suffering in personal injury cases. When jurors were provided with information about awards in similar cases (e.g., an award interval, the average award plus award interval, and example awards) the variability in awards was reduced, but the size was not affected, at least in conditions of medium- and high-severity injuries. Caps, on the other hand, had a much less predictable effect, although this effect can be understood in the context of anchoring and assimilation. For both low- and medium-severity injuries, caps actually increased both the size and the variability of the awards for pain and suffering, compared with a noncapped control condition. Mock jurors' awards were apparently hoisted up by the cap, at least in conditions where the plaintiff's injuries were not severe.

Another demonstration of the anchoring effect of caps on both compensatory and punitive damages comes from the work of Robbennolt and Studebaker (1999), who simulated a lawsuit in which the plaintiff sued a blood bank after contracting HIV subsequent to a blood transfusion. Caps on punitive damages were set at either the 10th percentile ($100,000), the 50th percentile ($5 million), or the 90th percentile ($50 million) of a normal distribution of awards, based on pilot testing of the scenario without any limits on punitive awards. Data showed that the caps functioned as anchors: The punitive damage awards in the condition with the highest cap were significantly higher than awards in the control condition in which punitive damages were not capped, and awards in the condition with the lowest cap were significantly less than those of the control group. The caps pulled punitive damage awards up or down, depending on the level of the cap. Robbennolt and Studebaker suspected that jurors who are given no limit on punitive damages may begin with an implicit anchor of zero and then adjust their awards upward. By contrast, jurors with a high cap might (a) assume that this award is appropriate to the worst-case situation, (b) decide how much the present case differs from that worst-case scenario, and (c) decide how much money should be deducted from that maximum amount to account for the differences. These distinctive reasoning processes could easily explain the differences in punitive awards.

Interestingly, Robbennolt and Studebaker (1999) found that the cap on punitive damages had an unexpected anchoring effect on compensatory damage awards as well. When punitive damages were capped at $100,000, the mean compensatory damage award was $1,435,000, but when punitive damages were capped at $50 million, the mean compensatory award jumped to $7,642,417! So, whereas the purpose of caps on damage awards is to reduce or limit the size and variability of awards, the results of this study showed several paradoxical effects. When caps were set above the level at which jurors would award punitive damages (in the absence of a cap), caps served to increase both the size and variability of the award. Furthermore, caps on punitive damages served as anchors for *compensatory* damage award decisions, in some instances raising them above the level they would have been in the absence of a cap.

The joint effects of *ad damnums* and caps were examined in a simulation study by Diamond and colleagues (Diamond, Ellis, Saks, & Landsman, 2000). The stimulus was a products liability trial in which some participants received no information about a cap but requests for either unspecified damages, $250,000, $500,000, or $1 million in damages for pain and suffering. Other mock jurors were told that a cap of $500,000 existed on damages for pain and suffering and that, in addition, the plaintiff had requested either unspecified damages, $250,000, or $500,000. The cap and *ad damnum* interacted to influence awards: Awards increased as the *ad damnum* increased, and the cap hoisted awards in all but the most extreme *ad damnum* condition.

As we have noted at several points, the task of attaching a dollar value to another person's losses, particularly on dimensions that defy quantification, such as pain and suffering, is a difficult one indeed. As these studies show, jurors appointed to make such decisions rely both on information that was intended for their use and information that was not. *Ad damnums* are likely to serve as anchors for jurors' judgments, functioning as a jumping-off point for discussions about appropriate compensation. Caps can substitute for *ad damnums* in situations where the latter are not offered and have the ability to dramatically increase awards for pain and suffering, at least in situations where the awards would naturally be low.

COMPONENTIAL APPROACH TO ASSESSING DAMAGES

Harry Kalven, who was among the first to scrutinize the workings of the civil jury, thought that jurors should be instructed to ascertain a series of component sums that could then be totaled to arrive at a damage award. Although Kalven (1958) doubted that this process matched jurors' natural inclinations (he surmised that jurors searched for a single sum that seemed appropriate—a point to which we return later in this chapter), it nonetheless merits some consideration as a means by which damages might reasonably be calculated.

A handful of accounts document jurors' use of a componential approach to damages assessment (see, e.g., Selvin & Picus, 1987). For example, Edward Walton received $2,166,736 as compensation for lost wages, loss of future earning capacity, pain and suffering, and loss of life's pleasures after he was diagnosed with mesothelioma, a terminal cancer the only known cause of which is asbestos exposure. According to Walton's attorney, the reason for the odd monetary figure is that the Philadelphia jury actually assigned dollar values for each item of damage and then added them together (Lichtman, 1999).

As another example, Vidmar (1995) recounted a jury's deliberation on damages in a wrongful-death case in which a 21-year-old North Carolina college student was killed when a tow truck driver swerved in front of her car. During the trial, an expert economist detailed the deceased's potential earnings as a teacher (her intended vocation) and the financial contributions she would have made to her parents in their old age. Based on consideration of present-day salaries for teachers, wage inflation, reductions to present value, tax rates, fringe benefits, self-maintenance, morbidity rates, and other assumptions, the economist gave the estimate of the deceased's economic worth to her mother as $188,663. The judge instructed jurors that under North Carolina law they were to consider "services, protection, care, and assistance" as well as reasonable funeral expenses, the loss of "society, companionship, guidance, and friendly office" and the pain and suffering of the deceased's family. Did they?

Lengthy interviews with jurors subsequent to their $205,866 verdict indicated that they engaged in detailed discussion about the appropriateness of the economist's figures, particularly his failure to take into account the deceased's plan to marry and raise children, and recalculated her economic loses at $64,866. After extended discussion about the ability of money to soothe grieving family members, the jury settled on a figure of $100,000 for pain and suffering, then opted to increase the award to cover attorney's fees, something that they are not expected to consider. After tentatively agreeing on the rounded figure of $200,000, they decided to add funeral expenses of approximately $6,000.

Kalven (1958) did not elaborate on his notion that jurors should be

instructed to consider a series of component factors in damages calculations, but we suspect that he had in mind something similar to what the
North Carolina jury did. They scrutinized the elements of economic loss
relating to income and services, raised concerns about legal fees, and considered the impact of the award on the defendant.

Jurors interviewed by Mott, Hans, and Simpson (2000) subsequent to
serving in tort and contract cases recounted a decision process that had
clear elements of componential analyses. When asked about the strategies
they had used to arrive at a final award amount, jurors frequently mentioned a component sums approach in which they considered specific case-
relevant factors (e.g., severity of the injury or loss, plaintiff's age, attorneys'
fees) and then adjusted the award using collective ideas about the appropriateness of the resulting sum. There obviously are elements of intuitive
reasoning in this strategy, as well—something that we consider in the next
section.

Many states use special verdict forms in which jurors are instructed
to answer specific questions relating to the material issues in the case and
to break down awards into a series of elements or components (Wiggins
& Breckler, 1990). The assumption underlying this procedure is that it will
force jurors to adopt a componential approach to damages calculations,
making discrete decisions about the value of each element of damages and
then summing those values.

Wiggins and Breckler (1990) tested the hypothesis that requiring the
jury to focus on individual elements of damages may cause awards to be
higher than if the jury is allowed to select a figure that "just seems right."
In a mock defamation case, jurors were given either a general verdict form
that asked them simply to find for the plaintiff or the defendant and award
the appropriate damages, or a special verdict form that required them to
answer several specific questions about the case. Mock jurors using special
verdict forms gave significantly higher compensatory damage awards than
did those who issued only general verdicts. The effect of attending to multiple and consecutive questions of fact was apparently to make the plaintiff's losses more highly compensable, perhaps because this form focused
their attention on discrete losses that, had a general verdict form been
used, would never have been considered.

As an alternative to the componential model, in which jurors assess
discrete elements of damages separately, Kalven (1958) proposed that they
instead may determine their award holistically and then work backward,
using arithmetic to determine the components. Zickafoose and Bornstein
(1999) tested a variation of the special verdict form and suggested that the
form of the computation (component factors vs. a more holistic approach)
may not much matter to the outcome. Mock jurors in a medical malpractice case were asked either to determine the total damage award first and
then divide this amount into its component parts (e.g., for medical ex-

penses, lost income, pain and suffering, and physical injury suffered) or to determine the amounts for the individual components before arriving at the total damage award. There were no differences in total award as a function of this variation, suggesting that jurors might not award more simply because their decision is broken down into a number of smaller steps. When asked how they determined the amount awarded, an overwhelming majority of participants (78% in one study) stated that they explicitly computed a number. They were more likely to make computations when asked to assess a total award first than when requested to determine the individual components first. What still remains to be determined, of course, is the extent to which jurors are naturally inclined to consider component factors and the ways that the resulting awards may be influenced by this strategy.

HOLISTIC APPROACH: ASSESSING A FIGURE THAT "SEEMS RIGHT"

In addition to the anchoring–adjustment and componential approaches we have alluded to a third means by which jurors may arrive at a damage award: by agreeing on a general figure that seems "about right." This reasoning process could take many forms. We suspect that its most frequent application is in the realm of noneconomic damages, where there are few benchmarks to use in decision making. Largely unaided, jurors might be likely to determine a pain and suffering award, for example, in the context of what seems fair and appropriate, given the facts of the case and the particular circumstances of the parties involved.

However, this strategy could also be used in discussions regarding the total compensation package that jurors favor and in the ways that the total is allocated among various kinds of damages. Consider, for example, the results of two recent studies showing that jurors who did not have the opportunity to award punitive damages inflated their compensatory damage awards (in comparison to jurors who could award both compensatory and punitive damages; Anderson & MacCoun, 1999; Greene, Coon, & Bornstein, 2001). When denied the opportunity to seek retribution against the defendant or to promote specific or general deterrence—all goals of punitive damage judgments—jurors apparently meet these goals by way of compensatory damage judgments.[3]

Anderson and MacCoun (1999) had mock jurors read the summary

---

[3]This possibility was alluded to by the Wisconsin Supreme Court in *Wangen et al. v. Ford et al.* (1980): "It is generally recognized that if punitive damages are not allowed, juries give vent to their desire to punish the wrongdoer under the guise of increasing the compensatory damages, particularly those awarded for pain and suffering" (p. 277; cited by Anderson & MacCoun, 1999).

of a products liability case. Some jurors were allowed to make both compensatory and punitive damage awards, and others were instructed to award compensatory damages only. Anderson and MacCoun found that jurors who did not have the opportunity to award punitive damages "compensated for this constraint" (p. 321) by inflating their award for pain and suffering. (The noneconomic portion of the compensatory award, because it is not tied to monetary guideposts, is a flexible alternative means to punish the defendant and to deter.) The authors suggested that this finding demonstrates either that jurors are unable to distinguish compensatory from punitive goals or that they consciously disregard the law that calls for such compartmentalization. We offer a third possibility: that jurors may have an intuitive sense of what a reasonable "package of compensation" looks like; they either explicitly or implicitly calculate an appropriate total award and then allocate that total among the various response options.

Another study supports this contention. In a study of the effects of capping punitive damages on compensatory damage award decisions, Greene, Coon, and Bornstein (2001) presented evidence to mock jurors in three different causes of action: (a) personal injury, (b) products liability, and (c) insurance bad faith. One fourth of mock jurors had punitive damages capped at $200,000 (a low limit imposed in at least one state), another fourth were told that their punitive damage award could not exceed their compensatory award (the rule used in at least one other state), a third group had no cap whatsoever on the amount of punitive damages they could award (as is true in approximately half the states), and the final fourth were not given any option to award punitive damages (as is the case in a handful of states). Like Anderson and MacCoun (1999), Greene, Coon, and Bornstein showed that jurors who had no opportunity to award punitive damages augmented the amount that they awarded in compensatory damages. In fact, the data showed that the compensatory damages awarded by these jurors were statistically equivalent to the total amount (compensatory plus punitive damages) awarded by jurors whose punitive damage awards were not limited in any way. These findings support the notion that jurors may have an overall impression of what an injury or loss is worth and, rather than concerning themselves with the damage components, as an accountant might, instead search for a sum that they feel is appropriate (Kalven, 1958).

Indeed, Mott et al.'s (2000) study of juries in 36 tort and contract cases showed that some level of intuitive reasoning was used by most of the groups. In approximately one third of juries the predominant strategy for determining damages was to pick an amount that seemed fair and just without explicit calculation. However, even the juries that assessed the value of separate components of the injury added a dash of holistic reasoning: In approximately 70% of the deliberations, jurors arrived at a starting number and then adjusted it because it seemed too high (frequently) or too low (infrequently). Obviously, they have some imprecise sense of what the losses are worth and impose their preferences on the final award. By and large, jurors appeared to engage in a certain amount of calculation and adjustment to arrive at a "just and fair" number—a melding of the componential and intuitive approaches.

EFFECTS OF TRIAL COMPLEXITY ON DECISIONS ABOUT DAMAGES

Claude Cimino was the named plaintiff in a complicated class-action asbestos case that involved a novel three-phase trial (*Cimino v. Raymark Industries, Inc.*, 1998). The first phase of the trial involved 2,298 individual claims against four defendants. The jury found against the defendants, apportioned liability, awarded $3.5 million in compensatory damages, and assessed punitive damages. In the next phase of the trial the jury determined verdicts and average damage awards in 160 sample claims. The judge then calculated the average award for five disease categories and applied these averages to the remaining untried claims (Mullenix, 1998).[4]

Various substantive and structural aspects of some trials make the assessments of damages especially difficult. In mass tort cases like the *Cimino* case, the issues being litigated are complex, the plaintiffs and defendants are many, the evidence is frequently technical, and the claimed losses are often immense. The tasks posed for jurors in the face of these complexities—determining causation and liability, distinguishing among the claims of various plaintiffs and the defenses of multiple defendants, and assigning monetary values to numerous claimed injuries—are arduous indeed. In fact, some commentators (e.g., Sugarman, 1990) have argued that lay juries are ill equipped to make decisions in certain kinds of complex lawsuits and that such cases would be more predictably and fairly decided by a judge.

Several empirical studies conducted by Horowitz and colleagues (e.g., Horowitz & Bordens, 1988) have assessed the effects of various aspects of trial complexity on decision making regarding damages in a toxic tort case.[5] An early study examined how the size of the nontrial plaintiff population and the presence of a plaintiff who was more severely injured than other plaintiffs would affect judgments of compensatory and punitive damages (Horowitz & Bordens, 1988; see chapter 3, this volume).

Horowitz and Bordens's (1988) study posed several intriguing psychological questions: When faced with multiple plaintiffs with differing degrees

---

[4]The 5th Circuit rejected the novel trial plan approximately 10 years after it was devised, reasoning in part that Texas tort law requires individual determination of causation and damages (*Cimino v. Raymark Industries, Inc.*, 1998).
[5]One structural aspect of complex lawsuits—whether they be tried in unitary or bifurcated format—although relevant to the present discussion, is discussed as a reform in chapter 9.

of injury, can jurors keep straight the unique information regarding each plaintiff? Do they average their responses to different plaintiffs, or do the injuries sustained by one unique plaintiff (i.e., the most severely injured) serve as an anchor that drives up the average award for other, less extreme claims? Will damage awards increase as the size of the nontrial population grows and jurors attribute more responsibility to the defendant?

The results show that structural variations in the trials affected judgments about damages. In other words, jurors assessed damages for any given individual in light of the information available regarding other plaintiffs. So, for example, the most severely injured plaintiff received lower damages when his case was aggregated with others, rather than tried separately, suggesting that the less severely injured plaintiffs pulled down jurors' responses to that outlier. In complementary fashion, the least severely injured plaintiff was helped significantly by being combined with others at trial, suggesting that the more severely injured plaintiffs pulled up responses to this individual. These findings support the notion that juries can derive damages decisions in a rational manner (Horowitz & Bordens, 1988).

Complex cases entail a number of other issues that may pose problems to the logical calculation of damages, however. More recently, Horowitz, ForsterLee, and Brolly (1996) focused on the effects of other factors in complex cases, namely information load (operationalized as the number of plaintiffs and witnesses who testify in a complex case; see chapter 3, this volume) and complexity of the testimony (defined as the technicality of the language used by these witnesses). Horowitz et al. posed a variety of interesting questions: Do increases in language complexity lead to suboptimal performance? Are jurors less able, in more complex trials, to process the facts that distinguish one plaintiff from another? If so, do their compensatory awards show a convergence of judgments rather than discrimination among plaintiffs who have differentially worthy claims?

Examination of jurors' compensatory award judgments showed that they were affected by the complexity of the language used during trial (commonly used, concrete words vs. vocabulary typically used in the legal system).[6] In general, less complex language apparently allowed jurors to discriminate more accurately among plaintiffs with differing degrees of injury. However, jurors were able to award damages commensurate with a plaintiff's injuries only when less complex language was combined with low information load. Only in this condition did jurors award significantly different amounts to plaintiffs who were differentially injured. This finding supports our contention that certain procedural elements of a damages trial negatively affect jurors' ability to think logically about awards.

---

[6]We offer the following example of the same idea expressed in complex and simple language, respectively: "Northern owed a duty of care to the plaintiffs as persons who foreseeably would be injured by its acts and omissions"; "Northern owed a duty of care to the plaintiffs as people whom it could see would be harmed by what it did or did not do."

There are many ways in which trials are complex: they may involve obtuse interpretations of law that are unclear even to people with legal education, multitudinous claims and counterclaims with accompanying variations in the burdens of proof, questions of a highly technical or scientific nature that are outside of the realm of most laypeople, requests for sums of money or evidence of financial worth that are difficult for jurors to apprehend, or protracted length. Often, several of these factors converge in the same case. Researchers have only the most rudimentary understanding of how these very difficult issues work—alone and in concert—to influence the damages judgments of jurors assigned the responsibility of making awards in such cases.

It is difficult even to gather data on these issues: Mock trials, by their very nature, condense the presentation of evidence and deliberative experience and thus are of limited utility in providing information about decision making in highly complex cases. Theoretically relevant variables can be identified and studied in isolation, but without the richness of the surrounding material their impact in complex cases may be concealed.[7] Posttrial interviews suffer from the often-observed concern that jurors may be unable to describe their decision-making process accurately and, furthermore, that jurors may have a difficult time separating their reasoning related to compensation from their thoughts about a number of other decisions they were required to make. Perhaps the best hope for eavesdropping on, and understanding, jurors' thoughts about compensation lies in various procedural modifications in place or under consideration across the country. In particular, if all parties agree, jury deliberations in selected cases in Arizona are now being videotaped (Diamond et al., 2002). Empirical analysis of these videotaped discussions may provide a window into the workings of actual juries as they grapple with various issues related to compensatory and punitive damage award decisions.

EFFECTS OF DELIBERATIONS ON DAMAGE AWARD ASSESSMENTS

Most of the studies that we have described to this point have examined individual jurors' notions of appropriate compensation in civil damage cases. The decision that is handed down by a jury, although informed by the viewpoints of 6, or 8, or 12 individual jurors, is obviously the result of a group process in which these individuals must reach a consensus on damages. Several years ago, writing about the effects of deliberation on damage award computations, Greene (1989) posited that "data

---

[7]Kramer and Kerr (1989) suggested, however, that findings from even highly artificial settings may be relevant to more realistic, complex situations.

on these issues are rudimentary and somewhat confusing" (p. 238). Unfortunately, more than 10 years later, the situation has changed little. Because of its inherent complexity, there have been few studies of the transformation of individual to group judgments in the context of civil damages cases.

We have some reason to believe that jury awards would be more predictable and less variable than individual jurors' awards. Jury deliberations make participants accountable for their decisions. Tetlock (1983) found that when research participants had to justify their views on an issue to another person, they "appeared to engage in preemptive self-criticism . . . to anticipate the counterarguments and objections that potential critics could raise to their positions" (p. 81). By contrast, participants who did not have to publicly air their views appeared to be "cognitively lazy," acting on their private assessment of the evidence and rendering a verdict consistent with these sentiments. If they know that they will need to discuss the facts and reach a consensus with other people, jurors may scrutinize the evidence and evaluate their reactions to it more thoroughly than they might in the absence of group deliberation.

There are other reasons to expect that jury awards would be more rational than individual verdicts. Misinterpretations of evidence and instructions can be detected and corrected during deliberations. Indeed, mock jurors generally show greater comprehension of trial testimony and less reliance on irrelevant facts after deliberations than before (Ellsworth, 1989; Greene & Johns, 2001). Finally, deliberations may enhance jurors' involvement in the case and may increase the seriousness and care with which they scrutinize the evidence. The act of deliberating requires people to become engaged with the facts and to formulate arguments about them—reasons to suspect that the outcomes of deliberation may be better (i.e., more thorough) than individual decisions.

One finding has emerged with some consistency from the relatively sparse literature on jury decisions regarding damages: There is a systematic inflation of award size as a result of group deliberation (Bourgeois, Horowitz, ForsterLee, & Grahe, 1995; Davis et al., 1993; Diamond & Casper, 1992; Diamond, Saks, & Landsman, 1998; Schkade, Sunstein, & Kahneman, 2000; Wasserman & Robinson, 1980; Zuehl, 1982).[8] Consider Diamond et al.'s (1998) study, which involved the mock trial of a products liability case in which the plaintiff claimed that he was injured by exposure

---

[8]An exception comes from a study conducted by Davis, Au, Hulbert, Chen, and Zarnoth (1997) showing that groups awarded marginally less in damages than individuals working alone. Davis et al. (1997) attributed this result to a change in social norms that affected the group deliberation. In the early 1990s, when these data were collected, a prevailing social sentiment, according to Davis et al. (1997), was that multimillion-dollar jury awards had been halted and that juries were becoming harsher on plaintiffs who sued doctors, insurance companies, and other deep-pocketed defendants. That explanation does not square with more recent findings that show inflation of awards from the individual to group levels, however.

to the airborne residue of a fireproofing material. The defendant, in turn, blamed the plaintiff's lung problems on his history of smoking. After watching the videotaped trial, mock jurors gave predeliberation damage awards, and some were then asked to deliberate in 6-person juries. The mean juror award for economic damages was $374,431, whereas the mean jury award was $412,291.

Earlier work by Diamond and Casper (1992) suggested several reasons for this inflation effect. First, deliberations apparently increase jurors' sense that the defendant's conduct was blameworthy. (Analysis of the content of the deliberations showed that mock jurors offered numerous examples of the inappropriateness of the defendant's conduct. These jurors gave higher ratings on questions related to defendant blameworthiness than did jurors who did not deliberate.) Deliberation apparently tends to increase the sense of blameworthiness, and this attitude, in turn, may be related to higher damage awards.

Second, analysis of the content of the deliberations revealed a surprising finding: Jurors who advocated higher damage award preferences were more likely than those who preferred a lower verdict to speak up at the beginning of the discussion. Thus, these early proposals provided a reference point, or anchor, for the subsequent discussion and tended to inflate the resulting jury award above the mean of the individual, predeliberation preferences.

Finally, when forepersons had expertise in the relevant subject area, they exercised greater influence on verdicts than did other jurors. This situation may have contributed to an inflation in awards, because forepersons came to the deliberations with award preferences that were on average $40,000 higher than the average of the group.

Some of these ideas were trumpeted by Schkade and colleagues (Schkade et al., 2000) in a large-scale study that assessed the outcome of group deliberation on damage awards (although their work primarily focused on how jurors assess punitive damages in 1 of 15 personal injury cases). Schkade et al. (2000) examined data from more than 3,000 mock jurors in more than 500 juries and noted that deliberations tended to inflate punitive damage awards over (often, far over) the median of individual judgments prior to deliberation. So, for example, among juries that reached a verdict on punitive damages,[9] 27% agreed on a monetary award that was as high or higher than the highest predeliberation assessment among that group. Schkade et al. termed this a *severity shift*.

To explain the so-called severity shift, Schkade et al. (2000) hypothesized that a feature of deliberation—something they termed *rhetorical asymmetry*—explains the one-way movement they observed. Simply put, after the jury has agreed to award punitive damages, the arguments for

---

[9]Approximately 82% of juries reached a verdict on punitive damages.

larger awards are more persuasive than arguments for smaller awards. As a result, the jury is drawn disproportionately toward the larger predeliberation judgments of its members. Jurors who argue for more money to punish the defendant have the upper hand.[10] This argument has something in common with the anchoring idea: Not only do jurors who advocate higher awards apparently speak first, but they may also speak louder.

One might wonder to what extent this so-called severity shift can explain awards for compensatory damages, where the moral objectives to punish and deter are theoretically absent and where losses are arguably easier to calculate. One also might wonder whether the severity shift might be mediated by the very decision to award punitive damages rather than by the rhetorical persuasiveness of certain verdict preferences. Indeed, the extreme shifts that Schkade et al. (2000) noted from predeliberation to group verdicts might be peculiar to punitive damage judgments.

Perhaps more interesting than data on the average awards, though, are data concerning the variability of awards and the presumed role of deliberations in reducing that variability. Is the range of jury awards around the mean award for that condition less than the range of juror awards? One might suspect that deliberations would reduce the variability in awards —at least for economic losses—because jurors can rely on the figures presented during the trial as benchmarks for discussion during deliberation.

Diamond et al. (1998) addressed this issue. Jurors in this study were given substantially more detailed instruction about the components of economic damages (e.g., for medical expenses and lost wages) than about noneconomic losses. (Past medical expenditures, as we have noted, can be relatively easily documented.) Also, although there is a substantial need for jurors to assess such issues as future medical care and the likely course of inflation (among other things), jurors receive at least some evidence and guidance to enable them to make these decisions in a reasoned way. By contrast, jurors are provided with no factual information and "precious little guidance from the law" (Diamond et al., 1998, p. 314) concerning damages for pain and suffering. Consequently, one would expect that individual damage awards for pain and suffering would be especially volatile and that deliberations would be only somewhat effective in reducing that variation.

Indeed, jurors were far more consistent in their assessments of damages for economic losses than in their estimates of how much the plaintiff should receive for pain and suffering (Diamond et al., 1998). Expressed as a percentage of the mean award, the variability among individual jurors

---

[10]In our opinion, this argument seems somewhat speculative and based primarily on a subsequent study involving law students who were asked whether, in deliberating about a punitive damages award, it would be harder to argue for a smaller or larger award. Schkade et al. (2000) have no independent measure of the rhetorical value of comments made during deliberations in the main study.

for economic damages was 84%, and for pain and suffering awards it was 179%.

Were jury verdicts less variable? Was the variability reduced just for economic awards or for the pain and suffering awards as well? Jury awards for both economic damages and for pain and suffering were substantially more concentrated around the mean than were juror awards, dropping to 78% for economic damages and to 147% for pain and suffering damages. These findings suggest that the pooling of damage estimates that occurs during the deliberation process can reduce the variability of individual awards for both quantifiable and less-quantifiable categories. Still, the variability across juries, particularly for pain and suffering awards and for punitive damages, remains relatively high.

Diamond et al. (1998) speculated on approaches to reducing undesirable variability. They suggested that restoring the jury to its traditional complement of 12 would reduce the idiosyncratic tendencies of any particular jury. Indeed, Davis et al. (1997) obtained data showing that the variance in awards is substantially less among juries of 12 than among juries of 6 people.[11]

As a second approach, Diamond et al. (1998) suggested that, especially in the realm of noneconomic damages, jurors would benefit by the provision of a set of reference points against which to assess damage awards. Yet we have already detailed the effects of one set of reference points—those provided by an *ad damnum*. Use of this guidepost with regard to pain and suffering damages may be especially problematic, given that the attorney's request may have only a limited relationship to the actual pain and suffering experienced by the plaintiff and that the attorney is not required to provide any evidence to justify the amount requested. An alternative proposed by Diamond et al. (1998)—presenting to the jury a set of pain and suffering awards that juries had made in comparable cases—has more merit in our minds, provided that the selection of appropriate comparables can be achieved.[12] We return to this idea in chapter 9.

EFFECTS OF "BLINDFOLDING" JURORS AND JURIES

One model of the civil justice system sees the jury as the conscience of the community with the objective to deliver just verdicts, even if this sometimes means that the jury must subvert the law (Leibman, Bennett, & Fetter, 1998). In jurisdictions that ascribe to this principle information

---

[11]These data also indicate that 12-person mock juries awarded a personal injury plaintiff less on average than did 6-person juries.

[12]Diamond et al. (1998) described the use of comparables in property tax appeals and condemnation proceedings and suggested that expert testimony can be used to support or challenge comparability.

about the consequences of a verdict is likely to be provided to jurors lest, in its absence, arbitrary and unintended verdicts result. In courts that remove the blindfold in order to "admit the sunshine of legal knowledge into the jury room" (Leibman et al., 1998, p. 351), the legal consequences of jury findings are made known to jurors by means of closing arguments, jury instructions, or both.

A competing model of the civil justice system sees juries as mere fact-finding tribunals that have no interest in the outcome of the lawsuit (Leibman et al., 1998). According to this perspective, jurors should consider only the facts in dispute and not be tempted to evaluate the evidence with a predetermined or desired outcome in mind. In jurisdictions that subscribe to this view, "blindfold" rules prohibit disclosure to the jury of information regarding the consequences of its findings. These courts are unlikely to disclose some information related to damages, including information pertaining to attorneys' fees, taxation of damage awards, insurance carried by the parties, who pays if a defendant is insolvent or immune, the potential reductions of awards by appellate courts, the effects of comparative negligence rules on awards,[13] the fact that damage awards in private antitrust lawsuits will automatically be tripled by the court, and limitations on noneconomic and punitive damages.

The rationale for blindfolding is threefold: that (a) the procedure will prevent bias that might be introduced by the undisclosed information, (b) some facts are so complex that they might confuse rather than educate the jury, and (c) certain evidence simply lacks probative value and wastes the jury's time (Diamond, Casper, & Ostergren, 1989). Are these valid reasons for withholding information? Is it appropriate to expect jurors to operate essentially as *tabulae rasae*, or blank slates, influenced only by what they see and hear in court? Is it reasonable to think that they will eschew reference to topics about which they have information, albeit limited or incorrect? Is it likely that they will disregard issues such as attorneys' fees and taxes that concern them? Most significant, is it correct to anticipate that blindfolding will *prevent* bias in decision making? Might failure to inform jurors about some of these matters *introduce* bias, because it allows jurors to fall back on their preconceptions and personal knowledge? Indeed, as we describe in the next few paragraphs, efforts to blindfold juries are often counterproductive, because jurors who lack information from the court will infer—rightly or wrongly—the economic consequences of their damage awards on the parties.

In our view, a blindfold may permit (rather than prevent) juries to reach verdicts based on misinformation. (As such, it constitutes yet another

---

[13]In chapter 7 we discussed a complementary problem: that in many cases in which the plaintiff has some percentage of fault, the jury—blindfolded to the fact that its award will be adjusted—reduces its award to reflect the plaintiff's wrongdoing. The result is double discounting.

example of how the system can stymie rational decision making on the part of jurors.) Some jurors may bring inaccurate "knowledge" with them to the deliberation room. Without legally correct information to challenge these erroneous beliefs, the misinformation could factor into the resulting verdict at the expense of all parties. So, for example, if jurors presume that a defendant has insurance to cover the total cost of the losses, they may inflate their award. As a result, defendants with little or no insurance will have to pay an inflated judgment, because the jury inaccurately believed that the insurance company would pay.

A complementary concern, which we described in chapter 5, is that individuals' prior beliefs and expectations influence how they evaluate the evidence and make decisions. When jurors come to the deliberation room with differing beliefs and expectations about issues such as attorneys' fees or limitations on awards, the blindfold effectively prevents the court and the parties from providing accurate information that might override these misconceptions. As a result, verdicts are uncertain and inconsistent. Some examples of varying expectations follow.

Evidence from archival studies, posttrial interviews, and mock jury experiments has indicated that jurors and juries consider some factors about which they are blindfolded, even though they are expected not to (Diamond et al., 1989; Diamond & Casper, 1992; Leibman et al., 1998; MacCoun, 1993; Mott et al., 2000). Sometimes, this occurs explicitly. For example, Goodman, Greene, and Loftus (1989) found that, when asked about the factors they considered in assessing damages, 20% of mock jurors said they considered that attorneys' fees would need to be paid, and 12% mentioned that the plaintiff would need to pay taxes on the amount awarded in damages. Real jurors interviewed subsequent to serving in tort and contract cases reported even more frequent discussion of attorneys' fees: Approximately 80% of jurors reported that their juries had either discussed or used the factor of attorneys' fees in their decision-making process, and more than one third reported that their jury engaged in discussion of the defendant's insurance (Mott et al., 2000)! On other occasions, the influence may be indirect and unspoken but may affect jurors' verdict preferences nonetheless. Thus, in the absence of explicit instructions, jurors' assessments of damages are likely to be inconsistent, haphazard and, on occasion, contrary to the intentions of the law (MacCoun, 1993).

We have some new evidence that jurors consider issues on which judges offer no instruction and that these considerations do indeed affect their judgments regarding damages. In some recent work, Greene and Dunaway (2002) videotaped mock jury deliberations in a case involving an automobile accident and analyzed the content of the deliberations to determine whether jurors mentioned three factors suspected to influence damages decisions but about which they receive no guidance: (a) attorneys' fees, (b) the role of insurance, and (c) any attempts at settlement. Notice the differing expectations in these discrete comments that jurors made about attorneys' fees:

- "Who knows if a million of this is going into the lawyers' pockets?"
- "I am going to assume that his lawyers will see something of this, so yeah, I'm increasing my award."
- "With the civil case I was on they wouldn't tell us what the lawyer was going to get so we figured that the lawyer's going to get at least 5–15% of that."
- "They get 30%."
- "Remember, the attorneys are going to get half."
- "Maybe it's his brother and he's doing it for free."

Some comments about insurance were as follows:

- "With a big truck like that, he (the defendant) is probably insured for a million."
- "Did anyone take into consideration what the limits are on physical injury?"
- (In response to the preceding question:) "I'm not really sure what they are. I think they are probably somewhere in the ballpark of a couple hundred thousand."

Given the tone of these statements, it seems likely that speculation and conjecture are invited, rather than avoided, when the jury is blindfolded to ways to handle these issues.

One blindfolding issue that has received considerable empirical attention is the unspoken trebling of compensatory damages in antitrust cases (Diamond & Casper, 1992). This information has historically been kept from the jury because of concerns that informed jurors may reduce their assessed award to an amount deemed sufficient to achieve direct compensation to the plaintiff but that this amount may not be sufficient to adequately penalize the defendant. On the other hand, jurors who are unaware of the trebling rule may augment their awards in order to punish the defendant and deter future conduct. In any event, blindfolding in this context is likely to produce undesired interjury variation.

Diamond and Casper (1992) designed a mock jury study to test the effectiveness of various sets of jury instructions related to blindfolding. In five conditions, jurors were instructed to compensate the plaintiff for any injury caused by the defendant's antitrust violations. (This is the amount that is automatically trebled by the judge.) The researchers varied the information that these jurors were given about the consequences of their decision: one group was told that their verdict would be trebled and that they should neither disregard nor consider this information; a second group was told that their verdicts would be trebled and that they should disregard this fact when making their assessments; the third group was told that their verdicts would be trebled and was given an explanation of the trebling provisions in antitrust statutes; a fourth group was not informed of the trebling rule but instead heard that the judge would add an amount for punishment and deterrence, if necessary; and the fifth group received no indication that the judge would add to their damage award. (This is the typical form of instruction in most courts.)

Analysis of the damage awards showed that jurors who were informed about trebling gave lower awards than did jurors who were not informed. Why? Two explanations are viable: either (a) the trebling information caused jurors to reduce their awards below what they believed would be necessary to compensate the plaintiff, or (b) the desire to punish and deter caused jurors not informed of the trebling rule to augment their awards above what they deemed necessary to compensate the plaintiff. Diamond and Casper (1992) were able to disentangle these possibilities by focusing on awards delivered by the group that was given an explanation for trebling. They found that these jurors gave higher awards than did those without an explanation, suggesting that the reduction in awards with trebling information is at least partially related to windfall avoidance and that jurors who understand why the award is trebled are less likely to reduce their verdicts.

How effective, then, are the present instructions related to damages in antitrust cases? The most commonly used instruction, which does not mention the trebling provision of the law, makes no attempt to control jurors' punitive impulses or to inform them of the consequences of their decisions (Diamond & Casper, 1992). As a result, jurors who come to the deliberation table either with no information or with misinformation about the trebling process may lead the group astray. Once the blindfold is removed, jurors' verdicts are likely to be more predictable and to be grounded in appropriate considerations regarding compensation and penalties.

As another example, there is question about whether to inform jurors of comparative negligence rules or whether to blindfold them to the consequences of their fault determinations (see chapter 7). Proponents of blindfolding argue that jurors should determine culpability unfettered by concerns about the effects of their determinations, that to provide information about the consequences of the fault allocations will invite sympathetic and biased judgments. Proponents of disclosure reason that the task of quantifying fault requires some degree of moral judgment and that decisionmakers should not be deprived of important information about the consequences of their fault determinations (Leibman et al., 1998).[14]

---

[14]When comparative fault standards were first devised in the 1930s, states blindfolded juries to the existence of the rule. A significant turnabout occurred in the late 1970s, when many jurisdictions opted to permit disclosure of the rule to juries. With the advent of tort reform in the late 1980s and early 1990s, however, the blindfold has reappeared in some states. For

What do the data say about the effects of blindfolding about comparative fault rules? Jordan Leibman and his colleagues conducted an empirical study to compare comparative fault verdicts of blindfolded jurors with verdicts from jurors who were informed about the rule (Leibman et al., 1998). They presented a realistic re-enactment of an automobile negligence case to 489 mock jurors who, after viewing the trial, deliberated in 6- or 7-person juries for up to 2 hours. At the conclusion of the deliberations the jury answered special interrogatories asking for the total amount of damages, the percentage of negligence attributable to each of three defendants, and the amount of damages attributable to each party (calculated by multiplying each party's percentage of fault by the total amount of damages suffered by the plaintiff).

The presence or absence of a blindfold was manipulated in the following way: for juries without a blindfold, the plaintiff's lawyer stated in his closing argument:

> So, in considering all of those causes, if you find that the fault of [the plaintiff] in proximately causing this accident was more than 50%, then she loses. If you find, however, that her fault was 50% or less, and the combined fault of [the defendants] more than 50%, then she is entitled to damages. That is the Indiana law concerning responsibility and liability. (Leibman et al., 1998, p. 382)

In addition, in this version of the videotaped trial the judge instructed jurors that if they determined that more than 50% of fault was attributable to the plaintiff, then no further deliberations were required. For juries with a blindfold in place, neither the plaintiff's attorney nor the judge referred to the comparative fault rule.

One can examine two facets of the data to assess the effects of the blindfold on jurors' judgments. First, Leibman et al. (1998) reasoned that if knowledgeable juries were motivated either by distaste for the concept of modified comparative fault or by sympathy for a severely injured plaintiff, then they would increase the percentage of fault attributable to the defendants in order to allow the plaintiff to recover. Indeed, the informed juries allocated significantly more fault to the defendant than did the blindfolded juries (44% vs. 34%). Second, in terms of damages awarded to the plaintiff, Leibman et al. found that damages awarded by jurors who were informed about the comparative fault rule tended to be smaller than damages awarded by blindfolded jurors ($2,606,234 vs. $3,164,273). So, although the plaintiff won more often when the blindfold was lifted, the payout to her was less. The authors concluded that even with the increased frequency of awards that accompany disclosure, the average recovery (and, presum-

---

example, the Illinois Assembly apparently concluded that "blindfolding would benefit the state's economy by reducing the liability exposure of businesses, professionals, governmental entities, and other constituencies often found to be defendants in tort cases" (Leibman et al., pp. 399–400).

ably, the total recovery as well) will be about the same under these different procedures. Tort reform proponents assert that a rule resulting in more frequent plaintiff wins would spur litigation. These findings—for example, that plaintiffs' victories are smaller when jurors are informed about comparative fault—suggest that blindfolding may not provide the correction for which tort reformers hope.

We argue that when jurors are left in the dark about how certain unspoken issues will affect the ultimate award, they concoct reasonable hypotheses and make a judgment about damage awards in light of these suppositions. It is better that jurors be respected as careful and methodical decisionmakers and that they be empowered by clear and frequent instruction about those features of damages that can be articulated. This policy has two advantages: (a) It acknowledges that jurors will intuitively use their prior knowledge to interpret the facts and attempt to reach consensus, and (b) when jurors are informed about how and what to discuss, more certain results will obtain.

CONCLUSION

Our understanding of how people translate an individual's misfortune into a monetary value is rudimentary and elusive. We know that certain features of the trial itself—the *ad damnum* and the presence of economic expert testimony—influence the outcome. We also know that decisions about compensation and punishment are affected by the complexity of the evidence, clarity of the language used to instruct jurors, presence of blindfolds, and jurors' opportunity to deliberate.

Understanding the psychological processes underlying these complex decisions is of significant import. In recent years, the concern about unpredictability and randomness in jury awards has alarmed professionals and laypeople alike. The research detailed in this chapter is relevant to debates currently underway in statehouses and reform commissions concerning the need for changes in civil damages cases. One would hope that individuals charged with any reform task would want to know what jurors *actually* do before suggesting changes in what they *apparently* do.

As we have often noted, our preference is for the policy to follow from the data, rather than the reverse. We believe that the data presented in this chapter—although sometimes tentative and occasionally contradictory—can begin to move us in that direction. It is clear that more and better studies are needed on how jurors make decisions about these difficult issues, but we are sanguine that our research foundation is a good one and that we are beginning to build an understanding of the transformation process.

9

REFORMING DAMAGE AWARD
DECISION MAKING

In chapter 1 we alluded to considerable controversy regarding jurors' and juries' abilities to establish fair, equitable, and predictable damage awards, particularly in the areas of noneconomic and punitive damages. We return to that theme again in this chapter as we consider the rhetoric, data, and policy implications flowing from a variety of proposals to reform traditional methods of damages assessments.

A number of factors have converged in the past 30 years to usher in these reforms: perceptions of excessiveness in the size and frequency of punitive damage awards (fed, in part, by media attention to exceptional cases and largely discredited by empirical research studies), concerns (also largely unfounded) that jurors and juries are untrustworthy in making decisions on damages, and suspicions that legal doctrines regarding damages may simply be inadequate. In a nutshell, the argument is this: The vagueness inherent in the common and statutory law regarding damages allows jurors' biases to operate largely unbounded, resulting in excessive and unpredictable awards.

Indeed, the lack of guidance on damage award decision making, detailed in chapter 1, has been decried by many (*Browning–Ferris Industries, Inc. v. Kelco Disposal, Inc.*, 1989; Chase, 1995; "The civil jury," 1997; Greene & Bornstein, 2000; Melsheimer & Stodghill, 1994; *TXO Production*

175

Corp. v. Alliance Resources Corp., 1993). As we have shown, jurors are typically given little assistance from the judge about how their assessments should be determined or about how to map their judgments onto a dollar scale. The following is an apt description:

> [The] law requires the monetization of a "product" for which there is no market and therefore, no market price. This largely explains the lamented fact that jurors who must undertake the monetization are given no absolute standard by which to do it. There is none to give them. Each juror must create or bring [his or her] own standard to the courtroom. (Chase, 1995, p. 765)

This mapping problem is especially apparent in areas of the law that lack precision and in which jurors are given virtually standardless discretion: in the setting of damages for libel actions, intentional infliction of emotional distress, and sexual harassment claims, among others.

Lacking guidance from the law, jurors and juries are forced to rely on the litigants' presentations, which may provide detailed information about every possible nuance of harm suffered and may also suggest a theory of how the jury should compute the value of these losses (Bovbjerg, Sloan, & Blumstein, 1989). However, as we have shown, those theories may be in conflict with one another, so even the assessment of economic damages is not straightforward. For instance, the parties in a civil trial typically argue for and against various ways to determine losses and various methods to discount an award to its present value. In the realm of noneconomic damages, subjectivity is even more likely, as attorneys can present a variety of ways for juries to compute awards for pain and suffering, for example.

In response to these issues, the majority of states have implemented legislative reforms aimed at corralling juries' discretion and curbing so-called runaway verdicts. Among the reform proposals are capping damage awards, providing guidance to jurors in the form of damages scheduling, bifurcating the evidence in certain civil trials, clarifying the instructions provided to the jury, requiring that some or all of a damage award be paid to the state, and removing punitive damage decisions entirely from the hands of the jury.[1] We now discuss each of these proposals, how they are likely to affect jury verdicts (if at all), and the corresponding empirical work on each reform.

---

[1]State legislatures have enacted a number of other tort reforms that are not discussed here because they do not involve juries. These include statute of limitation changes, establishment of pretrial screening panels, provisions for arbitration, limitations on contingency fees, laws that allow courts to make the losing party pay court costs, and new rules concerning evidence of compensation received from collateral sources, among other things (Sloan, Mergenhagen, & Bovbjerg, 1989).

CAPPING DAMAGE AWARDS

In response to concerns about the variability and size of damage awards, caps, or maximum limits on allowable damages, have been imposed in a majority of states (Saks, Hollinger, Wissler, Evans, & Hart, 1997). Capping schemes assume many different forms; some pertain to all civil cases, and others apply to only certain causes of action, such as products liability or medical malpractice. Damage caps typically limit only the size of noneconomic and punitive awards. In the realm of punitive damages, some states impose an absolute upper limit on the amount of money that can be awarded. For example, Alabama imposes a $250,000 cap (Ala. Code §§ 6-11-21, 1994). Other states (e.g., Florida; Fla. Stat. Ann. § 768.73, 1995) impose a maximum permitted ratio under which punitive damages may be awarded in some ratio to the compensatory damages (typically 2:1 or 3:1, although punitive awards in Colorado may not exceed the compensatory award; Colo. Rev. Stat. §§ 13-21-102, 2000). Still other states (e.g., Nevada; Nev. Rev. Stat. § 42.005, 1993) simultaneously impose both kinds of limits. Finally, in some states (e.g., Nebraska, New Hampshire, Louisiana, Washington), jurors are not allowed to award any punitive damages (Hurd & Zollers, 1994, Koenig & Rustad, 1993). In general, legislation allows the cap on punitive damages to be exceeded if the defendant's behavior is especially egregious (Koenig & Rustad, 1993).[2]

Consider the situation of Jessie and Karla Sellers—plaintiffs in a deceptive trade practices lawsuit against Chrysler and a Dallas car dealership. In the fall of 2000, a Dallas jury awarded the couple $83.5 million, apparently believing that they had been misled about the towing capacity of a Dodge Ram pickup truck. Specifications in a Chrysler brochure indicated that the truck had adequate capacity to tow their 9,000-lb horse trailers. The Sellers bought the truck but apparently encountered problems immediately after purchase. They claimed that the "bucking truck" lost contact with the road while pulling trailers and that Mr. Sellers lost control of the truck while driving in Missouri. Mechanics at the dealership apparently tried without success to fix the problem. The Sellers were unable to afford a vehicle with more towing power offered to them by Chrysler. They eventually stopped driving the truck, lost their business, and now live in one of the horse trailers they used to haul (Fisk, 2000).

At trial, the plaintiffs alleged that Chrysler destroyed "key documents" relating to bucking problems on the Dodge Ram, and indeed, the trial court issued an instruction to the jury noting that "Chrysler negligently caused harm to the plaintiff." The jury awarded just under $1 million

---

[2]Also note, though, that many state courts have recently begun to overturn all or parts of laws that attempt to limit damage awards, typically reasoning that such limitations violate the constitutional right of plaintiffs to trial by jury and to court-sanctioned remedies (Smith, 1999).

in compensatory damages, $80 million in punitive damages against Chrysler, and $2.5 million in punitive damages against the dealer. But Texas law in effect at the time capped punitive damages at three times the economic damages, reducing the Sellers's award by 97%, to $2.4 million (a sizable chunk by working people's standards, but still a far cry from the original).

Caps on punitive damage awards are widely perceived to be the most important of all legislative tort reforms, yet they are also highly controversial. Galanter and Luban (1993) argued, for example, that punitive damages should be linked to the heinousness of the wrongful act and have nothing to do with the amount of compensatory damages awarded to an injured party.[3] Thus, they oppose proposals that explicitly cap the punitive award at some multiple of the compensatory award. Others contend that ratio-based caps dismantle the desired sting of punitive damages in cases with fortuitously low compensatory awards ("The civil jury," 1997). Owen (1994) suggested that such arbitrary methods of measurement deprive the decisionmaker of the ability to tailor the punishment to fit the particular wrongdoer and the wrongful act.

Reform proponents, on the other hand, claim that these caps will reduce the size, variability, and unpredictability of punitive damage awards. Caps have been touted as providing "unmistakable guidance to juries, trial courts and appellate courts" (*Crookston v. Fire Insurance Exchange*, 1991, p. 809), thereby removing any possibility of wildly excessive awards, informing defendants about the maximum amount they might have to pay, and reducing administrative and litigation costs.

On occasion, these limits are communicated directly to jurors in the form of judicial instructions. For example, the punitive damages instruction in Colorado states explicitly:

> If you find . . . that the injury complained of was attended by circumstances of willful and wanton conduct, then in addition to actual damages, you may also assess a reasonable sum as exemplary [punitive] damages *not to exceed the amount awarded as actual damages* [italics added]. (*Colorado Jury Instructions 3d: Civil*, 1989, p. 14)

It is more typical that jurors are not instructed about limits imposed on their decisions; rather, courts impose these limits on any award that exceeds the maximum allowable. Over time, however, some or many members of the jury may become aware of such provisions (Saks et al., 1997), either because they are familiar with local legislative debates that surround this issue or because they have general knowledge about attempts at tort reform. In this light, jurors are again blindfolded: Some of them may come to the deliberation table with a lay understanding of capping provisions but receive no explicit guidance from the judge to support their intuitions.

---

[3]In fact, though, Eisenberg and Wells (1998) showed that the mass of punitive awards are indeed significantly correlated with the corresponding compensatory award.

Until recently, little of the debate about the effects of caps on damages was informed by empirical investigation. Now researchers have begun to inquire about the effects of awareness of such caps on resulting awards. Because early capping schemes applied only to medical malpractice cases, a body of work has focused on that domain. Danzon (1986) found that caps reduced the value of paid medical malpractice claims between 1975 and 1984 by 23%, but Gronfein and Kinney (1991) found that the value of paid medical malpractice claims *increased* after a cap was imposed in Indiana, compared with Ohio and Michigan, where there were no caps.[4]

At least three simulation studies have examined the impact of restricting punitive damage awards on the process of jurors' decision making (Anderson & MacCoun, 1999; Greene, Coon, & Bornstein, 2001; Robbennolt & Studebaker, 1999). In addition, one study has looked at the impact of capping damages for pain and suffering (Saks et al., 1997). In terms of caps on pain and suffering awards, Michael Saks and his colleagues (Saks et al., 1997) found that in cases involving low or moderate injuries such limits increased both the size and variability of the plaintiffs' awards. So much for the hypothesized ameliorative effects of capping damage awards, at least in the realm of noneconomic damages!

We turn now to the studies of caps on punitive damages. Are caps on punitive awards any more effective at reining in these assessments? As we described in chapter 8, capping punitive damages has an obvious effect on the level of punitive damages awarded (Robbennolt & Studebaker, 1999). However, it can also have a surprising and significant effect on the amount of the compensatory award; it acted as an anchor for the compensatory awards as well as for the punitive awards. Robbennolt and Studebaker (1999) found that as the level of the cap on punitive damages increased, the size and variability of the compensatory award increased as well.

A related issue is what happens to the compensatory awards when jurors are prohibited from awarding punitive damages in cases that might warrant them. (One might call this the ultimate cap, yet, as we noted previously, several states have adopted this policy.) That question was addressed by Anderson and MacCoun (1999) in a mock products liability case. Some jurors in their study were allowed to make compensatory and punitive damage awards, and others were allowed to award compensatory damages only. Anderson and MacCoun found that jurors who did not have the opportunity to award punitive damages "compensated for this constraint" (p. 321) by inflating their compensatory damage award.

There also are data showing that mock jurors who were not given the opportunity to award punitive damages in three kinds of cases (personal

---

[4]No distinction was made between claims disposed of through settlement and those resolved at trial, so the extent to which jurors' decision making is implicated in these findings is unclear.

injury, products liability, and insurance bad faith) augmented the amount that they awarded in compensatory damages (Greene, Coon, & Bornstein, 2001). Jurors who had no option to award punitive damages inflated their compensatory damage award to serve punitive ends.[5] In fact, data show that the compensatory damages awarded by these jurors were statistically equivalent to the total amount (compensatory plus punitive) awarded by jurors whose punitive damage awards were not limited in any way.

Why might jurors inflate their compensatory damage award when punitive damages are limited? The task of assessing damages involves multiple and seemingly conflicting goals. Jurors must first focus on the plaintiff and determine an appropriate compensatory award to that plaintiff regardless of its impact on the defendant. In theory, it should not matter whether the defendant is Jerry's Auto Repair, a small locally owned automobile repair shop, or the Ford Motor Corporation.[6] Jurors are to award compensatory damages that fully and fairly repay the plaintiff for his or her losses related to, say, defective brake pads. Jurors may then turn to the defendant and assess punitive damages against that defendant with little regard for the plaintiff or his or her needs. It should not matter, at this point, whether the plaintiff is Billy Joe Smith or Bill Gates. A defendant–manufacturer who opted to forego adequate testing in the interests of saving money should be assessed a reasonable punitive damage award.

Jurors' instructions do not make these distinctions and directions clear (Greene & Bornstein, 2000). Rather, the instructions tend to explain the intended function of each kind of award but tend not to guide jurors in how to address these complementary functions. The instructions make no distinction, for example, between the plaintiff and defendant focus that implicitly underlies the two kinds of damage awards. Under these circumstances, defendant-focused concerns can cross over into the assessment of compensatory damages, and plaintiff-focused concerns can cross over into the assessment of punitive damages.[7]

What can one make of these data—limited though they are—in terms of policy recommendations? These data support the assumption that limitations on punitive damage awards will reduce the size of punitive awards. That's the easy part. Of significantly greater concern is the prospect

---

[5]Interestingly, jurors who had no option to award punitive damages did not tell the researchers that they intended the compensatory award to punish and deter, however. It may be that they augmented their compensatory awards without clearly distinguishing compensatory goals from punitive goals. Perhaps they lacked awareness of the factors that influenced their awards (Wilson, 1985).

[6]As we noted in chapter 4, a number of studies have shown that corporate defendants pay greater compensation than individual defendants in both actual (Chin & Peterson, 1985) and simulated trials (Hans & Ermann, 1989; Wasserman & Robinson, 1980), although what might appear on the surface as a deep-pocket effect may actually be a defendant-identity effect (MacCoun, 1996). Wealthy defendants were not necessarily at a disadvantage, unless they were corporations as well.

[7]However, see Cather, Greene, and Durham's (1996) article, which we described in chapter 7.

that limits on punitive damages (or their prohibition in cases where jurors might deem them appropriate) may affect the size and variability of compensatory awards.

Like others (e.g., Baldus, MacQueen, & Woodworth, 1995; Galanter & Luban, 1993), we are concerned that legislative caps also raise serious ethical and policy questions. Because of inconsistencies across states in laws limiting punitive damages, similarly injured plaintiffs may receive radically different compensation in different locales. Furthermore, serious inequities may exist in how tortfeasors are dealt with. Wildly malicious defendants may escape significant sanction in some jurisdictions but not others. Because legislative caps may bear little relation to the amount of money actually required to punish and deter, they may undercut the very premise of punitive damages (Baldus et al., 1995). So, although legislative caps may simplify courts' review of the amount of the awards in additur and remittitur (adding to, or subtracting from, the jury's award; Baldus et al., 1995), we question their effectiveness and worry that they may lead to further inequities in awards. We advocate further empirical research along these lines, tempered by careful and thoughtful applications of the research findings in setting future policy.

PROVIDING JURY GUIDANCE IN THE FORM OF DAMAGES SCHEDULING

As we have stated, substantive law provides no objective benchmarks for valuing noneconomic and punitive damages; it is decidedly imprecise. In fact, as Bovbjerg et al. (1989) noted, "Conventional wisdom seems almost to revel in the imprecision of valuation" (p. 913). These authors cited a jury instruction that tells jurors that "the law cannot give you a precise formula or yardstick . . . but the law contemplates that twelve intelligent jurors, exercising common sense and calling upon their experiences in life, can satisfactorily fix and determine a proper award of money" (*American Jurisprudence Pleading and Practice Forms*, 1982, p. 278). No wonder there is considerable variation in awards!

Must it be so, however? Is there really no objective measure of an appropriate award? Bovbjerg et al. (1989) have proposed the present tort recovery system be replaced by one in which noneconomic damages are uniformly "scheduled."[8] Scheduling, according to Bovbjerg et al., can provide rational standards in the form of dollar values based on prior jury

---

[8]Other authors have proposed guidepost systems as well (e.g., Baldus et al., 1995; Schuck, 1993).

awards.[9] More specifically, they suggested three scheduling models that can be applied to ordinary cases of bodily harm and mental distress.

One scheduling proposal involves the creation of an award matrix in which every injury is classified by its severity and the age of the plaintiff. (Bovjberg et al. [1989] suggested that severity and age are "intuitively and empirically related to subjective assessments of the extent of pain and suffering likely to have been experienced, yet they are sufficiently objective to facilitate their application in particular cases," pp. 945–946.) Each resulting cell of the matrix would be given a value for pain and suffering awards, based on an average of previous awards for such injuries. Juries would use their discretion to determine what cell a given injury falls into but would be required to award the amount indicated by the matrix.

A second version of Bovjberg et al.'s (1989) scheduling proposal would give juries a limited number (10 or fewer) of standardized "injury scenarios" with associated dollar values related to noneconomic losses. The described injuries would range from less severe to more severe, relative to the injury in question, and the range of awards would serve as benchmarks to assist jurors in assessing noneconomic damages in their case. Bovbjerg et al. (1989) claimed that this approach takes advantage of people's natural inclination, when faced with difficult valuation problems, to make comparisons with other situations.

A third proposal involves setting flexible upper and lower limits on jury awards using prior award averages based, again, on age and injury severity. These boundaries would affect only outlier awards and would not be applied in all cases, as schedules would be. Thus, juries could use their discretion to fit their award to the circumstances but would be prevented from going either too high or too low in their assessments.

Significant practical difficulties must be surmounted before these proposals could see their way into a courtroom. One obvious concern is the need for a reliable database of prior awards: Who can say that those prior awards—determined in the absence of clear guidelines—can serve as an objective foundation for scheduling future awards? A second concern is that valuations fluctuate over time and across jurisdictions, so truly comparable cases may be difficult to discover. Finally, these plans may not respond to the needs of an especially worthy (or unworthy) plaintiff or to a plaintiff's individual circumstances, geared as they are to reaching fair and predictable results across cases rather than to providing particularized justice in any specific case. In short, scheduling of damages has enormous practical difficulties (and would be politically contentious as well).

Yet the scheduling of noneconomic losses fits with current efforts to better equip juries with the tools necessary to do their job (Marder, 1998).

---

[9]Bovbjerg et al. (1989) noted that a similar approach is taken by workers' compensation programs and disability plans that make award determinations in an administrative forum.

After all, jurors at present get concrete information about economic losses (in the form of past medical expenses and lost wages). The proposed system would provide a foundation for their thinking about nonpecuniary losses (and, perhaps, punitive damages) as well. In addition, it may also increase the consistency of awards across cases—certainly a worthy goal.

What does the empirical evidence suggest regarding the value of schedules for determining noneconomic damage awards? As we noted in chapter 8, Saks et al. (1997) tested a variant of damages scheduling that most closely approximates the first plan offered by Bovbjerg et al. (1989). In the Saks et al. study, some mock jurors were provided with a small cluster of dollar values for noneconomic losses resulting from a personal injury similar to the one they were assessing—specifically, awards at the 10th, 35th, 65th, and 90th percentiles of the distribution of awards determined in a pilot study. These jurors were told that they were being given guidance in the form of awards from similar cases involving the same type of injury. The main result was that jurors' pain and suffering awards were less variable when these prototype awards were presented than when they were not (at least in cases involving moderate and severe injuries). It is important to note that the size of the mean award was not affected by the examples. These findings suggest that damages scheduling—complicated as it will prove to be—may be worth the effort if it can effectively reduce the wide disparity in awards for similar noneconomic losses. It is certainly worthy of further scrutiny.

BIFURCATING THE EVIDENCE

In federal courts and most state courts the judge has the option of separating the issues put before the jury. This procedure, known as *bifurcation*, is assumed to have multiple benefits. One important reason to bifurcate issues is to increase efficiency. In unitary (nonbifurcated) tort cases, for example, a jury hears all of the evidence and decides all the issues in the same deliberation. For the vast majority of cases in which the jury finds for the defendant on liability (and in which damages will not be awarded), all of the time spent presenting evidence on damages has been wasted. In bifurcated cases, on the other hand, the jury would have heard only evidence related to liability but no information related to the awarding of damages.

Another suggested benefit of bifurcation—and one that is more relevant to decisions regarding damages—is that it enhances fairness. As we have pointed out, in a unitary trial in which the issues are not separated, juries may improperly consider evidence that has no bearing on the particular decision they are asked to make (e.g., they may weigh the severity of the plaintiff's injury into their liability judgment or consider the defendant's conduct in determining compensation). In a bifurcated trial, on the other hand, they receive only the evidence that is directly related to the decision at hand, so presumably they would make more just decisions.

A third rationale for bifurcation is that it may increase jurors' comprehension by narrowing the range of issues (and accompanying testimony and instruction) that jurors must consider. Bifurcation may allow them to focus on fewer issues at a time (Gensler, 2000).

Several forms of bifurcation exist. The most common form involves structuring the trial so that evidence regarding the extent of damages is not included in the liability phase of personal injury and other tort cases. Here, the jury hears evidence related to liability (or causation), is instructed on how to resolve those claims, and determines a verdict on those issues before hearing any evidence or instruction relevant to damages.

A slip-and-fall case tried in New Jersey provides an example. Louis Diodata sued the Roy Rogers restaurant, alleging that he was injured when he slipped and fell on the wet floor of the bathroom in the restaurant. In the liability phase of the bifurcated trial, the plaintiff called the restaurant manager to testify. He acknowledged that the restaurant was busy on the day that Diodata fell, that it had been raining, that there were no mats in the men's room or in the hallway leading to the men's room, and that the floor of the bathroom was slippery when the tiles were wet. He further acknowledged that mops were used interchangeably in the kitchen, bathroom, and dining areas, despite the fact that the kitchen floor was sometimes greasy and slippery. On direct examination, the plaintiff testified that he suffered a concussion in the fall. Because of the decision to bifurcate, the judge sustained an objection to the concussion testimony and instructed the jury that neither party was allowed to present medical testimony during this phase of the trial. By a vote of 5–1, the jury found in favor of the restaurant (Liskow, 1999).[10]

A second, less common form of bifurcation involves separation of the compensatory and punitive damages phases of the trial so that evidence relevant to punitive damages (e.g., the defendant's wealth and prior bad acts) is not made known to jurors until after they have determined liability for and assessed compensatory damages.[11] That way, evidence that is legally irrelevant to compensation cannot inappropriately influence the compensatory judgment. We first describe empirical research on bifurcation of the liability and damages phases and then turn to work on the separation of compensatory and punitive decisions.

---

[10]To complete the story, Diodata moved for a new trial, arguing that without the medical testimony his credibility was put into doubt. The judge agreed and ordered a new, combined trial.

[11]On occasion, trials are bifurcated to separate the determination of whether punitive liability is appropriate from consideration of the amount of a punitive award.

Separation of Liability and Damages Phases of the Trial

It has long been believed that evidence regarding the plaintiff's injuries in personal injury cases would influence jury decisions about compensatory liability (i.e., that defendants would be more likely to be found liable in unitary trials, when jurors know about the extent of the plaintiff's injuries, than in bifurcated trials, when they do not). Support for that notion comes from an early study by Zeisel and Callahan (1963) that examined the effects of unitary and bifurcated trial proceedings in tort cases in federal courts in northern Illinois. Defendants prevailed in 79% of bifurcated trials but in only 42% of unitary trials. Zeisel and Callahan interpreted this difference as indicating that in unitary trials jurors use evidence about the extent of the plaintiff's losses in making a decision about liability. Thus, the plaintiff is advantaged. In bifurcated trials, where the decision about liability is made before any evidence of damages is presented, this spillover does not occur, thereby advantaging defendants.

The results of Zeisel and Callahan's (1963) study raise several questions. First, precisely why does this spillover occur? Jonathan Casper (1993) correctly noted that the advantages to plaintiffs in unitary trials could be the product of two diverse processes: (a) The increased blame jurors assign to the defendant after hearing about the serious consequences of his or her actions may spill over and influence thoughts about that defendant's liability, and (b) evidence about injuries to the plaintiff may cause jurors to lower their standard of proof for the liability judgment in order to compensate a needy plaintiff. Bornstein (1998) showed that evidence of serious injury arouses emotions in jurors that are associated with motivations to alleviate the plaintiff's suffering through compensation. In particular, severe injuries are likely to arouse sympathy in others. Jurors who feel more sympathy for the injured plaintiff are more likely than unsympathetic jurors to find causation and liability, even when the evidence regarding liability is the same for all jurors. As further proof, many mock jurors in an automobile negligence case reported that their liability judgments were motivated in part by their desire to compensate the plaintiff for his economic losses and pain and suffering (Greene, Johns, & Bowman, 1999). Obviously, when liability and damages are tried separately, the sympathy factor is muted.

Another unanswered question regarding Zeisel and Callahan's (1963) data concerns the effects of bifurcation on verdict size. Stephen Landsman and his colleagues (Landsman, Diamond, Dimitropoulos & Saks, 1998) noted that without data on the *size* of jurors' verdicts it is impossible to assess the overall consequences of bifurcation. They pointed out that bifurcation may result in fewer plaintiff verdicts but that the size of the judgments against defendants in bifurcated cases may still be substantial.

In chapter 7 we described the effects of liability-related evidence on judgments regarding damage awards. Here we ponder the effectiveness of bifurcation to reduce any such unwanted effects. Some data on verdict size and bifurcation come from the work of Irwin Horowitz and Kenneth Bordens (1990), who exposed all mock jurors in a toxic tort trial to the same evidence but varied the structure of the trial and compared verdicts and compensatory damage awards as a function of trial structure. Juries in unitary trials heard all the trial elements before making any decisions, whereas juries in the bifurcated trials heard evidence about and made decisions about liability before they were given information on damages. Horowitz and Bordens (1990) found, surprisingly, that although most unitary juries decided for the plaintiff (and most bifurcated juries voted for the defendant), the average award in a unitary trial was actually lower than its counterpart in a bifurcated trial.[12]

So the picture is not at all clear, and indeed, other studies have reached different conclusions. Greene and Smith (2002) recently explored the effects of bifurcation in an automobile negligence case in which mock jurors assessed damages for both economic and noneconomic losses and found that jurors who had no evidence regarding the defendant's liability (i.e., those in bifurcated trial conditions who heard only evidence relating to the plaintiff's injuries) gave smaller awards than did jurors who had heard evidence about the defendant's liability (i.e., in unitary trials). Follow-up questioning revealed some motivational explanations of this effect. For example, mock jurors who heard only evidence regarding the plaintiff's injuries were less likely than jurors who also heard liability-relevant evidence to say that their awards were motivated by the desire to punish or blame the defendant. Evidence regarding the defendant's conduct also influenced jurors' perceptions of the plaintiff's injuries. So, for example, mock jurors who heard evidence regarding the defendant's conduct rated the plaintiff's physical suffering, mental suffering, and overall severity of injury as more extreme than did their counterparts in the bifurcated trial conditions who had no conduct-related evidence. This is further indication that jurors may misuse evidence intended for one purpose to inform their decisions about other issues (Greene, Johns, & Smith, 2001).

Another recent look at the effects of bifurcation of liability and damages evidence was undertaken by Roselle Wissler and her colleagues (Wissler, Rector, & Saks, 2001). Using a mock personal injury trial that followed from an automobile accident, Wissler et al. (2001) also compared compensatory awards in unitary and bifurcated trial formats. In the former condition jurors were given all the evidence in the case (i.e., concerning the defendant's liability and the plaintiff's injuries) and then decided liability and awarded damages. In the latter condition they had the same

---

[12]This result is surprising (and somewhat difficult to interpret) in light of the differences in procedures in the unitary and bifurcated trials. Jurors in the unitary trials also had evidence regarding punitive liability and damages, whereas jurors in the bifurcated trials did not (Wissler, Rector, & Saks, 2001).

information, but its timing was changed: First, they had evidence about the defendant's actions and judged liability, and only then did they learn about the plaintiff's injuries and award compensation.

Like other studies of bifurcation, the results here are complicated. The question they address is whether jurors' awards in the unitary trial conditions are influenced by evidence of the defendant's conduct and whether bifurcation is effective in reducing that misuse of evidence. In the unitary trial format (and without special instructions to use the evidence in the prescribed way), mock jurors were *somewhat* influenced by evidence of the defendant's conduct. For instance, they gave higher awards for general damages (i.e., pain and suffering) when the defendant was highly responsible (vs. less responsible) for causing the accident, suggesting a lack of independence between information about the defendant's actions and jurors' award judgments. Their awards for lost earnings and medical expenses were not significantly affected by the level of defendant responsibility, however.

What happened when the trial format was bifurcated? Were jurors less likely to rely on conduct-related evidence when they assessed general damages? No. Jurors still used evidence regarding the defendant's level of responsibility in their decisions about general damages. They awarded more when his responsibility was greater. In addition, though, mock jurors in the bifurcated conditions also awarded more in lost earnings when the defendant's responsibility was high—something they had not done in the unitary trial conditions! So, paradoxically, bifurcation seemed to exacerbate, rather than reduce, the impact of liability evidence on awards for lost earnings. In general, Wissler et al. (2001) concluded that separating the liability and damages evidence does not succeed in eliminating the effect of the former on judgments of the latter.

These discrepancies suggest that the *form* of the bifurcation may matter. Recall that jurors in Wissler et al.'s (2001) study received evidence about the defendant's responsibility and assessed liability in an earlier phase of the mock trial. Jurors in the bifurcated trials of Greene and Smith's (2002) study had no evidence whatsoever concerning the defendant's actions in causing the accident. (Both are valid replications of real world events.) Greene and Smith found that their jurors gave lower damage awards than did jurors in unitary trial conditions. Wissler et al. (2001) found no such diminution as a result of bifurcation, suggesting that jurors who heard evidence about both liability and damages—even when presented in separate stages of the trial—apparently relied on the conduct-related evidence to buttress their decisions about damages.

What can one conclude about the effectiveness of bifurcation on judgments concerning compensation? The data seem to suggest that bifurcation may be of some, albeit limited, usefulness. It may be effective in reducing the impact of injury-related information on judgments of liability for compensatory damages (Greene & Smith, 2002). This stands to reason, because jurors in bifurcated proceedings typically have little knowledge about anyone's injuries when they make decisions regarding liability (although they may have suspicions that stem from seeing the plaintiff in the courtroom during the liability phase). Bifurcation is less effective in reducing the impact of conduct-related information on monetary damage awards, at least in situations where jurors have previously heard this evidence. Some mock jurors apparently rely on this evidence to inform their judgments regarding the size of the damage award, even in bifurcated proceedings.

Separation of Compensatory and Punitive Damages Phases

In a unitary trial all the evidence is presented to the jury at one time, and the jury then retires to make several decisions in the same deliberation session. It has long been suspected that evidence of the defendant's net worth, relevant only to the size of the punitive damages award,[13] may inappropriately affect judgments about compensatory liability and about the size of the compensatory damage award. In a bifurcated trial, on the other hand, the presentation of evidence relevant to punitive damages (e.g., concerning net worth) is presented if, and only if, the jury has already found the defendant liable for compensatory damages, has determined what that compensation should be, and has also found him or her liable for punitive damages.

Several states have enacted statutes that require bifurcation of this sort. The California statute is particularly clear. It provides that

> the court shall, on application of any defendant, preclude the admission of evidence of that defendant's profits or financial condition until after the trier of fact returns a verdict for plaintiff awarding actual [i.e., compensatory] damages and finds that a defendant is guilty of malice, oppression or fraud. (California Civil Code, § 3295 (d), 1987)

In this situation, bifurcation is assumed to prevent evidence that is relevant only to punitive damages from prejudicing the jury's determinations of compensatory liability and damages.

Another recent study (Greene, Woody, & Winter, 2000) examined the effects of bifurcation of compensatory and punitive damages decisions. Across three tort cases (medical malpractice, automobile negligence, and products liability), Greene et al. (2000) manipulated the structure of the trial so that jurors in unitary trials heard all of the evidence (concerning

---

[13]Recall that evidence regarding the defendant's financial condition is essential to punitive damages decisions, because the jury's goal is to assess punitive damages that are large enough to be felt but not so large as to bankrupt the defendant. However, evidence of financial condition should be considered only for that purpose.

compensatory liability and damages and punitive liability and damages) and then assessed compensatory and punitive damages. Jurors in bifurcated trials, on the other hand, made judgments of compensatory damages before hearing any evidence related to defendant reprehensibility and wealth.

What effect did this variation in trial structure have on damage awards? Surprisingly, it had no effect on compensatory awards. In other words, jurors in unitary trials awarded no more in compensatory damages than did jurors in bifurcated trials. However, trial structure had an unexpected effect on punitive damage awards: Punitive damages were higher in bifurcated trials than in unitary trials. We ponder these results again later.

Landsman et al. (1998) also assessed the impact of bifurcation on awards for compensatory and punitive damages in a jury analogue study. They used a products liability case to address several questions about differences between unitary and bifurcated trials: (a) Are jurors in unitary and bifurcated trials differentially likely to find compensatory liability? (b) Do they use evidence differently? (c) Do they make awards of different sizes? These researchers edited the transcript from an asbestos case and manipulated two variables (trial structure: unitary or bifurcated, and strength of the plaintiff's case: weak or moderate) to yield four versions of the mock trial. In addition, jurors in the unitary trial heard either low or high net-worth information regarding the defendant.

Apparently, jurors were differentially likely to find liability for compensatory damages. Jurors in unitary trials were more likely to find the defendant liable than were jurors in bifurcated trials (55% vs. 43%). Despite instructions to the contrary, the former group apparently made improper use of punitive damages case facts in assessing liability for compensation.

Do jurors in unitary trials award more in compensatory damages? It depends. When the evidence favoring the plaintiff on liability was moderately strong, jurors in unitary trials awarded more in compensation than did jurors in bifurcated trials ($722,500 vs. $612,000). (When the evidence was weak, damage awards in unitary and bifurcated trials did not differ.) This finding suggests that the punitive damages evidence led jurors in at least some cases to respond with higher compensatory awards. In this context, evidence related to punitive damages improperly influenced judgments of compensatory damages. According to these data, trying punitive damages issues separately from compensatory damages issues will reduce the likelihood of evidence being misused (Gensler, 2000).

Surprisingly, a different picture emerges with respect to the size of punitive damage awards (although the details are consistent with the findings of Greene et al., 2000). Larger punitive awards came from bifurcated juries than from unitary juries. Landsman et al. (1998) offered the following explanation of this apparent reversal of fortune. They suggested that in bifurcated trials the only juries that decide punitive damages are those that already favored the plaintiff in the area of compensation. In a bifurcated proceeding, prodefense juries would never get to the punitive damages phases of a trial. So, in a unitary trial, prodefense jurors who were unable to prevail on compensation can still assert some restraint when the size of the punitive award is fixed. This explanation accounts for Landsman et al.'s finding—where juries determined liability as well as damage awards. It does not explain the augmented punitive damage awards in Greene et al.'s (2000) study, where liability was stipulated and only damages were awarded and where jurors did not drop out as the trial proceeded.

As we noted at the beginning of this section, one hypothesized advantage of bifurcation is that it may enhance jury comprehension and reduce jury confusion (Gensler, 2000). One would suspect that the task for any jury is simplified significantly when fewer issues are to be decided. Fewer witnesses testify, fewer exhibits are displayed, less trial time is required, the issues are more narrowly focused, the jury instructions are fewer, and the relevance of the evidence to a particular issue is more obvious. (In fact, jurors in the bifurcated versions of Landsman et al.'s [1998] study may have augmented their punitive damage awards because evidence of the defendant's wealth and reprehensible conduct were presented closer to the decision point and may have been more salient.) Finally, bifurcation may also reduce the problem of differing standards of proof on liability. (Typically, compensatory liability is determined by a "preponderance of the evidence," whereas punitive liability is determined by "clear and convincing evidence.")

Although preliminary data (Landsman et al., 1998) indicate no comprehension benefits from bifurcation, Gensler (2000) correctly noted that the real test would come from lengthy, complex cases (as opposed to abbreviated simulation cases) in which bifurcation could significantly reduce the amount of evidence, number of issues, and delay between hearing the evidence and fact finding.

Taken together, these findings suggest a rather complicated picture of the interrelationship of compensatory damages evidence and punitive damages evidence and of the role of bifurcation in separating the two and enhancing fairness. As Landsman et al.'s (1998) data show, bifurcation apparently affects decisions about compensatory and punitive award decision making in variable ways. Bifurcation can effectively reduce the improper usage of punitive damages evidence in compensatory award decision making, but it may also result in augmented punitive damage awards.

We make one final note regarding bifurcation: Some have argued that the procedure artificially constrains jurors' decision making because it withholds selected portions of the evidence (Hannaford, Dann, & Munsterman, 1998). In so doing, bifurcation removes the ability of juries to inject community values into their deliberations (as, e.g., when jurors might want to use evidence of the defendant's conduct to augment or decrease damages).

The extent to which community values *should* play a role in jury decisions is, of course, open to debate.

CLARIFYING INSTRUCTIONS ON DAMAGE AWARDS

There is little doubt that punitive damages instructions, in particular, provide little guidance about how much to award. If the jury finds that the defendant's conduct warrants punitive liability, then courts usually ask jurors to assess punitive damages sufficient to punish and to deter and, in so doing, to consider the defendant's conduct and (in some jurisdictions) his or her wealth. However, the instructions are often no more specific than that.[14] As a result, "the jury is given no guidepost with which to measure whether 1 million or 100 million is the appropriate punishment. . . . These sort of general instructions are little better than advising the jury to 'do the right thing'" (Melsheimer & Stodghill, 1994, p. 337). Unclear instructions increase the risk that passion and prejudice will inform punitive damage awards: "The lack of clear guidance heightens the risk that arbitrariness, passion, or bias will replace dispassionate deliberation as the basis for the jury's verdict" (*TXO Production Corp. v. Alliance Resources Corp.*, 1993, p. 475, Justice O'Connor, dissenting).[15]

In addition to concerns about the vagueness of instructions, critics have noted other issues related to judicial instructions. Cases that may warrant punitive damage judgments typically involve many complicated issues, and jurors may have difficulty tracking and responding to the instructions relevant to these various debates. The instructions may do little to help jurors factor the social costs and benefits of the defendant's conduct into the equation. Finally, as Sunstein, Kahneman, and Schkade (1998) noted, jurors may lack the ability to translate their punitive intent into a dollar value; most ordinary people, they argued, would not know what a given dollar amount would do to, or mean to, a particular defendant or corporation.[16]

Some courts and commentators have devised solutions to these problems that incorporate changes in the ways that jurors are instructed. For

[14]In some jurisdictions jury instructions are supplemented with criteria used by appellate courts in posttrial review. For example, jurors may be admonished that the award bear some reasonable relationship to the compensatory award, that it not bankrupt the defendant, and that jurors not be motivated by passion or prejudice ("The civil jury," 1997).
[15]The argument may be equally applicable to compensatory damage award decisions in ordinary tort cases in which jurors also receive imprecise guidance, particularly about noneconomic damages. The debate is perhaps more vociferous in the realm of punitive damages, because the stakes are usually higher.
[16]Sunstein et al. (1998) argued that the jury's task should be restricted to ranking the case in comparison to a set of preselected cases or to assessing a number on a bounded scale and that some "translating institution" (p. 2121), knowledgeable about the effects of dollar awards on both individuals and firms and about their wealth, could then convert this judgment into an award.

example, Melsheimer and Stodghill (1994) urged courts to give "detailed and intelligent instructions" that clearly explain the purposes of punitive damages and to "provide conceptual benchmarks by which such damages should be calculated" (p. 349). Justice O'Connor, dissenting in *Pacific Mutual Life Insurance Company v. Haslip* (1991), encouraged courts to provide jurors with a list of standards against which their punitive damages judgments would be reviewed. Perczek (1993) offered a sample jury instruction that she claimed would limit discretion and provide appropriate guidance to the jury in punitive damages cases. Excerpts of the instruction follow:

> Punitive damages are damages exceeding the amount of money necessary to compensate the plaintiff for his/her injury and loss. You may award punitive damages for two purposes only: to punish the defendant for his/her willful conduct or conduct evincing a reckless disregard for probable consequences and to make him/her an example so as to warn and deter others from engaging in similar misconduct. . . . In deciding whether to award punitive damages, you must consider the following factors: 1) the degree of reprehensibility of the defendant's conduct and the grievousness of his/her acts; 2) the duration of that conduct and the degree of the defendant's awareness that the conduct would harm the plaintiff; 3) the attitude and conduct of the defendant upon discovery of his/her misconduct and any actions taken by the defendant to remedy the misconduct once it became known to him/her; 4) the defendant's concealment; and 5) the existence and frequency of similar misconduct in the past. . . . There are certain factors that will aid you in determining the amount of punitive damages . . . and you must consider them in deciding a just and fair amount. . . . You must consider the following: 1) the likelihood, at the time of the defendant's misconduct, that serious harm would result from it; 2) the seriousness of the hazard to the public arising from the defendant's misconduct; 3) the duration of that hazard and its excessiveness; 4) the profitability of the misconduct to the defendant; 5) the desirability of removing that profit from the defendant. . . . There is one last factor that you may consider in assessing the punitive damages award, and that is the defendant's wealth and financial condition. You have heard evidence pertaining to the defendant's wealth and financial condition. This evidence was admitted for your consideration only with reference to the question of what amount of punitive damages is necessary to punish the defendant in view of his/her financial condition. (pp. 868–872)

Finally, the Model Punitive Damages Act (Uniform Law Commissioners, 1997) lists a number of factors that reformers believe are relevant to jury decisions about punitive damages and that judges should deliver in these cases. Among the factors are

- the nature of the defendant's wrongful conduct and the effect on the claimant and others;
- the amount of compensatory damages awarded;

- fines, penalties, damages, or other restitution to be paid by the defendant arising from this wrongful conduct;
- the defendant's present and future financial condition and the effect of the award on these conditions;
- any profit or gain obtained by the defendant through his or her wrongful conduct;
- any adverse effect of the award on innocent persons;
- any remedial measures taken or not taken by the defendant since the wrongful conduct;
- any compliance or noncompliance with applicable standards governing these actions; and
- any other aggravating or mitigating factors relevant to the amount of the award.

Clearly, these proposed instructions provide more specific guidelines than present directives. However, the extent to which such revisions would cabin jurors' discretion and result in more predictable awards is an empirical question. Are the proposed instructions likely to enhance juror comprehension and award consistency, or would such lengthy lists give jurors tacit permission to consider a wider range of factors and ultimately result in more disparate verdicts and awards? Because neither of the instructions detailed previously has been evaluated empirically, we can, at present, only guess at their effectiveness.

It is worth noting that some modest success has been achieved in using instructions to focus jurors on the evidence that is relevant to their damages decisions. Wissler, Kuehn, and Saks (2000) found that jury instructions not to discount awards for medical expenses and noneconomic damages to reflect any uncertainty about the defendant's liability were effective in reducing those tendencies. Instructions not to increase awards to reflect the defendant's egregious conduct were similarly effective. Wissler et al. suspected that when the law explains to jurors both *how* to treat the evidence and *why*—explaining that doing otherwise would result in under- or overcompensation of the plaintiff—such instructions enhance the likelihood that jurors will correctly apply that evidence.

PAYING PUNITIVE DAMAGE AWARDS TO THE GOVERNMENT

Several states have adopted a plan by which all or some of a punitive damage award is paid to the state treasury or state agencies (e.g., Iowa: Iowa Code 668A.1).[17] The rationale is that punitive damages are not intended to be compensatory; their purpose is not to further enrich the plain-

---

[17]For example, in Georgia, 75% of any punitive damages award, less the cost of litigation, is allocated to the state treasury (cited by Anderson & MacCoun, 1999).

tiff. Indeed, when punitive damages are large—as, for example, in cases against wealthy corporate defendants—the plaintiff may receive a windfall (and critics of punitive damages have further ammunition to attempt to curtail or eliminate these awards). When punitive damages are treated as fines paid to the government, however, the windfall problem is eliminated, and the actual intent of the award—to punish and to deter but not to compensate—is restored. U.S. Supreme Court Chief Justice Rehnquist put it this way:

> Punitive damages are generally seen as a windfall to plaintiffs, who are entitled to receive full compensation for their injuries—but no more. Even assuming that a punitive fine should be imposed after a civil trial, the penalty should go to the State, not to the plaintiff—who by hypothesis is fully compensated. (*Smith v. Wade*, 1982, p. 59)

One wonders, though, whether jurors, as taxpaying residents of the state, might assess punitive damages at an unreasonably high level so that they, and other residents, may indirectly profit from the state's receipt of a large award. Jurors might also award higher amounts because they approve of the money going to a good cause ("The civil jury," 1997).

Fortunately, we have some empirical data on the effects of sharing a portion of a punitive damage award with the state. Anderson and Mac-Coun (1999) used jury analogue methodology to test the notion that jurors in a products liability lawsuit would be more likely to award punitive damages, and in greater amounts, when the award would go either to the state treasury or a consortium of state agencies[18] rather than to the plaintiff. They found, unexpectedly, that respondents were more likely to award punitive damages when the plaintiff would have been the recipient, rather than the state. The authors offered two explanations for this counterintuitive result. Jurors may have opted to use the punitive damage award to offer further compensation to the plaintiff, or they may have intended the award to serve—in addition to deterrent and punishment functions—as a form of restitution. As Anderson and MacCoun noted, "many citizens feel that fair punishment for wrongdoing requires acts of restitution for restorative, rather than compensatory purposes. The offender has torn the social fabric, and acts of restitution serve to repair that damage" (p. 327). If this finding can be generalized to other jurisdictions and fact patterns, the obvious policy implication is that awarding any punitive damages to the state or other neutral third party may actually reduce the number of punitive damage awards.

---

[18]Some examples include the California Breast Cancer Research Fund, the State Children's Trust Fund for the Prevention of Child Abuse, and the California Public School Library Protection Fund. (These agencies are apparently hypothetical.)

ELIMINATING JURIES

Although it may seem incongruous—in a book about juries and damage awards—to discuss removing damages decisions from juries altogether, we raise that possibility here because it has been mentioned as a reform to the current system, particularly in the realm of punitive damages. Some critics (e.g., Schkade, Sunstein, & Kahneman, 2000; Sunstein et al., 1998) suggest that because juries are ill equipped to carry out the task of assigning punitive damages that produce optimal deterrence, the task should be relegated instead to judges or to specialized regulatory agencies. Sunstein et al. (1998) cited two real-world precedents in support of this proposal: (a) the workers' compensation system, in which a fixed dollar value is placed on an injury through a predetermined schedule produced by the legislature or an administrative agency, and (b) federal sentencing guidelines, in which case-by-case judgments have been replaced by standardized sentences for comparably situated criminal defendants.

A handful of states now have judges assess punitive damages. In these jurisdictions the jury determines compensatory damages and decides whether the defendant is liable for punitive damages, and the judge then determines their amount. However, as Sunstein et al. (1998) noted, although a system of judge-imposed punitive damages might well reduce the variability and unpredictability of these awards, judges, too, may have difficulty mapping normative judgments onto dollar amounts. (Sunstein et al. suggested that some form of scheduling should accompany the move from jury to judicial control of punitive damage awards.)

How do jurors compare with judges on the task of assessing punitive damages? Data come from two recent studies: one that used experimental methodology and a second that tracked actual case outcomes. Unfortunately, their take-home messages differ: The former concluded that jurors' assessments were more prone to error than judges', whereas the latter showed that jurors' awards are not substantively different from judges'.

In the former study, Harvard Law professor W. Kip Viscusi asked whether mock jurors would assess damages properly, based on the actual losses incurred when an oil well blew out, or whether they would focus on the worst-case scenario instead—a sort of "what might have been" analysis (Viscusi, 2000). His analysis of assessed damages from approximately 500 jury-eligible adults and 90 state court judges who read the same scenarios showed that jurors' awards were considerably more variable than judges' awards and that jurors were more likely than judges to assess damages in excess of the actual losses incurred. This finding may be relevant to situations where the worst-case scenario is either known to jurors or is hinted at by attorneys during the trial, but it may be of limited usefulness in the vast majority of damages cases where the focus is on the particular plaintiff seated in the courtroom.

The most comprehensive study of jury–judge agreement, conducted by Eisenberg and colleagues (Eisenberg, LaFountain, Ostrom, Rottman, & Wells, 2002), analyzed data from nearly 9,000 trials that ended in 1996 from 45 of the nation's largest trial courts. The primary finding was a negative one—that judges and juries do not behave substantially differently in these cases; they award punitive damages at about the same rate, and punitive awards bear approximately the same relationship to compensatory awards. The range of jury awards was somewhat more spread out than judicial awards, but only a few jury awards were outside the ranges of what judges would award in similar cases. These results call into question the notion that because judges would perform better than juries they should displace juries in setting punitive damage levels.

CONCLUSION

Our analyses of these proposed and enacted reforms lead to two conclusions. First, although a handful of empirical studies tell us something about the likely effects of capping and bifurcation on jurors' judgments, enough may not yet be known to make scientifically supported recommendations regarding their implementation in court. It is not known, for example, whether awards in cases where liability and damages evidence are separated are likely to be larger or smaller than awards in cases where jurors hear all the evidence at once. Neither is it known exactly how those variations affect the jurors' tasks. Researchers do not know, for example, whether bifurcation will enhance juror comprehension and reduce confusion (and whether it should be trumpeted for these suspected benefits alone). They also do not know why awards for noneconomic losses become larger and more variable when a cap is placed on them and whether these effects might be reduced by clearer instructions from the judge.

What is more, little is known about the likely implications for juries of other reform proposals—damages scheduling, instruction revision, and allocating damages to the state—and researchers have a scant foundation for recommending their use or nonuse in court. For example, researchers have very little knowledge about the real-world appropriateness of damages scheduling and only a rudimentary understanding of the complicated issues involved in situations where plaintiffs must share punitive damage awards with the state. Researchers know nothing about the impact of more detailed instructions on jurors' judgments regarding damages and have only the slightest reason to suspect that judges will render more predictable and equitable punitive damage awards than would juries.

Our second conclusion correlates with the first. Because so little is known about the likely consequences of these reforms in court, and because some of what we have learned has been altogether unexpected (e.g., that caps on pain and suffering damages actually increase variability of awards, that compensatory awards are generally larger when punitive damages are limited, that bifurcation exacerbates the impact of liability evidence on some types of damage awards, and that punitive awards are more likely when the recipient is the plaintiff rather than the state), we sound a loud, cautionary note. In our opinion, most of these reforms are not yet ready for "prime time"; their enactment may do little to enhance the predictability and fairness of jurors' verdicts on damages. Worse, they may have profound and wholly unexpected side effects and may actually impair jurors' abilities to give wise and reasoned judgments. Therefore, our main points are as follows. First, because our knowledge is in a tentative and fragmentary state, we urge empirical researchers to continue to probe inside the "black box" (MacCoun, 1993) to examine the behavioral effects of these reforms. Second, because we simply do not yet know enough, we urge policymakers and court reformers to tread lightly over this ground that seems ever-shifting and decidedly unstable.[19]

---

[19]By contrast, we are highly supportive of some of the more general kinds of reforms that have been empirically examined and are gradually being instituted in civil trials across the country. These reforms—for example, allowing jurors to ask questions of witnesses (Penrod & Heuer, 1997) and to discuss the case before the end of trial (Diamond et al., 2002; Hannaford, Hans, & Munsterman, 2000)—recognize the fact that many jurors are active, probing decisionmakers who may wish to seek clarification or explanation from witnesses or from each other.

10

FINAL REMARKS AND RECOMMENDATIONS[1]

We reiterate that jurors' task in assessing damages is exceedingly difficult. Jurors are presented with an enormous amount of evidence, much of which may be pertinent to one damages-related decision but not to another (e.g., characteristics of the injury should influence compensatory but not punitive damages, whereas the opposite is true for information relating to the defendant's wealth). The awarding of damages is contingent on a prior finding of liability, which is predicated on an overlapping yet distinct constellation of evidentiary factors. Jurors often are not permitted to take notes. They receive minimal guidance, especially in the damages phase of the trial. They are asked to check their assumptions and prior experiences at the door. And for $10 per day and the satisfaction of having done their civic duty, they put their lives on hold for days or weeks on end and may be vilified in the press for having reached the "wrong" decision, even though there is no objective metric of what the "right" decision might be.

---

[1]We chose the title for this final chapter after careful reflection. We deliberately avoided terms like *summary* and *conclusions*, because we feel it would be impossible to summarize an entire book in one short chapter. Readers who have turned to this chapter in the hope of finding a pithy take-home message should not despair but should turn instead to the concluding comments at the end of the individual chapters. For readers who have already read those chapters, rather than simply rehashing the major findings contained therein, we revisit some of the themes laid out at the beginning of the book.

IS THE GLASS OF JURY BEHAVIOR HALF EMPTY
OR HALF FULL?

Our analysis of jurors' behavior under these trying circumstances leads us to the conclusion that the glass is decidedly half full (if not even three quarters full). Our many years of conducting research on jury decision making, and our recent immersion in the literature while writing this book, have given us a healthy respect and appreciation for how well jurors generally do their job. Do jurors always get it right? Of course not. Do jurors sometimes arrive at outlandish decisions that bear little relation to the evidence? Certainly. For the most part, however, jury damage awards reflect proper attention to the factors that are supposed to influence those decisions, and even when they do not, other objectives (e.g., equity or commonsense notions) may be at work. More important, when jurors do fall short they tend to do so in systematic, predictable ways. As we stated at the beginning of this book, we are moved more by data than by rhetoric —and the data show fairly convincingly that although the rhetoric about incompetent juries and arbitrary, illogical verdicts might grab headlines, it tends to be a gross exaggeration of the truth. We now consider a few examples.

Are Jury Damage Awards Too Large?

The data indicate that the average jury award has indeed increased over the years. In particular, there are more very large (i.e., multimillion dollar) awards than there used to be. Nonetheless, the vast majority of jury damage awards are fairly modest and have not increased more than the rate of inflation. Moreover, who is to say what is too large? Archival studies indicate that, on average, injured plaintiffs are undercompensated compared with their projected costs (e.g., Sloan & van Wert, 1991; Viscusi, 1986), suggesting that most jury awards are perhaps not large enough. Compensable costs, especially for medical care, have increased dramatically in the past generation, and one could also argue that in an age of ever more varied leisure opportunities, the costs of intangible, nonpecuniary losses— that is, the sorts of things for which pain and suffering awards are designed to compensate—have increased as well. Are jury awards often quite large? Yes, definitely. Are they *too* large? Obviously, this question is hard to answer in the abstract, but we suspect that in the overwhelming majority of cases, the answer is probably "no."

Are Jury Damage Awards Too Unpredictable?

With respect to the predictability of jury awards, we again see jurors behaving largely in a sensible and predictable manner. Although plaintiffs with similar injuries may indeed receive widely (some would say "wildly") divergent awards (e.g., Diamond, Saks, & Landsman, 1998; Saks, Hollinger, Wissler, Evans, & Hart, 1997), and high variability characterizes pain and suffering awards in particular, natural variation in a system of compensation such as American tort law is inevitable and, arguably, even desirable. Such variation allows juries to tailor their awards to subtle, idiosyncratic case characteristics and to their gut instincts about what is fair. It is difficult to determine at what point any horizontal inequity, which undeniably exists, crosses the line from normal sampling error to misguided caprice.

Three observations lead us to conclude that the degree of variability that exists in jury awards is not cause for great concern. First, although there is some horizontal inequity in compensation, there is far more vertical equity. The single best predictor of compensation awards is injury severity (e.g., Bovbjerg, Sloan, Dor, & Hsieh, 1991): Plaintiffs who are hurt worse receive more money for their injuries. If this were not the case, jurors would be derelict in their duty; however, the strong predictive utility of injury severity suggests that jurors are properly sensitive to this salient and legally paramount criterion. Despite claims to the contrary, punitive damages are highly predictable as well (Daniels & Martin, 1990; Eisenberg, Goerdt, Ostrom, Rottman, & Wells, 1997). More than anything else, they reflect the defendant's wealth and the egregiousness of the defendant's conduct, both of which are factors that the law explicitly instructs jurors to consider.

Second, the variability that exists in awards for similar injuries is reduced by the deliberation process. Thus, although individual jurors may reach judgments that appear to be inconsistent across a sample of cases with similar characteristics, these inconsistencies tend to be ironed out in the deliberation room.

Third, jurors' damage awards generally show a proper consideration of normatively relevant factors and a proper exclusion of normatively irrelevant factors. Injury severity affects compensation awards but generally does *not* affect punitive awards. Defendants' wealth and reprehensible conduct affect punitive awards but generally do *not* affect compensation. Irrefutable evidence of a deep-pocket effect for compensation awards simply does not exist (MacCoun, 1996; Vidmar, 1995). Background and demographic characteristics of all of the parties (plaintiffs, defendants, jurors) have little appreciable effect on any aspect of jurors' decisions, with the exception of defendants' corporate status (Hans, 2000). Overall, then, jurors do a good job of adhering to legal precepts under difficult circumstances in a complex situation.

Do Jurors Treat Different Classes of Defendants Differently?

Some of the loudest hue and cry over the purported arbitrariness of jury damage awards revolves around the alleged mistreatment of medical defendants that supposedly drives up the costs of malpractice insurance and health care, among other evils. However, the fact of the matter is that malpractice defendants win more often than other types of defendants (Bovbjerg et al., 1991; Danzon, 1985; Gross & Syverud, 1991; Metzloff, 1991), and when case characteristics such as the nature and the severity of the injury are held constant, they do not have to pay more in compensation (Vidmar, 1995). Furthermore, punitive damages in malpractice cases are exceedingly rare (Daniels & Martin, 1990; Eisenberg et al., 1997; Rustad, 1998), and when they are levied they probably reflect the fact that medical defendants are (or are perceived to be, which amounts to the same thing in the jury's eyes) wealthier than comparable nonmedical defendants.

WHAT CAN BE DONE TO HELP JURORS DECIDE BETTER?

Despite jurors' relatively high degree of success at applying the law, they are far from perfect arbiters of interpersonal disputes. For example, jurors' verdicts are influenced by their attitudes toward both the civil justice system in general and certain types of defendants (e.g., corporations) in particular (Hans, 1996, 2000). Contributorily negligent plaintiffs receive less compensation for the same injury than do non-negligent plaintiffs (Hammitt, Carroll, & Relles, 1985; Zickafoose & Bornstein, 1999). The *ad damnum* is capable of arbitrarily pulling damage awards up or down, even when it bears no relationship to the factual issues raised at trial.

What prescriptive steps could be taken to improve jurors' performance and make their verdicts comport even more with applicable legal norms? In awarding damages, jurors face two major stumbling blocks: (a) a lack of guidance, and (b) the legal system's unrealistic expectations about how people make decisions.

Lack of Guidance

If interviews with civil jurors make anything clear, it is their frustration and confusion at how (and why) they are left to their own devices in determining an appropriate monetary award (Hans, 2000; Mott, Hans, & Simpson, 2000). Instructions on other substantive matters of law, such as the criteria for determining negligence, or the standard of proof, can be quite elaborate, but when it comes to determining damages, jurors are essentially told to "pick a fair number" (Greene & Bornstein, 2000). It should come as no surprise that jurors employ a diverse set of strategies in attempting to do so, and there seems little doubt that the high variability in awards can be attributed, at least in part, to this lack of guidance. Some support for this contention comes from research indicating that the use of special verdict forms that delineate more clearly what is expected of jurors enhances their attention to legally appropriate factors (Wiggins & Breckler, 1990). Jurors could also be provided with some sort of tool to use in attempting to quantify the unquantifiable, such as a schedule for awarding damages (e.g., Bovbjerg, Sloan, & Blumstein, 1989), which has proven effective at reducing some of the variability in awards (Saks et al., 1997). We advocate for further study, and possible adoption, of this and other promising innovations.

How People Make Decisions: The Legal Versus the Psychological Perspective

Jurors make decisions in situations where they have to assimilate a great deal of evidence, weigh competing hypotheses, and reach a final judgment (i.e., their verdict) when there is no objectively correct answer. The task's complexity is compounded by the fact that the decisions of 12 (or 10, or 6) individuals must then be melded into a single consensus. Such complex decision-making situations are prime candidates for the expression of cognitive shortcuts, or heuristics, that are usually helpful and efficient but sometimes result in subpar decisions (D. E. Bell, Raiffa, & Tversky, 1988; Tversky & Kahneman, 1974). There is ample evidence that such heuristics are at work in jurors' decision making (Arkes, 1989; Saks & Kidd, 1980). For example, the pronounced influence of the *ad damnum* reflects the *anchoring heuristic*, and jurors' inability to ignore certain evidence that is relevant to one judgment but not another reflects the *hindsight effect*. Decision-making researchers (e.g., D. E. Bell et al., 1988) stress that these heuristics are not necessarily good or bad (although for the most part, they are adaptive); rather, they are simply the outcome of how people's minds work in complex, uncertain situations.

Legal guidelines have a tendency to make assumptions that are at odds with these fundamental psychological processes—that is, the "normative" is out of synchrony with the "descriptive." For example, jury instructions presume that jurors will be able to ignore information to which they are blindfolded or that is outside the formally admitted evidence (such as pretrial publicity or their personal beliefs) and that they can apply certain evidence to one type of decision while ignoring it in making other decisions. In truth, these requirements set to jurors an incredibly difficult task. It is possible, of course, that legal policymakers know the limitations of human reasoning and judgment and that the instructions serve merely as a reminder for jurors to try and remain impartial and objective. The fact that jurors succeed at following the law as well as they do suggests that the instructions are somewhat successful in this respect.

But why, we ask, not revise the instructions, or modify the process, in order to serve the same goals while also conforming better to jurors' natural inclinations and thought processes? Research suggests that clarifying jury instructions, or explaining to jurors the rationale behind certain requirements, enhances the instructions' efficacy (e.g., Diamond & Casper, 1992). Bifurcation is another procedure that has the potential to minimize the problem of jurors fusing discrete judgments together, as it reduces the demands to use evidence selectively, applying it in some contexts but ignoring it in others. Although the scant research on bifurcation has been rather mixed as to its effectiveness, it makes so much sense from a psychological perspective that we view it as one of the more promising potential reform measures and encourage future research on its effects.

WHAT CAN SOCIAL SCIENCE RESEARCH DO FOR THE LEGAL SYSTEM?

Many commentators (e.g., Diamond, 1997; Saks, 1992; Vidmar, 1998) have noted the often-uneasy alliance between law and social science. On the one hand, social science data and conclusions are appearing ever more frequently in the courts, and policymakers are actively soliciting empirical data to guide their decision making and agenda setting. On the other hand, many social scientists feel that the courts make inadequate use of the knowledge that they have to offer, and some legal theorists feel that expert witnesses are flooding the courts with junk science (e.g., Huber, 1988, 1991). Much of the controversy surrounds the matter of method: The experimental approaches favored by social scientists may be good exemplars of scientific methodology, but it is unclear how well, or how directly, these approaches speak to the operation of the legal system, which proceeds, as it has for centuries, by precedent and argument.

There are a number of sound reasons why relatively artificial simulation studies, in which mock jurors make hypothetical decisions, are often not very informative from a legal perspective (Davis, Bray, & Holt, 1977; Diamond, 1997). On the other hand, there are equally sound arguments for why tightly controlled experimental studies are highly relevant and informative to real world contexts such as jury behavior (Diamond, 1997; Vidmar, 1994b). Psycholegal researchers are often encouraged by studies finding that the degree of experimental verisimilitude used in various research methodologies has little effect on the research's substantive conclusions (Bornstein, 1999; Kramer & Kerr, 1989; Wilbanks, 2001). Nonetheless, the point is moot if, as is typically the case, courts are reluctant to rely on jury research that is lacking in realism (Diamond, 1997). Even if jury researchers were to win the battle over the scientific merits of simulation methodology, they would lose the war over whether those findings can ultimately be put to any practical use in the world of legal policy.

Thus, we cannot overemphasize the desirability of conducting sophisticated psycholegal research that mirrors jurors' actual task demands as closely as possible. Ideal research on the jury would observe jury behavior *in situ*; that is, while real jurors deliberated to real verdicts. Since the groundbreaking University of Chicago Jury Project (Broeder, 1959; Kalven, 1958; Kalven & Zeisel, 1966), such observations have simply not been feasible (or legal). Recently, however, legal constraints have begun to loosen somewhat, and some states (e.g., Arizona) have allowed the observation and recording of jury deliberations in actual cases. There have been no reports, that we know of, indicating that any of the participants in these courtroom dramas (jurors, litigants, attorneys, or judges) have been harmed in any way by having trials and deliberations recorded, and the procedure can only be an enormous boon to researchers. We hope that in jurisdictions where juries may be observed researchers will be able to use the available data to further their understanding of the fundamental psychological processes involved in decision making on damages and related issues.

Whether researchers choose experimental laboratory-based methods, naturalistic field methods, or something in between, we close (as so many research reports do) with a call for more data. Our call for more research is partly an invitation to test our own objectivity. We do not deny having our own theoretical biases (although we have tried to hide them as much as possible). We are not immune—as jurors themselves are not immune —from having our beliefs and expectations color our assessment of the evidence (in our case, the evidence is the literature on jury decisions regarding damages, rather than trial testimony). We hope that if, with more data, the preponderance of the evidence shifted away from our beliefs, we would recognize the shift and modify our stance accordingly.

Our call for more (and better) research also reflects a desire to get the evidence out in the open and to let legal policy be influenced by data rather than by unfounded assumptions.[2] Policies enacted in the absence of data are lucky if they turn out to be right and wasteful or harmful if they turn out to be wrong. In the domain of jury research, policy implications range from how jurors are chosen during *voir dire* to the decision rule they use in reaching a verdict, with other policies guiding everything that happens in between: evidence presentation, trial structure, instructions, and so on. Our reading of the data is that jurors do quite well at the difficult task of awarding damages. There is, nonetheless, obvious room for improvement, and our hope is that good research can find the best ways to help jurors function in their important and demanding task.

---

[2]Professor Michael Saks (1989) forcefully made the case for the importance of basing legal policy on empirical data. An instructive example is the recently popular statutory reform of imposing caps on punitive or pain and suffering awards. Caps have been enacted primarily to reduce variability and curb excessive awards. However, research has shown that in some circumstances caps actually have the opposite effect and may paradoxically increase award size and variability (Robbennolt & Studebaker, 1999; Saks et al., 1997; see chapter 9, this volume).

ONE FINAL REMARK

Professor Harry Kalven, whom we have acknowledged throughout this book as one of the earliest and foremost authorities on the civil jury, entitled one of his articles "The Dignity of the Civil Jury" (Kalven, 1964). The harsh criticism that has been heaped on the civil jury over the past few decades has sought to rob it of its dignity. Some commentators have advocated curtailing or restricting the jury's license. Others have favored abolishing the jury altogether, at least for the performance of some tasks (e.g., the awarding of punitive damages). Although we are loath to cast ourselves as defenders of the jury—principally because we feel it does not need defending—we are confident in our assessment that, by and large, jurors are up to the task in awarding damages. Where they fail, they fail for understandable reasons, due largely to the incompatibility between what the law proposes and what the mind disposes. In our opinion, the civil jury's dignity survives intact.

REFERENCES

Abraham, K. S., & Jeffries, J. C. (1989). Punitive damages and the rule of law: The role of defendant's wealth. *Journal of Legal Studies, 18,* 415–425.

Abramson, E. M. (1989–1990). The medical malpractice imbroglio: A non-adversarial suggestion. *Kentucky Law Journal, 78,* 293–310.

Adler, S. J. (1994). *The jury: Trial and error in the American courtroom.* New York: Times Books/Random House.

American Bar Association. (1991). *Jury comprehension in complex cases.* Washington, DC: Author.

American Jurisprudence Pleading and Practice Forms. (Vol. 8). (1982). Rochester, NY: Lawyers Co-operative.

American Tort Reform Association. (2002). Retrieved July 17, 2002, from http://www.atra.org

Anderson, M. C., & MacCoun, R. J. (1999). Goal conflict in juror assessments of compensatory and punitive damages. *Law and Human Behavior, 23,* 313–330.

Andrews, P., Meyer, R. G., & Berlá, E. P. (1996). Development of the Lost Pleasure of Life Scale. *Law and Human Behavior, 20,* 99–111.

Arkes, H. R. (1989). Principles in judgment/decision making research pertinent to legal proceedings. *Behavioral Sciences and the Law, 7,* 429–456.

Astolfo, T. (1991). *Attitudinal predictors in a negligence case.* Unpublished master's thesis, Florida International University, Miami.

Bailis, D. S., & MacCoun, R. J. (1996). Estimating liability risks with the media as your guide: A content analysis of media coverage of tort litigation. *Law and Human Behavior, 20,* 419–429.

Baldus, D., MacQueen, J., & Woodworth, G. (1995). Improving judicial oversight of jury damages assessments: A proposal for the comparative additur/remittitur of awards for nonpecuniary harms and punitive damages. *Iowa Law Review, 80,* 1109–1267.

Baron, J., & Ritov, I. (1993). Intuitions about penalties and compensation in the context of tort law. *Journal of Risk and Uncertainty, 7,* 17–33.

Bell, D. E., Raiffa, H., & Tversky, A. (Eds.). (1988). *Decision making: Descriptive, normative, and prescriptive interactions.* Cambridge, MA: Cambridge University Press.

Bell, P. A. (1984). The bell tolls: Toward full tort recovery for psychic injury. *University of Florida Law Review, 36,* 333–412.

Belli, M. (1982). *Modern trials* (2nd ed.). St. Paul, MN: West.

Bezanson, R., Cranberg, G., & Soloski, J. (1987). *Libel law and the press: Myth and reality.* New York: Free Press.

Biskind, E. (1954). *How to prepare a case for trial.* Englewood Cliffs, NJ: Prentice Hall.

Bodenhausen, G., & Lichtenstein, M. (1987). Social stereotypes and information-processing strategies: The impact of task complexity. *Journal of Personality and Social Psychology, 48*, 267–282.

Bonanti, R. (2000, August). Tort "reform" in the states. *Trial, 36*, 28–34.

Bordens, K. S., & Horowitz, I. A. (1998). The limits of sampling and consolidation in mass tort trials: Justice improved or justice altered? *Law and Psychology Review, 22*, 43–66.

Bornstein, B. H. (1994). David, Goliath, and Reverend Bayes: Prior beliefs about defendants' status in personal injury cases. *Applied Cognitive Psychology, 8*, 233–258.

Bornstein, B. H. (1998). From compassion to compensation: The effect of injury severity on mock jurors' liability judgments. *Journal of Applied Social Psychology, 28*, 1477–1502.

Bornstein, B. H. (1999). The ecological validity of jury simulations: Is the jury still out? *Law and Human Behavior, 23*, 75–91.

Bornstein, B. H., & Rajki, M. (1994). Extra-legal factors and product liability: The influence of mock jurors' demographic characteristics and intuitions about the cause of an injury. *Behavioral Sciences and the Law, 12*, 127–147.

Bornstein, B. H., Rung, L. M., & Miller, M. K. (2002). The effects of defendant remorse on mock juror decisions in a malpractice case. *Behavioral Sciences and the Law, 20*, 339–409.

Bornstein, B. H., Whisenhunt, B. L., Nemeth, R. J., & Dunaway, D. L. (2002). Pretrial publicity and civil cases: A two-way street? *Law and Human Behavior, 26*, 3–17.

Bourgeois, M. J., Horowitz, I. A., ForsterLee, L., & Grahe, J. (1995). Nominal and interactive groups: Effects of preinstruction and deliberations on decisions and evidence recall in complex trials. *Journal of Applied Psychology, 80*, 58–67.

Bovbjerg, R. R., Sloan, F. A., & Blumstein, J. F. (1989). Valuing life and limb in tort: Scheduling "pain and suffering." *Northwestern University Law Review, 83*, 908–976.

Bovbjerg, R. R., Sloan, F. A., Dor, A., & Hsieh, C. R. (1991). Juries and justice: Are malpractice and other personal injuries created equal? *Law and Contemporary Problems, 54*, 5–42.

Bragg, R. (2000, July 15). *Tobacco lawsuit in Florida yields record damages.* Retrieved July 17, 2002, from http://www.nytimes.com

Bray, R., & Noble, A. (1978). Authoritarianism and decisions of mock juries: Evidence of jury bias and group polarization. *Journal of Personality and Social Psychology, 36*, 1424–1430.

Breslo, J. A. (1992). Taking the punitive damage windfall away from the plaintiff: An analysis. *Northwestern University Law Review, 86*, 1130–1168.

Broder, A. J. (1994, January 3). Judges, juries and verdict awards. *New York Law Journal*, p. 3.

Broeder, D. W. (1959). The University of Chicago jury project. *Nebraska Law Review, 38*, 744–760.

Burger, J. M. (1981). Motivational biases in the attribution of responsibility for an accident: A meta-analysis of the defensive-attribution hypothesis. *Psychological Bulletin, 90,* 496–512.

Byrne, D., Clore, G., & Smeaton, G. (1986). The attraction hypothesis: Do similar attitudes affect anything? *Journal of Personality and Social Psychology, 51,* 1167–1170.

Calfee, J. E., & Rubin, P. H. (1992). Some implications of damage payments for nonpecuniary losses. *Journal of Legal Studies, 21,* 371–411.

California jury instructions: Civil, book of approved jury instructions (8th ed.). St. Paul, MN: West.

Casper, J. (1993). Restructuring the traditional civil jury: The effects of changes in composition and procedures. In R. Litan (Ed.), *Verdict: Assessing the civil jury system* (pp. 414–459). Washington, DC: Brookings Institution.

Casper, J., Benedict, K., & Perry, J. (1989). Juror decision making, attitudes, and the hindsight bias. *Law and Human Behavior, 13,* 291–310.

Cather, C., Greene, E., & Durham, R. (1996). Plaintiff injury and defendant reprehensibility: Implications for compensatory and punitive damage awards. *Law and Human Behavior, 20,* 189–205.

Centers for Disease Control. (2001). Divisions of HIV/AIDS Prevention surveillance report (Vol. 13, No. 1). Retrieved July 17, 2002, from http://www.cdc.gov/hiv/stats/hasr1301.htm

Chapman, G. B., & Bornstein, B. H. (1996). The more you ask for, the more you get: Anchoring in personal injury verdicts. *Applied Cognitive Psychology, 10,* 519–540.

Charfoos, L. S., & Christensen, D. W. (1986). Measuring damages. *American Bar Association Journal, 72,* 74–77.

Chase, O. G. (1995). Helping jurors determine pain and suffering awards. *Hofstra Law Review, 23,* 763–790.

Chin, A., & Peterson, M. (1985). *Deep pockets, empty pockets: Who wins in Cook County jury trials.* Santa Monica, CA: RAND.

Chitty, J. (1809). *Pleading and parties to actions, with precedents.* New York: Publisher unknown.

Citizens Against Lawsuit Abuse. (n.d.). *Believe it or not.* Retrieved from http://www.cala.com/cala10.htm

The civil jury. (1997). *Harvard Law Review, 110,* 1408–1536.

Clermont, K. M., & Eisenberg, T. (1992). Trial by jury or judge: Transcending empiricism. *Cornell Law Review, 77,* 1124–1177.

Colorado jury instructions 3d: Civil. (1989). San Francisco: Bancroft-Whitney.

Coyle, M. (2001, April 9). Updating "hedonic" damages. *National Law Journal,* pp. A1, A15.

Dane, F. C., & Wrightsman, L. (1982). Effects of defendants' and victims' characteristics on jurors' verdicts. In N. L. Kerr & R. M. Bray (Eds.), *The psychology of the courtroom* (pp. 83–115). New York: Academic Press.

Daniels, S., & Martin, J. (1990). Myth and reality in punitive damages. *Minnesota Law Review, 75,* 1–64.

Daniels, S., & Martin, J. (1997). Persistence is not always a virtue: Tort reform, civil liability for health care, and the lack of empirical evidence. *Behavioral Sciences and the Law, 15,* 3–19.

Danzon, P. M. (1985). *Medical malpractice: Theory, evidence, and public policy.* Cambridge, MA: Harvard University Press.

Danzon, P. M. (1986). The frequency and severity of medical malpractice claims: New evidence. *Law and Contemporary Problems, 49,* 57–79.

Danzon, P. M. (1990). The "crisis" in medical malpractice: A comparison of trends in the United States, Canada, the United Kingdom and Australia. *Law, Medicine and Health Care, 18,* 48–58.

Darden, W. R., DeConinck, J. B., Babin, B. J., & Griffin, M. (1991). The role of consumer sympathy in product liability suits. *Journal of Business Research, 22,* 65–89.

Davis, J. H., Au, W. T., Hulbert, L., Chen, X., & Zarnoth, P. (1997). Effects of group size and procedural influence on consensual judgments of quantity: The example of damage awards and mock civil juries. *Journal of Personality and Social Psychology, 73,* 703–718.

Davis, J. H., Bray, R., & Holt, R. (1977). The empirical study of decision processes in juries: A critical review. In J. L. Tapp & F. J. Levine (Eds.), *Law, justice, and the individual in society: Psychological and legal issues* (pp. 326–361). New York: Holt, Rinehart & Winston.

Davis, J. H., Stasson, M. F., Parks, C. D., Hulbert, L., Kameda, T., Zimmerman, S. K., et al. (1993). Quantitative decisions by groups and individuals: Voting procedures and monetary awards by mock civil juries. *Journal of Experimental Social Psychology, 29,* 326–346.

DeFrances, C. J., & Litras, M. F. (1999, September). Civil trial cases and verdicts in large counties, 1996 (NCJ Rep. No. 173246). *Bureau of Justice Statistics Bulletin.* Retrieved July 17, 2002, from http://www.ojp.usdoj.govbjs/pub/pdf/ctcvlc96.pdf

DeMay, J. (1977). *The plaintiff's personal injury case: Its preparation, trial and settlement.* Englewood Cliffs, NJ: Prentice Hall.

Diamond, S. (1997). Illuminations and shadows from jury simulation. *Law and Human Behavior, 21,* 561–571.

Diamond, S., Brown, M., Ellis, L., Hannaford, P., Rose, M., & Vidmar, N. (2002, March). The impact of juror discussions during trial: The Arizona Jury Project. In S. Diamond (Chair), *The impact of juror discussions during trial: The Arizona Jury Project.* Symposium conducted at meeting of the American Psychology–Law Society, Austin, TX.

Diamond, S., & Casper, J. D. (1992). Blindfolding the jury to verdict consequences: Damages, experts, and the civil jury. *Law and Society Review, 26,* 513–563.

Diamond, S., Casper, J. D., Heiert, C. L., & Marshall, A. (1996). Juror reactions to attorneys at trial. *Journal of Criminal Law and Criminology, 87,* 17–47.

Diamond, S., Casper, J. D., & Ostergren, L. (1989). Blindfolding the jury. *Law and Contemporary Problems, 52,* 247–267.

Diamond, S., Ellis, L., Saks, M. J., & Landsman, S. (2000, March). *Ad damnums and caps: Assistance or merely influence?* Paper presented at meeting of American Psychology–Law Society, New Orleans, LA.

Diamond, S., Saks, M. J., & Landsman, S. (1998). Juror judgements about liability and damages: Sources of variability and ways to increase consistency. *DePaul Law Review, 48,* 301–325.

Dobbs, D. B. (1973). *Handbook on the law of remedies.* St. Paul, MN: West.

Douthwaite, G. (1988, 1992 Cum. Suppl.). *Jury instructions on damages in tort actions* (2nd ed.). Charlottesville, VA: Michie.

Eagly, A., & Wood, W. (1991). Explaining sex differences in social behavior: A meta-analytic perspective. *Personality and Social Psychology Bulletin, 17,* 306–315.

Eisenberg, T., Goerdt, J. A., Ostrom, B., Rottman, D., & Wells, M. T. (1997). The predictability of punitive damages. *Journal of Legal Studies, 26,* 623–660.

Eisenberg, T., LaFountain, N., Ostrom, B., Rottman, D., & Wells, M. T. (2002). Juries, judges, and punitive damages: An empirical study. *Cornell Law Review, 87,* 743–782.

Eisenberg, T., & Wells, M. T. (1998). Punitive awards after BMW, a new capping system, and the reported opinion bias. *Wisconsin Law Review, 1998,* 387–425.

Elliott, E. D. (1989). Why punitive damages don't deter corporate misconduct effectively. *Alabama Law Review, 40,* 1053–1072.

Ellis, D. D. (1989). Punitive damages, due process, and the jury. *Alabama Law Review, 40,* 975–1008.

Ellis, L. (2002, March). *Don't find my client liable, but if you do . . . Defense award recommendations.* Paper presented at the meeting of the American Psychology–Law Society, Austin, TX.

Ellsworth, P. (1989). Are twelve heads better than one? *Law and Contemporary Problems, 52,* 205–224.

Epstein, R. A. (2000). *Cases and materials on torts* (7th ed.). New York: Aspen Law and Business.

Eustis, R. (2001, March 8). $1.6 million punitive award peeled from stripper's legal victory. *Fulton County Daily Report.* Retrieved July 17, 2002, from http://www.law.com

Feigenson, N. (2000). *Legal blame: How jurors think and talk about accidents.* Washington, DC: American Psychological Association.

Feigenson, N., Park, J., & Salovey, P. (1997). Effects of blameworthiness and outcome severity on attributions of responsibility and damage awards in comparative negligence cases. *Law and Human Behavior, 21,* 597–617.

Feigenson, N., Park, J., & Salovey, P. (2001). The role of emotions in comparative negligence judgments. *Journal of Applied Social Psychology, 31,* 576–603.

Feild, H. S. (1978). Juror background characteristics and attitudes toward rape: Correlates of jurors' decisions in rape trials. *Law and Human Behavior, 2,* 73–93.

Felstiner, W., Abel, R., & Sarat, A. (1980–1981). The emergence and transformation of disputes: Naming, blaming, claiming ... *Law and Society Review, 15,* 631–654.

Fincham, F. D., & Jaspars, J. M. (1980). Attribution of responsibility: From man the scientist to man as lawyer. *Advances in Experimental Social Psychology, 13,* 81–138.

Finkel, N. (1995). *Commonsense justice.* Cambridge, MA: Harvard University Press.

Finkel, N. (1997). Commonsense justice, psychology and the law: Prototypes that are common, senseful, and not. *Psychology, Public Policy, and Law, 3,* 461–489.

Fischel, D. R., & Sykes, A. O. (1996). Corporate crime. *Journal of Legal Studies, 25,* 319–349.

Fischhoff, B. (1975). Hindsight ≠ foresight: The effect of outcome knowledge on judgment under uncertainty. *Journal of Experimental Psychology: Human Perception and Performance, 1,* 288–299.

Fischhoff, B. (1982). Debiasing. In D. Kahneman, P. Slovic, & A. Tversky (Eds.), *Judgment under uncertainty: Heuristics and biases* (pp. 422–444). Cambridge, England: Cambridge University Press.

Fishbein, M., & Ajzen, I. (1975). *Belief, attitude, intention, and behavior: An introduction to theory and research.* Reading, MA: Addison-Wesley.

Fishfader, V. L., Howells, G. N., Katz, R. C., & Teresi, P. S. (1996). Evidential and extralegal factors in juror decisions: Presentation mode, retention, and level of emotionality. *Law and Human Behavior, 20,* 565–572.

Fisk, M. (2000, October 5). Jury tags Chrysler for $83 million (but state cap law in force at filing time trims award to $2.4 million). *National Law Journal.* Retrieved July 17, 2002, from http://web.lexis-nexis.com/universe/

Foley, L. A., & Pigott, M. A. (1997). Race, age and jury decision in a civil rape trial. *American Journal of Forensic Psychology, 15,* 37–55.

ForsterLee, L., Horowitz, I. A., Athaide-Victor, E., & Brown, N. (2000). The bottom line: The effects of written expert witness statements on juror verdicts and information processing. *Law and Human Behavior, 24,* 259–270.

Fox, D. R. (1996). The law says corporations are persons but psychology knows better. *Behavioral Sciences and the Law, 14,* 339–360.

Frank, J. (1945). *Courts on trial.* Princeton, NJ: Princeton University Press.

Fulero, S. M., & Penrod, S. D. (1990). Attorney jury selection folklore: What do they think and how can psychologists help? *Forensic Reports, 9,* 233–259.

Galanter, M. (1983). Reading the landscape of disputes: What we know and don't know (and think we know) about our allegedly contentious and litigious society. *UCLA Law Review, 31*, 4–71.

Galanter, M. (1990). The civil jury as regulator of the litigation process. *University of Chicago Legal Forum, 1990*, 201–271.

Galanter, M., & Luban, D. (1993). Poetic justice: Punitive damages and legal pluralism. *American University Law Review, 42*, 1393–1463.

Geistfeld, M. (1995). Placing a price on pain and suffering: A method for helping juries determine tort damages for nonmonetary injuries. *California Law Review, 83*, 773–852.

Gensler, S. S. (2000). Bifurcation unbound. *Washington Law Review, 75*, 705–784.

Glaberson, W. (1998, July 30). Plaintiff is awarded $345,000 in Brawley defamation case. *New York Times*. Retrieved July 17, 2002, from http://www.nytimes.com

Goodman, J., Greene, E., & Loftus, E. F. (1989). Runaway verdicts or reasoned determinations: Mock juror strategies in awarding damages. *Jurimetrics Journal, 29*, 285–309.

Goodman, J., Loftus, E. F., & Greene, E. (1990). Matters of money: *Voir dire* in civil cases. *Forensic Reports, 3*, 303–329.

Goodman, J., Loftus, E. F., Miller, M., & Greene, E. (1991). Money, sex, and death: Gender bias in wrongful death damage awards. *Law and Society Review, 25*, 263–285.

Goodman-Delahunty, J., & Foote, W. E. (1995). Compensation for pain, suffering, and other psychological injuries: The impact of *Daubert* on employment discrimination claims. *Behavioral Sciences and the Law, 13*, 183–206.

Graddy, E. (1997). Compensation, damages, and functional form in tort liability research. *Jurimetrics, 37*, 269–283.

Greene, E. (1989). On juries and damage awards: The process of decision making. *Law and Contemporary Problems, 52*, 225–246.

Greene, E., & Bornstein, B. H. (2000). Precious little guidance: Jury instruction on damage awards. *Psychology, Public Policy, and Law, 6*, 743–768.

Greene, E., Coon, D., & Bornstein, B. (2001). The effects of limiting punitive damage awards. *Law and Human Behavior, 25*, 215–232.

Greene, E., & Dodge, M. (1995). The influence of prior record evidence on juror decision making. *Law and Human Behavior, 19*, 67–78.

Greene, E., Downey, C., & Goodman-Delahunty, J. (1999). Juror decisions about damages in employment discrimination cases. *Behavioral Sciences and the Law, 17*, 107–121.

Greene, E., & Dunaway, K. (2002, August). *Do jurors talk about "silent factors" during deliberation?* Paper presented at the meeting of the American Psychological Association, Chicago.

Greene, E., Goodman, J., & Loftus, E. F. (1991). Jurors' attitudes about civil litigation and the size of damage awards. *American University Law Review, 40*, 805–820.

Greene, E., & Johns, M. (2001). Jurors' use of instructions on negligence. *Journal of Applied Social Psychology, 31*, 840–859.

Greene, E., Johns, M., & Bowman, J. (1999). The effects of injury severity on jury negligence decisions. *Law and Human Behavior, 23*, 675–693.

Greene, E., Johns, M., & Smith, A. (2001). The effects of defendant conduct on jury damage awards. *Journal of Applied Psychology, 86*, 228–237.

Greene, E., & Smith, A. (2002, March). *Debiasing techniques: Reducing the impact of hindsight bias in civil jury trials.* Paper presented at the meeting of the American Psychology–Law Society, Austin, TX.

Greene, E., Woody, W. D., & Winter, R. (2000). Compensating plaintiffs and punishing defendants: Is bifurcation necessary? *Law and Human Behavior, 24*, 187–205.

Gronfein, W., & Kinney, E. (1991). Controlling large malpractice claims: The unexpected impact of damage caps. *Journal of Health Politics, Policy and Law, 16*, 441–464.

Gross, S. R., & Syverud, K. D. (1991). Getting to no: A study of settlement negotiations and the selection of cases for trial. *Michigan Law Review, 90*, 319–393.

Gross, S. R., & Syverud, K. D. (1996). Don't try: Civil jury verdicts in a system geared to settlement. *UCLA Law Review, 44*, 1–64.

Hammitt, J. K., Carroll, S. J., & Relles, D. A. (1985). Tort standards and jury decisions. *Journal of Legal Studies, 14*, 751–762.

Haney, C. (1993). Psychology and legal change: The impact of a decade. *Law and Human Behavior, 17*, 371–398.

Haney, C. (1997). Commonsense justice and capital punishment: Problematizing the "will of the people." *Psychology, Public Policy, and Law, 3*, 303–337.

Hannaford, P., Dann, B. M., & Munsterman, G. T. (1998). How judges view civil juries. *DePaul Law Review, 48*, 247–263.

Hannaford, P., Hans, V. P., & Munsterman, G. T. (2000). Permitting jury discussions during trial: Impact of the Arizona reform. *Law and Human Behavior, 24*, 359–382.

Hans, V. P. (1989). The jury's response to business and corporate wrongdoing. *Law and Contemporary Problems, 52*, 177–203.

Hans, V. P. (1992). Jury decision making. In D. K. Kagehiro & W. S. Laufer (Eds.), *Handbook of psychology and law* (pp. 56–76). New York: Springer-Verlag.

Hans, V. P. (1996). The contested role of the civil jury in business litigation. *Judicature, 79*, 242–248.

Hans, V. P. (2000). *Business on trial: The civil jury and corporate responsibility.* New Haven, CT: Yale University Press.

Hans, V. P., & Ermann, M. D. (1989). Responses to corporate versus individual wrongdoing. *Law and Human Behavior, 13*, 151–166.

Hans, V. P., & Lofquist, W. S. (1992). Jurors' judgments of business liability in tort cases: Implications for the litigation explosion debate. *Law and Society Review, 26,* 85–115.

Hans, V. P., & Lofquist, W. S. (1994). Perceptions of civil justice: The litigation crisis attitudes of civil jurors. *Behavioral Sciences and the Law, 12,* 181–196.

Hans, V. P., & Vidmar, N. (1986). *Judging the jury.* New York: Plenum.

Harrington, D., & Dempsey, J. (1969). Psychological factors in jury selection. *Tennessee Law Review, 37,* 173–178.

Hart, A. J., Evans, D. L., Wissler, R. L., Feehan, J. W., & Saks, M. J. (1997). Injuries, prior beliefs, and damage awards. *Behavioral Sciences and the Law, 15,* 63–82.

Hart, H. L. A., & Honore, T. (1985). *Causation in the law* (2nd ed.). Oxford, England: Clarendon.

Hastie, R. (1991). Is attorney conducted *voir dire* an effective procedure for the selection of impartial juries? *American University Law Review, 40,* 703–726.

Hastie, R., Penrod, S., & Pennington, N. (1983). *Inside the jury.* Cambridge, MA: Harvard University Press.

Hastie, R., Schkade, D., & Payne, J. (1998). A study of juror and jury judgments in civil cases: Deciding liability for punitive damages. *Law and Human Behavior, 22,* 287–314.

Hastie, R., Schkade, D., & Payne, J. (1999). Juror judgments in civil cases: Effects of plaintiff's request and plaintiff's identity on punitive damage awards. *Law and Human Behavior, 23,* 445–470.

Hawkins, S. A., & Hastie, R. (1990). Hindsight: Biased judgments of past events after the outcomes are known. *Psychological Bulletin, 107,* 311–327.

Hayden, G., Senna, J., & Seigel, L. (1978). Prosecutorial discretion in peremptory challenges: An empirical investigation of formatical use in the Massachusetts jury selection process. *New England Law Review, 13,* 768–791.

Hensler, D. R., Marquis, M. S., Abrahamse, A. F., Berry, S. H., Ebener, P. A., Lewis, E. G., et al. (1991). *Compensation for accidental injuries in the United States.* Santa Monica, CA: RAND.

Hinsz, V. B., & Indahl, K. E. (1995). Assimilation to anchors for damage awards in a mock civil trial. *Journal of Applied Social Psychology, 25,* 991–1026.

Horowitz, I. A. (1997). Reasonable doubt instructions: Commonsense justice and standard of proof. *Psychology, Public Policy, and Law, 3,* 285–302.

Horowitz, I. A., & Bordens, K. S. (1988). The effects of outlier presence, plaintiff population size, and aggregation of plaintiffs on simulated civil jury decisions. *Law and Human Behavior, 12,* 209–230.

Horowitz, I. A., & Bordens, K. S. (1990). An experimental investigation of procedural issues in complex tort trials. *Law and Human Behavior, 14,* 269–285.

Horowitz, I. A., & Bordens, K. S. (2000). The consolidation of plaintiffs: The effects of number of plaintiffs on jurors' liability decisions, damage awards, and cognitive processing of evidence. *Journal of Applied Psychology, 85,* 909–918.

Horowitz, I. A., ForsterLee, L., & Brolly, I. (1996). Effects of trial complexity on decision making. *Journal of Applied Psychology, 81*, 757–768.

Horowitz, I. A., & Kirkpatrick, L. C. (1996). A concept in search of a definition: The effects of reasonable doubt instructions on certainty of guilt standards and jury verdicts. *Law and Human Behavior, 20*, 655–670.

Huber, P. (1988). *Liability: The legal revolution and its consequences*. New York: Basic Books.

Huber, P. (1991). *Galileo's revenge: Junk science in the courtroom*. New York: Basic Books.

Hurd, S. N., & Zollers, F. E. (1994). State punitive damages statutes: A proposed alternative. *Journal of Legislation, 20*, 191–212.

Izzett, R., & Leginski, W. (1974). Group discussion and the influence of defendant characteristics in a simulated jury setting. *Journal of Social Psychology, 93*, 271–279.

Jacowitz, K. E., & Kahneman, D. (1995). Measures of anchoring in estimation tasks. *Personality and Social Psychology Bulletin, 21*, 1161–1166.

Jaffe, L. L. (1953). Damages for personal injury: The impact of insurance. *Law and Contemporary Problems, 18*, 219–240.

Johnson, J. T., & Drobny, J. (1987). Happening soon and happening later: Temporal cues and attributions of liability. *Basic and Applied Social Psychology, 8*, 209–234.

Kagehiro, D. K., Taylor, R. B., Laufer, W. S., & Harland, A. T. (1991). Hindsight bias and third-party consent to warrantless police searches. *Law and Human Behavior, 15*, 305–314.

Kahneman, D., Schkade, D., & Sunstein, C. (1998). Shared outrage and erratic awards: The psychology of punitive damages. *Journal of Risk and Uncertainty, 16*, 47–84.

Kalven, H. (1958). The jury, the law, and the personal injury damage award. *Ohio State Law Journal, 19*, 159–178.

Kalven, H. (1964). The dignity of the civil jury. *Virginia Law Review, 50*, 1055–1075.

Kalven, H., & Zeisel, H. (1966). *The American jury*. Boston: Little, Brown.

Kamin, K. A., & Rachlinski, J. J. (1995). Ex post ≠ ex ante: Determining liability in hindsight. *Law and Human Behavior, 19*, 89–104.

Kang, M. S. (1999). Don't tell juries about statutory damage caps: The merits of nondisclosure. *University of Chicago Law Review, 66*, 469–493.

Kassin, S. M., & Sommers, S. R. (1997). Inadmissible testimony, instructions to disregard, and the jury: Substantive versus procedural considerations. *Personality and Social Psychology Bulletin, 23*, 1046–1054.

Kerr, N., Hymes, R., Anderson, A., & Weathers, J. (1995). Defendant–juror similarity and mock juror judgments. *Law and Human Behavior, 19*, 545–567.

Klan must pay $37 million for inciting church fire. (1998, July 25). *New York Times*. Retrieved July 17, 2002, from http://www.nytimes.com

Koenig, T., & Rustad, M. (1993). The quiet revolution revisited: An empirical study of the impact of state tort reform of punitive damages in products liability. *Justice System Journal, 16,* 21–44.

Kramer, G. P., & Kerr, N. (1989). Laboratory simulation and bias in the study of juror behavior. *Law and Human Behavior, 13,* 89–99.

Kraus, N., Malmfors, T., & Slovic, P. (1992). Intuitive toxicology: Expert and lay judgments of chemical risks. *Risk Analysis, 8,* 435–455.

Kritzer, J., Bogart, W., & Vidmar, N. (1991). The aftermath of injury: Cultural factors in compensation seeking in Canada and the United States. *Law and Society Review, 25,* 499–543.

LaBine, S. J., & LaBine, G. (1996). Determinations of negligence and the hindsight bias. *Law and Human Behavior, 20,* 501–516.

Landes, W. M., & Posner, R. A. (1987). *The economic structure of tort law.* Cambridge, MA: Harvard University Press.

Landsman, S., Diamond, S., Dimitropoulos, L., & Saks, M. J. (1998). Be careful what you wish for: The paradoxical effects of bifurcating claims for punitive damages. *Wisconsin Law Review, 1998,* 297–342.

Leebron, D. W. (1989). Final moments: Damages for pain and suffering prior to death. *New York University Law Review, 64,* 256–284.

Leibman, J. H., Bennett R. B., Jr., & Fetter, R. (1998). The effect of lifting the blindfold from civil juries charged with apportioning damages in modified comparative fault cases: An empirical study of the alternatives. *American Business Law Journal, 35,* 349–402.

Leibson, D. J. (1976–1977). Recovery of damages for emotional distress caused by physical injury to another. *Journal of Family Law, 15,* 163–211.

Lempert, R. (1999). Juries, hindsight, and punitive damage awards: Failures of a social science case for change. *DePaul Law Review, 48,* 867–894.

Lichtman, L. (1999). Jury awards nearly $4 million in cases. *The Legal Intelligencer.* Retrieved July 12, 2002, from http://web.lexis-nexis.com/universe/

Lieberman, J., & Sales, B. (1997). What social science teaches us about the jury instruction process. *Psychology, Public Policy, and Law, 3,* 589–644.

Linz, D., & Penrod, S. D. (1982, March). *A meta-analysis of the influence of research methodology on the outcomes of jury simulation studies.* Paper presented at the Academy of Criminal Justice Sciences, Louisville, KY.

Linz, D., & Penrod, S. D. (1984). Increasing attorney persuasiveness in the courtroom. *Law and Psychology Review, 8,* 1–47.

Liskow, M. (1999, April 26). The bifurcated trial plaintiff in a slip-and-fall case, requiring new, combined trial. *The New Jersey Lawyer.* Retrieved July 19, 2002, from http://web.lexis-nexis.com/universe/

Litras, M. F., Gifford, S., DeFrances, C., Rottman, D., LaFountain, N., & Ostrom, B. (2000). Tort trials and verdicts in large counties, 1996 (NCJ Rep. No. 179769). *Bureau of Justice Statistics Bulletin.* Retrieved July 19, 2002, from http://www.ojp.usdoj.gov/bjs

Livingston, K. (2001, April 24). California study: Punitive damages hit $6 billion in 1990s. *The Recorder.* Retrieved July 19, 2002, from http://www.law.com

Loss of enjoyment of life as a separate element of damages. (1981). *Pacific Law Journal, 12,* 965–986.

Lupfer, M., Cohen, R., Bernard, J., & Smalley, D. (1985). An attributional analysis of jurors' judgments in civil cases. *Journal of Social Psychology, 125,* 743–751.

MacCoun, R. J. (1993). Getting inside the black box: What empirical research tells us about civil jury behavior. In R. E. Litan (Ed.), *Verdict: Assessing the civil jury* (pp. 137–180). Washington, DC: Brookings Institution.

MacCoun, R. J. (1996). Differential treatment of corporate defendants by juries: An examination of the "deep-pockets" hypothesis. *Law and Society Review, 30,* 121–161.

MacCrimmon, K., & Wehrung, D. (1986). *Taking risks: The management of uncertainty.* New York: Free Press.

Macrae, C. N. (1992). A tale of two curries: Counterfactual thinking and accident-related judgments. *Personality and Social Psychology Bulletin, 18,* 84–87.

Macrae, C. N., & Milne, A. B. (1992). A curry for your thoughts: Empathic effects on counterfactual thinking. *Personality and Social Psychology Bulletin, 18,* 625–630.

Malouff, J., & Schutte, N. S. (1989). Shaping juror attitudes: Effects of requesting different damage amounts in personal injury trials. *Journal of Social Psychology, 129,* 491–497.

Marder, N. S. (1998). Juries and damages: A commentary. *DePaul Law Review, 48,* 427–452.

Marques, J., & Yzerbyt, V. (1988). The black sheep effect: Judgmental extremity towards ingroup members in inter- and intragroup situation. *European Journal of Social Psychology, 18,* 287–292.

Marti, M. W., & Wissler, R. L. (2000). Be careful what you ask for: The effect of anchors on personal injury damages awards. *Journal of Experimental Psychology: Applied, 6,* 91–103.

Mazzella, R., & Feingold, A. (1994). The effects of physical attractiveness, race, socioeconomic status, and gender of defendants and victims on judgments of mock jurors: A meta-analysis. *Journal of Applied Social Psychology, 24,* 1315–1344.

McCaffery, E. J., Kahneman, D., & Spitzer, M. L. (1995). Framing the jury: Cognitive perspectives on pain and suffering awards. *Virginia Law Review, 81,* 1341–1420.

Melsheimer, T. M., & Stodghill, S. H. (1994). Due process and punitive damages: Providing meaningful guidance to the jury. *SMU Law Review, 47,* 329–350.

Melton, G. B., Petrila, J., Slobogin, C., & Poythress, N. G. (1997). *Psychological evaluations for the courts: A handbook for mental health professionals and lawyers* (2nd ed.). New York: Guilford Press.

Metzloff, T. B. (1991). Resolving malpractice disputes: Imaging the jury's shadow. *Law and Contemporary Problems, 54,* 43–129.

Miller, D. T., & McFarland, C. (1986). Counterfactual thinking and victim compensation: A test of norm theory. *Personality and Social Psychology Bulletin, 12*, 513–519.

Mills, C., & Bohannan, W. (1980). Juror characteristics: To what extent are they related to jury verdicts? *Judicature, 64*, 23–31.

Moller, E. (1996). *Trends in civil jury verdicts since 1985.* Santa Monica, CA: RAND.

Moller, E., Pace, N., & Carroll, S. (1999). Punitive damages in financial injury jury verdicts. *Journal of Legal Studies, 28*, 283–339.

Moran, G., & Comfort, J. (1986). Neither "tentative" nor "fragmentary": Verdict preference of impaneled felony jurors as a function of attitude toward capital punishment. *Journal of Applied Psychology, 71*, 146–155.

Moran, G., Cutler, B. & Loftus, E. F. (1990). Jury selection in major controlled substance trials: The need for extended *voir dire. Forensic Reports, 3*, 331–348.

Morris, C. (1959). Liability for pain and suffering. *Columbia Law Review, 59*, 476–485.

Morrison, D. (1989). Predicting contraceptive efficacy: A discriminant analysis of three groups of adolescent women. *Journal of Applied Social Psychology, 19*, 1431–1452.

Mott, N. L., Hans, V. P., & Simpson, L. (2000). What's half a lung worth? Civil jurors' accounts of their award decision making. *Law and Human Behavior, 24*, 401–419.

Mullenix, L. (1998, September 21). Complex litigation. *National Law Journal*, p. B5.

Murphy, C. P. (1993). Integrating the constitutional authority of civil and criminal juries. *George Washington Law Review, 61*, 724–805.

Murphy, S. W. (1991). Contributory negligence in medical malpractice: Are the standards changing to reflect society's growing health care consumerism? *University of Dayton Law Review, 17*, 151–179.

Nagel, S. S., & Weitzman, L. J. (1971). Women as litigants. *Hastings Law Journal, 23*, 171–198.

Nagel, S. S., & Weitzman, L. J. (1972). Sex and the unbiased jury. *Judicature, 56*, 108–111.

Narby, D., Cutler, B., & Moran, G. (1993). A meta-analysis of the association between authoritarianism and jurors' perceptions of defendant culpability. *Journal of Applied Psychology, 78*, 34–42.

National Highway Traffic Safety Administration. (2000). *Traffic safety facts 2000.* Retrieved July 17, 2002, from http://www-nrd.nhtsa.dot.gov/pdf/nrd-30/ncsa/tsf2000/2000ovrfacts.pdf

O'Connell, J., & Bailey, T. (1972). The history of payment for pain and suffering. *University of Illinois Law Forum, 1972*, 83–109.

O'Connell, J., & Simon, R. J. (1972). Payment for pain and suffering: Who wants what, when and why? *University of Illinois Law Forum, 1972*, 1–82.

Olczak, P. V., Kaplan, M. F., & Penrod, S. D. (1991). Attorneys' lay psychology and its effectiveness in selecting jurors: Three empirical studies. *Journal of Social Behavior and Personality, 6*, 431–452.

Olsen-Fulero, L., & Fulero, S. (1997). Commonsense rape judgments: An empathy-complexity theory of rape juror story making. *Psychology, Public Policy, and Law, 3*, 402–427.

Opatrny, D. (2000, June 14). Jurors getting smarter and stingier: Judges in San Francisco seeing rise in juror education levels, drop in sympathy. *The Recorder.* Retrieved July 17, 2002, from http://www.law.com

Ostrom, B., Rottman, D., & Goerdt, J. A. (1996). A step above anecdote: A profile of the civil jury in the 1990s. *Judicature, 79*, 233–241.

Ostrom, B., Rottman, D., & Hanson, R. (1992). What are tort awards really like? The untold story from the state courts. *Law and Policy, 14*, 77–106.

Owen, D. G. (1994). A punitive damages overview: Functions, problems and reform. *Villanova Law Review, 39*, 353–413.

Padawer-Singer, A., & Barton, A. (1975). The impact of pretrial publicity on jurors' verdicts. In R. J. Simon (Ed.), *The jury system in America: A critical review* (pp. 125–139). Beverly Hills, CA: Sage.

Penrod, S. (1990). Predictors of jury decision making in criminal and civil cases: A field experiment. *Forensic Reports, 3*, 261–277.

Penrod, S., & Heuer, L. (1997). Tweaking commonsense: Assessing aids to jury decision making. *Psychology, Public Policy, and Law, 3*, 259–284.

Pepper, J. (1996, June 5). Forget about panning for gold; buy a car in Alabama and sue for a bad paint job. *The Detroit News.* Retrieved March 20, 2001, from http://detnews.com/menu/stories/50868.htm

Perczek, J. (1993). On efficiency, deterrence, and fairness: A survey of punitive damages law and a proposed jury instruction. *Suffolk University Law Review, 27*, 825–904.

Perrin, G., & Sales, B. D. (1993). Artificial legal standards in mental/emotional injury litigation. *Behavioral Sciences and the Law, 11*, 193–203.

Peterson, M. A. (1984). *Compensation for injuries: Civil jury verdicts in Cook County.* Santa Monica, CA: RAND.

Peterson, M. A. (1986). *A summary of research results: Trends and patterns in civil jury verdicts.* Santa Monica, CA: RAND.

Peterson, M. A., Sarma, S., & Shanley, M. (1987). *Punitive damages: Empirical findings.* Santa Monica, CA: RAND.

Phares, E., & Wilson, K. (1972). Responsibility attribution: Role of outcome severity, situational ambiguity, and internal–external control. *Journal of Personality, 40*, 392–406.

Plant, M. L. (1958). Damages for pain and suffering. *Ohio State Law Journal, 19*, 200–211.

Polinsky, A. M., & Shavell, S. (1998). Punitive damages: An economic analysis. *Harvard Law Review, 111*, 869–962.

Poser, S., Bornstein, B. H., & McGorty, E. K. (in press). Measuring damages for lost enjoyment of life: The view from the bench and the jury box. *Law and Human Behavior.*

Priest, G. L. (1987). The current insurance crisis and modern tort law. *Yale Law Journal, 96*, 1521–1590.

Prosser, W. L. (1953). Comparative negligence. *Michigan Law Review, 51*, 465–508.

Rachlinski, J. (1998). A positive psychological theory of judging in hindsight. *University of Chicago Law Review, 65*, 571–625.

Raitz, A., Greene, E., Goodman, J., & Loftus, E. F. (1990). Determining damages: The influence of expert testimony on jurors' decision making. *Law and Human Behavior, 14*, 385–395.

Reskin, B., & Visher, C. (1986). The impacts of evidence and extralegal factors in jurors' decisions. *Law and Society Review, 20*, 423–438.

Restatement (second) of torts. (1965). St. Paul, MN: American Law Institute.

Restatement (third) of torts: Apportionment of liability. (2000). St. Paul, MN: American Law Institute.

Ritov, I., & Baron, J. (1994). Judgements of compensation for misfortune: The role of expectation. *European Journal of Social Psychology, 24*, 525–539.

Robbennolt, J. K. (2000). Outcome severity and judgments of "responsibility": A meta-analytic review. *Journal of Applied Social Psychology, 12*, 2575–2609.

Robbennolt, J. K., & Sobus, M. S. (1997). An integration of hindsight bias and counterfactual thinking: Decision-making and drug courier profiles. *Law and Human Behavior, 21*, 539–560.

Robbennolt, J. K., & Studebaker, C. A. (1999). Anchoring in the courtroom: The effects of caps on punitive damages. *Law and Human Behavior, 23*, 353–373.

Rodgers, G. B. (1991). Factors contributing to compensatory damage awards in product liability cases involving personal injury. *Journal of Products Liability, 13*, 19–29.

Rodriguez, L., & Bogett, W. R. (1989). Societal considerations in scaling injury severity and effects. *Journal of Safety Research, 20*, 73–83.

Roese, N. J. (1997). Counterfactual thinking. *Psychological Bulletin, 121*, 133–148.

Rohrlich, T. (2001, February 1). We aren't seeing you in court. *Los Angeles Times*, p. A1. Retrieved July 17, 2002, from http://www.latimes.com

Rubin, P., Calfree, J., & Grady, M. (1997). *BMW v. Gore*: Mitigating the punitive economics of punitive damages. In H. Demsetz, E. Gelhorn, & N. Lund (Eds.), *Supreme Court economic review* (Vol. 5, pp. 179–216). Chicago: University of Chicago Press.

Rustad, M. (1992). In defense of punitive damages in products liability: Testing tort anecdotes with empirical data. *Iowa Law Review, 78*, 1–88.

Rustad, M. (1998). Unraveling punitive damages: Current data and further inquiry. *Wisconsin Law Review, 1998,* 15–69.

Rustad, M., & Koenig, T. (1995). Reconceptualizing punitive damages in medical malpractice: Targeting "moral corporations" not "moral monsters." *Rutgers Law Review, 47,* 975–1082.

Saks, M. J. (1989). Legal policy analysis and evaluation. *American Psychologist, 44,* 1110–1117.

Saks, M. J. (1992). Do we really know anything about the behavior of the tort litigation system—And why not? *University of Pennsylvania Law Review, 140,* 1147–1292.

Saks, M. J. (1997). What do jury experiments tell us about how juries (should) make decisions? *Southern California Interdisciplinary Law Journal, 6,* 1–53.

Saks, M. J. (1998). Comments on the Vidmar and Diamond studies. *DePaul Law Review, 48,* 423–426.

Saks, M. J., Hollinger, L. A., Wissler, R. L., Evans, D. L., & Hart, A. J. (1997). Reducing variability in civil jury awards. *Law and Human Behavior, 21,* 243–256.

Saks, M. J., & Kidd, R. F. (1980). Human information processing and adjudication: Trial by heuristics. *Law and Society Review, 15,* 123–160.

Sand, L. B., Siffert, J. S., Loughlin, W. P., Reiss, S. A., & Batterman, N. (1984, 2000 Suppl.). *Modern federal jury instructions: Civil.* New York: Matthew Bender.

Sanders, J. (1998). *Bendectin on trial.* Ann Arbor: University of Michigan Press.

Sanders, J., & Joyce, C. (1990). Off to the races: The 1980's tort crisis and the law reform process. *Houston Law Review, 27,* 207–295.

Satter, R. (1990). *Doing justice: A trial judge at work.* New York: American Lawyer Books/Simon and Schuster.

Schkade, D., Sunstein, C., & Kahneman, D. (2000). Deliberating about dollars: The severity shift. *Columbia Law Review, 100,* 1139–1175.

Schuck, P. (1993). Mapping the debate on jury reform. In R. Litan (Ed.), *Verdict: Assessing the civil jury system* (pp. 306–340). Washington, DC: Brookings Institution.

Schwartz, V. E. (1994, 1999 Cum. Suppl.). *Comparative negligence* (3rd ed.). Charlottesville, VA: Michie.

Schwartz, V. E., Behrens, M. A., & Mastrosimone, J. (1999). Reining in punitive damages "run wild": Proposals for reform by courts and legislatures. *Brooklyn Law Review, 65,* 1002–1035.

Selvin, M., & Picus, L. (1987). *The debate over jury performance: Observations from a recent asbestos case.* Santa Monica, CA: RAND.

Shanley, M. G. (1985). *Comparative negligence and jury behavior.* Santa Monica, CA: RAND.

Shanley, M. G., & Peterson, M. A. (1983). *Comparative justice: Civil jury verdicts in San Francisco and Cook Counties, 1959–1980.* Santa Monica, CA: RAND.

Shanley, M. G., & Peterson, M. A. (1987). *Posttrial adjustments to jury awards*. Santa Monica, CA: RAND.

Shaw, J. I., & Skolnick, P. (1996). When is defendant status a shield or a liability? Clarification and extension. *Law and Human Behavior, 20*, 431–442.

Sivacek, J., & Crano, W. (1982). Vested interest as a moderator of attitude-behavior consistency. *Journal of Personality and Social Psychology, 43*, 210–221.

Sloan, F. A., & Hsieh, C. R. (1990). Variability in medical malpractice payments: Is the compensation fair? *Law and Society Review, 24*, 997–1039.

Sloan, F. A., & Hsieh, C. R. (1995). Injury, liability, and the decision to file a medical malpractice claim. *Law and Society Review, 29*, 413–435.

Sloan, F. A., Mergenhagen, P., & Bovbjerg, R. (1989). Effects of tort reforms on the value of closed medical malpractice claims: A microanalysis. *Journal of Health Politics, Policy and Law, 14*, 663–687.

Sloan, F. A., & van Wert, S. S. (1991). Cost and compensation of injuries in medical malpractice. *Law and Contemporary Problems, 54*, 131–168.

Smith, W. C. (1999). Prying off tort reform caps: States striking down limits on liability and damages, and statutes of limitation. *American Bar Association Journal, 85*, 28–29.

Snyder, E. C. (1970). Sex role differential and juror decisions. *Sociology and Social Research, 55*, 442–448.

Sommer, K. L., Horowitz, I. A., & Bourgeois, M. J. (2001). When juries fail to comply with the law: Biased evidence processing in individual and group decision making. *Personality and Social Psychology Bulletin, 27*, 309–320.

Spranca, M., Minsk, E., & Baron, J. (1991). Omission and commission in judgment and choice. *Journal of Experimental Social Psychology, 27*, 76–105.

Stephan, C. (1974). Sex prejudice in jury simulation. *Journal of Personality, 88*, 305–312.

Stephan, C. (1975). Selective characteristics of jurors and litigants. In R. Simon (Ed.), *The jury system in America: A critical overview* (pp. 97–121). Beverly Hills, CA: Sage.

Sugarman, S. D. (1990, May). The need to reform personal injury law leaving scientific disputes to scientists. *Science, 248*, 823–827.

Sunstein, C., Kahneman, D., & Schkade, D. (1998). Assessing punitive damages (with notes on cognition and valuation in law). *Yale Law Journal, 107*, 2017–2153.

Swann, W. B., Langlois, J. H., & Gilbert, L. A. (Eds.). (1999). *Sexism and stereotypes in modern society: The gender science of Janet Taylor Spence*. Washington, DC: American Psychological Association.

Swim, J. (1993). In search of gender bias in evaluations and trait inferences: The role of diagnosticity and gender stereotypicality of behavioral information. *Sex Roles, 29*, 213–237.

Taragin, M. I., Willet, L. R., Wilczek, A. P., Trout, R., & Carson, J. L. (1992).

The influence of standard of care and severity of injury on the resolution of medical malpractice claims. *Annals of Internal Medicine, 117,* 780–784.

Tate, E., Hawrish, E., & Clark, S. (1974). Communication variables in jury selection. *Journal of Communication, 24,* 130–139.

Taylor, S., & Mettee, D. (1971). When similarity breeds contempt. *Journal of Personality and Social Psychology, 20,* 75–81.

Terman, S. A. (1995). Emotional damages due to wrongful death—What are they worth? *Behavioral Sciences and the Law, 13,* 43–59.

Tetlock, P. (1983). Accountability and complexity of thought. *Journal of Personality and Social Psychology, 45,* 74–83.

Thomas, E. A. C., & Parpal, M. (1987). Liability as a function of plaintiff and defendant fault. *Journal of Personality and Social Psychology, 53,* 843–857.

Tversky, A., & Kahneman, D. (1974, September). Judgment under uncertainty: Heuristics and biases. *Science, 185,* 1124–1131.

Ugwuegbu, D. (1979). Racial and evidential factors in juror attribution of legal responsibility. *Journal of Experimental Social Psychology, 15,* 133–146.

Uniform Law Commissioners. (1997). *Model punitive damages act.* Chicago: Author.

U.S. General Accounting Office. (1989). *Product liability: Verdicts and case resolution in five states* (Report to the Chairman, Subcommittee on Commerce, Consumer Protection, and Competitiveness, Committee on Energy and Commerce, House of Representatives). Washington, DC: Author.

Van Dyke, J. (1977). *Jury selection procedures.* Cambridge, MA: Ballinger.

Vidmar, N. (1992). The unfair criticism of medical malpractice juries. *Judicature, 76,* 118–124.

Vidmar, N. (1993). Empirical evidence on the deep pockets hypothesis: Jury awards for pain and suffering in medical malpractice cases. *Duke Law Journal, 43,* 217–266.

Vidmar, N. (1994a). Are juries competent to decide liability in tort cases involving scientific/medical issues? Some data from medical malpractice. *Emory Law Journal, 43,* 885–911.

Vidmar, N. (1994b). Making inferences about jury behavior from jury verdict statistics: Cautions about the Lorelei's Lied. *Law and Human Behavior, 18,* 599–617.

Vidmar, N. (1995). *Medical malpractice and the American jury: Confronting the myths about jury incompetence, deep pockets, and outrageous damage awards.* Ann Arbor: University of Michigan Press.

Vidmar, N. (1998). The performance of the American civil jury: An empirical perspective. *Arizona Law Review, 40,* 849–899.

Vidmar, N., Gross, F., & Rose, M. (1998). Jury awards for medical malpractice and post-verdict adjustments of those awards. *DePaul Law Review, 48,* 265–299.

Vidmar, N., Lee, J., Cohen, E., & Stewart, A. (1994). Damage awards and jurors' responsibility ascription in medical versus automobile negligence cases. *Behavioral Sciences and the Law, 12,* 149–160.

Vidmar, N., & Rice, J. J. (1993). Assessments of non-economic damage awards in medical negligence: A comparison of jurors with legal professionals. *Iowa Law Review, 78*, 883–911.

Viscusi, W. K. (1986). The determinants of the disposition of product liability claims and compensation for bodily injury. *Journal of Legal Studies, 15*, 321–346.

Viscusi, W. K. (1988). Pain and suffering in product liability cases: Systematic compensation or capricious awards? *International Review of Law and Economics, 8*, 203–220.

Viscusi, W. K. (2000). Corporate risk analysis: A reckless act? *Stanford Law Review, 52*, 547–597.

Wagner, W. (1989). *Art of advocacy: Jury selection.* New York: Matthew Bender.

Walster, E. (1966). Assignment of responsibility for an accident. *Journal of Personality and Social Psychology, 3*, 73–79.

Wasserman, D. T., & Robinson, J. N. (1980). Extra-legal influences, group processes, and jury decision-making: A psychological perspective. *North Carolina Central Law Journal, 12*, 96–159.

Weiler, P. C. (1991). *Medical malpractice on trial.* Cambridge, MA: Harvard University Press.

Werchick, J. W. (1965). Unmeasurable damages and a yardstick. *Hastings Law Journal, 17*, 263–300.

Wexler, D. B., & Schopp, R. F. (1989). How and when to correct for juror hindsight bias in mental health malpractice litigation: Some preliminary observations. *Behavioral Sciences and the Law, 7*, 485–504.

Whalen, D. H., & Blanchard, F. A. (1982). Effects of photographic evidence on mock juror judgment. *Journal of Applied Social Psychology, 12*, 30–41.

White, A. (1952). Selecting a jury. In J. Appleman (Ed.), *Successful jury trials: A symposium.* Indianapolis, IN: Bobbs-Merrill.

Wiener, R. L., Gaborit, M., Pritchard, C. C., McDonough, E. M., Staebler, C. R., Wiley, D. C., et al. (1994). Counterfactual thinking in mock juror assessments of negligence: A preliminary investigation. *Behavioral Sciences and the Law, 12*, 89–102.

Wiggins, E., & Breckler, S. (1990). Special verdicts as guides to decision making. *Law and Psychology Review, 14*, 1–41.

Wilbanks, J. C. (2001). *The defendant, the evidence, the trial, and the damages: A meta-analysis of civil jury decision making.* Unpublished master's thesis, University of Nebraska.

Williams, C. W., Lees-Haley, P. R., & Price, J. R. (1996). The role of counterfactual thinking and causal attribution in accident-related judgments. *Journal of Applied Social Psychology, 26*, 2100–2112.

Williams, J. E., & Best, D. L. (1990). *Measuring sex stereotypes: A multination study.* Newbury Park, CA: Sage.

Wilson, T. D. (1985). Strangers to ourselves: The origins and accuracy of beliefs about one's own mental states. In J. Harvey & G. Weary (Eds.), *Attributions in contemporary psychology* (pp. 9–36). New York: Academic Press.

Winter, G. (2001, January 30). Jury awards soar as lawsuits decline on defective goods. *New York Times*. Retrieved July 17, 2002, from http://www.nytimes.com

Wissler, R. L., Evans, D. L., Hart, A. J., Morry, M. M., & Saks, M. J. (1997). Explaining "pain and suffering" awards: The role of injury characteristics and fault attributions. *Law and Human Behavior, 21*, 181–207.

Wissler, R. L., Hart, A. J., & Saks, M. J. (1999). Decision-making about general damages: A comparison of jurors, judges, and lawyers. *Michigan Law Review, 98*, 751–826.

Wissler, R. L., Kuehn, P., & Saks, M. J. (2000). Instructing jurors on general damages. *Psychology, Public Policy, and Law, 6*, 712–742.

Wissler, R. L., Rector, K. A., & Saks, M. J. (2001). The impact of jury instructions on the fusion of liability and compensatory damages. *Law and Human Behavior, 25*, 125–139.

Woman gets $6.5 million in plane crash suit. (2001, April 20). Retrieved April 21, 2001, from http://wire.ap.org/APnews

Zebrowitz, L. A., & McDonald, S. M. (1991). The impact of litigants' baby-facedness and attractiveness on adjudications in small claims courts. *Law and Human Behavior, 15*, 603–623.

Zeisel, H., & Callahan, T. (1963). Split trials and time-saving: A statistical analysis. *Harvard Law Review, 76*, 1606–1625.

Zeisel, H., & Diamond, S. (1976). The jury selection in the Mitchell–Stans conspiracy trial. *American Bar Foundation Research Journal, 1*, 151–170.

Zickafoose, D. J., & Bornstein, B. H. (1999). Double discounting: The effects of comparative negligence on mock juror decision making. *Law and Human Behavior, 23*, 577–596.

Zuehl, J. J. (1982). *The ad damnum, jury instructions, and personal injury damage awards*. Unpublished manuscript, University of Chicago.

TABLE OF AUTHORITIES

Case citations are to the West regional reporter series, with the exception of U.S. Supreme Court citations, which are to U.S. Reports.

7 U.S.C. § 18 (a)(1)(B), (1994), 15
10 U.S.C. § 2207 (a)(2), (1994), 15
42 U.S.C.A. 1981a(b)(3) (West, 1994), 110 n.8
Ala.Code §§ 6-11-21, 1994, 177
Barry v. Edmunds, 116 U.S. 550 (1886), 7
BMW of North America v. Gore, 517 U.S. 559 (1996), 8, 11, 75
Botta v. Bruner, 138 A.2d 713 (N.J. 1958), 115 n.12
Brown v. Van Braam, 3 U.S. 344 (1797), 7
Browning-Ferris Industries, Inc. v. Kelco Disposal, Inc., 492 U.S. 257 (1989), 20, 175
California Civil Code, § 3295 (d), 1987, 188
Capelouto v. Kaiser Foundation Hospitals, 103 Cal. Rptr. 856 (1972), 111
Cimino v. Raymark Industries, Inc., 151 F.3d 297 (1998), 161
Colo. Rev. Stat. §§ 13-21-102, 2000, 177
Crisci v. Security Insurance Co., 58 Cal. Rptr. 13 (1967), 111 n.9
Crookston v. Fire Insurance Exchange, 1991, 178
Danculovich v. Brown, 593 P.2d 187 (Wyo. 1979), 140
Danner v. Mid-State Paving Co., 173 So.2d 608 (Miss. 1965), 114 n.11
Day v. Woodworth, 54 U.S. 363 (1851), 7
DeHanes v. Rothman, 158 N.J. 90; 727 A.2d 8 (1999), 151

Dimick v. Schiedt, 293 U.S. 474 (1935), 7

Dunlap v. Lee, 126 S.E.2d 62 (N.C. 1962), 114 n.11

Fla. Stat. Ann. § 768.73, 1995, 177

Huckle v. Money, 95 Eng. Rep. 768 (1763), 6

Huff v. Tracy, 129 Cal. Rptr. 551 (1976), 110 n.7

Kemezy v. Peters, 79 F.3d 33 (7th Cir. 1996), 65, 66 n.3, 75

Kozar v. Chesapeake & Ohio Railway Co., 320 F. Supp. 335 (W.D. Mich. 1970), 140

Li v. Yellow Cab Co. of California, 532 P.2d 1226 (Cal. 1975), 128, 132, 133

McDougald v. Garber, 536 N.E.2d 372 (N.Y. 1989), 106 n.3, 110

Molzof v. U.S., 112 S. Ct. 711 (1992), 110 n.7

Nev. Rev. Stat. § 42.005, 1993, 177

O'Shea v. Riverway Towing Co., 677 F.2d 1194 (7th Cir. 1982), 12, 14, 108

Pacific Mutual Life Insurance Company v. Haslip, 400 U.S. 1 (1991), 192

Petition of Kinsman Transit Co., 338 F.2d 708 (2d Cir. 1964), 141 n.14

Scott v. Sheperd, 95 Eng. Rep. 1124 (1773), 6

Sherrod v. Berry, 629 F. Supp. 159 (N.D. Ill. 1985), rev'd, 856 F.2d 802 (7th Cir. 1988), 110 n7

Smith v. Wade, 461 U.S. 30 (1982), 194

Thompson v. National Railroad Passenger Corp., 621 F.2d 814 (6th Cir. 1980), 110

Twyman v. Twyman, 855 S.W.2d 619 (Tex. 1993), 111

TXO Production Corp. v. Alliance Resources Corp., 509 U.S. 443 (1993), 20, 116 n.14, 175–176, 191

United States Football League v. National Football League, 842 F.2d 1335 (2nd Cir. N.Y. 1988), 70

Vanskike v. ACF Industries, Inc., 665 F.2d 188 (8th Cir. 1981), 115 n.12

Wangen et al. v. Ford et al., 97 Wis. 2d 260 (1980), 159 n.3

INDEX

Ad damnum figure, 151–153, 156, 167,
 202, 203
Additur, 18
Age
 of jurors, 82–83
 of plaintiff, 58–59
 of victim, as factor in damages scheduling, 182
Amount of damage awards
 in antitrust cases, 170–171
 appropriateness of, 200
 based on defendant's ability to pay,
 25–26, 37–38, 39–41, 65–70,
 75–77
 in bifurcated trial, 185–187, 189–190
 caps on, 150–151, 155–156, 177–181
 comparative negligence assessment,
 128–133, 172–173
 concerns about, 23, 24–25, 175
 corporate risk assessment and, 25
 corporate status of defendant and, 67–
 72, 77
 data sources, 33–34
 delay between cause and effect as factor in, 123–124
 descriptive analysis, 31, 34–39
 distribution by size and frequency, 34–
 35
 economic status of jurors as factor in,
 84–85
 educational attainments of jurors as
 factor in, 85–86
 effects of jury deliberations, 164–165
 equity in, 24, 51, 79, 107, 125, 201
 for fatalities, 104–106
 gender of jurors as factor in, 86–87, 88
 influence of amount requested by litigants, 151–155, 156, 167
 juror attitudes and beliefs about, 90–92
 juror characteristics as factor in, 93–94
 juror perception of exorbitance in, 14
 juror–litigant similarity and, 88, 89
 in malpractice cases, 73–75
 nominal or none, 70
 political beliefs of jurors as factor in,
 85

predictability of, 24–25, 200–201
prescriptive approach, 31
punitive awards, 15–16, 37
schedule of damages, 181–183
severity of injury as factor in, 103,
 112–113, 116–118, 124–125,
 201
tort reform efforts, 8–9, 23, 175, 176,
 196–197
trends, 7–9, 24, 32, 34, 35–36, 37,
 200
typicality of injury as factor in, 120–
 123, 125
variability in, 24, 79, 181, 201
variation by case type, 73–77
for various degrees of injury among
 multiple plaintiffs, 161–162
when punitive damages paid to state,
 194
See also Determination of damage
 amounts
Anchoring and adjustment heuristic,
 150–156, 203
Antitrust law, 170–171
Arbitration and mediation, 9
Attitudes and perceptions of jurors, 89–
 92
Authoritarian personality, 82, 90
Automobile accidents, 16–18, 33, 35
 consideration of defendant's conduct
 in, 135–136
 punitive damages, 76
 trial outcomes, 73–74

Babylonian law, 6
Bias and prejudice in jurors, 20–21, 23
 attorneys' theories of jury selection, 81
 against corporate defendant, 70–72, 90
 defendant's ability to pay, 25–26
 gender, 55–58
 goals of jury blindfolding, 168
 in malpractice cases, 73
 proplaintiff/antidefendant, 64
 racial, 54–55, 65

Bifurcated trial, 43, 143, 183–191, 196, 204
Bot, 6
Brain damage, 112
Brennan, William, 20
Bush (George H. W.) administration, 8
Bush (George W.) administration, 8

Cause of injury, 119–123
Class action suits, 60–61
Clinton administration, 8
Cognitive functioning in awards determi-
     nations, 10–11
  assessment of plaintiff's comparative
     negligence, 129–133
  attitudinal factors, 89–92
  benefits of bifurcated trial, 184, 190
  complex cases, 20, 161–163
  components, 149
  counterfactual thinking, 121–122, 123
  decision-making strategies, 147–148,
     149, 203–204
  expectancy beliefs, 92–93, 120–121,
     123
  group processes in jury deliberations,
     163–167
  inability to disregard information, 142,
     143
  individual differences among jurors,
     79–80
  influence of litigant characteristics,
     48–49
  instructions to jury on damage awards,
     18–21, 202–204
  juror–litigant similarity and, 88–89
  mapping normative judgments to eco-
     nomic compensation, 21, 176
  perception of pain and suffering, 111,
     112–113
  research needs, 204–205
  significance of, 125
  three-part analytical model, 29–31
  trial procedure as obstacle to fair deci-
     sion making, 5, 11
  See also Determination of damage
     amounts
Commercial law, 33, 52–53
  compensatory damages, 12
  defective products cases, 24
  punitive damages, 37
Commission, injury by, 119–120

Comparative negligence standard, 17, 74
  current practice, 128
  double discounting effect, 129–130,
     131, 132–133
  evaluation of plaintiff behavior in,
     130–133
  instructions to jury, 129–130, 131
  jury instructions, 171–173
  punitive damage awards and, 140–141
  shared liability of plaintiff and defen-
     dant, 139–141
  trial outcomes, 128–129
  use of special verdict forms, 132–133
Compensatory damage awards
  amount of punitive damages related to,
     37
  in bifurcated trial, 184, 188–191
  caps on, 155, 156, 177, 179
  conduct of defendant as factor in,
     135–136, 137–138
  conduct of litigant as factor in, 98
  corporate status of defendant and, 66–
     72
  descriptive analysis, 32–36
  economic, 12–13
  financial status of defendant as factor
     in, 39, 40, 66–70, 72
  historical evolution of legal concepts,
     6–7
  instructions to jury on, 18–19, 68
  nominal or none, 70
  noneconomic. *See* Pain and suffering
     awards
  punitive damages included in, 159–
     160, 179–181
  rationale, 3, 11, 15, 119
  severity of injury as factor in, 98, 101,
     103–116, 139, 140, 201
  in shared liability of plaintiff and de-
     fendant, 139–141
  size of plaintiff population as factor in,
     60–61
Contract law, 32, 33, 37
Contributory negligence, 127–128
Corporations
  amount of damage awards assessed
     against, *vs.* individuals, 65–70,
     77
  as defendants, jury response to, 38,
     70–72
  juror attitudes and beliefs, 90

risk assessment in product development, 25

Counterfactual thinking, 121–122, 123

Damage awards
  determinants of jury decision making, 3–4, 5
  historical evolution of legal concepts, 6–9
  popular perception and understanding, 21–23
  rationale, 3, 11
  See also Amount of damage awards; Determination of damage amounts

Death
  compensatory damage awards, 104–106
  punitive damage awards, 116

Defendant characteristics
  ability to pay damages, 25–26, 37–38, 39–41, 65–70, 75–77
  behavior in causing injury, 134–138
  behavior in court, 138–139
  case type and, 72–75
  corporate identity, 65–72, 77
  insurance coverage, 72
  juror–litigant similarity, 87–89
  physical appearance, 64–65
  punitive damage assessments and, 75–77
  race, 65
  shared negligence with plaintiff, 139–141
  significance of, in juror decision making, 63–66, 77
  See also Litigant status

Determination of damage amounts
  assimilation and contrast effects, 150–151
  behavior of defendant as factor in, 134–139, 143
  behavior of plaintiff as factor in, 127–133, 143
  in bifurcated trial, 183–191
  calculating for inflation and interest rate effects, 14–15
  case type and, 72–77
  challenges for jurors, 13, 14–15, 175–176, 199, 202
  characteristics of defendant as factor in, 64–72, 75–77

characteristics of plaintiff as factor in, 51, 53–62
componential approach, 147–148, 157–159
contextual factors, 3–4, 5, 27
current system performance, 200
descriptive analysis of juror behavior, 30
economic compensation, 12
effects of award caps, 179
effects of jury blindfolding, 167–173
effects of jury deliberations, 163–167
effects of pretrial publicity, 138
extralegal influences, 47–49
future losses, 12–13
historical evolution of legal concepts, 6–9
holistic approach, 159–161
influence of amount requested by litigants, 151–155
instructions to jury, 17, 18–21, 42–43, 202–203
judge's authority, 17–18
as judicial precedent, 10
juror bias against wealthy defendants in, 25–26
juror characteristics as factor in, 79–80, 82–94
jury simulation methodology, 26–27, 68, 82, 117, 163, 204
legal strategies for influencing, 13–14
legal system as obstacle to good decision making in, 5
liability determination and, 41, 42–43
nonjury mechanisms, 195–196
normative judgment in, 30, 39–42
opportunities for improving jury decision making, 5, 30–31, 42–43, 148, 202–204
for pain and suffering, 13–14, 113–116
performance of juries in, 4, 7–8
psychological factors, 10–11, 82, 173
reform strategies, 176, 196–197
in shared liability of plaintiff and defendant, 139–141
significance of, as research topic, 9–11, 173, 204–205
use of damages schedules, 181–183, 196
use of evidence in, 97–99
videotaped jury deliberations, 163

Determination of damage amounts
(*continued*)
See also Amount of damage awards;
Cognitive functioning in awards
determinations
Deterrence
defendant's ability to pay as basis for
damages, 38, 39–40, 65–66
punitive damages rationale, 15, 16,
116, 134
Disability cases, 53, 104–106, 112–113
Double discounting, 129–130, 131, 132–
133

Economic compensation, 12–13
calculating for inflation and interest
rate effects, 14–15
defendant's wealth as factor in juror
decision making, 25–26, 37–38,
39–41, 65–70
for future losses, 12–13
gender differences, 55–58
obstacles to jury decision making, 21
severity of injury and, 104
Educational attainments of jurors, 85–
86
English law, 6
Evidence
in bifurcated trial, 183–184, 188–189
complex cases, 161–163
of defendant's conduct, 135–136
of defendant's wealth, 188
instructions to jury on uses of, 142–
143
jury deliberations, 164
jury's ability to disregard, 142, 143
misuses of, by jurors, 98–99
for pain and suffering evaluation, 114–
115
pretrial publicity, 138
significance of, in jury decision making, 97–98
See also Litigant conduct; Severity of
injury
Exemplary damages. *See* Punitive awards
Expectancy beliefs of jurors, 92–93, 120–
123, 169
Expert testimony, 13–14, 17
on *ad damnum* figure, 154–155
for pain and suffering determination,
114–115
Extralegal factors, 26–27
significance of, 47–49, 97

See also Defendant characteristics; Juror
characteristics and behavior;
Litigant status; Plaintiff characteristics

Filing of lawsuits
by individuals, 53
legal basis, 52–53
trends, 8–9, 32–33
Fusion of judgment, 41, 137, 141–143
Future losses, 12–13, 106, 108

Gender
juror–litigant similarity, 88
of jurors, 81, 86–87
of plaintiff, 55–58
Geographic home of litigants, 59–60
Government, lawsuits against, 73
paying awards to, 193–194

Haney, Craig, 42
Hebrew Covenant Code of Mosaic Law,
6
Hedonic damages, 110
Hindsight bias, 141–142, 203
Hindu law, 6
Historical development of damage awards
concepts, 6–9
Hittite law, 6
Horizontal inequity, 24, 62, 107, 125,
129, 201

Inflation, 14–15
Instructions to jury, 17, 42–43, 196
on comparative negligence, 129–130,
131, 171
on compensatory damages, 18–19, 68
on consequences of verdict, 167–173
on consideration of defendant's wealth,
66–67, 68
on damages caps, 178
on pain and suffering deliberations,
113–114, 167
pretrial, 5, 31
problems in, 18–21
on punitive damages, 19–20, 68
reform strategies, 176, 191–193
on uses of evidence, 142–143

Insurance coverage, 169–170
  for defendants, as factor in jury deci-
    sion making, 72
Insurance industry, 33
  risk assessment, 25
Interest rates, 14–15

Judge(s)
  application of comparative negligence
    finding, 128–129
  as arbiters of damage awards, 17–18,
    195–196
  disagreement with jury decisions, 63–
    64, 196
  See also Instructions to jury
Judicial procedure
  administrative handling of damages
    cases, 31
  bifurcated trial, 43, 143, 183–191
  civil liability system, 9
  defendant's conduct during trial, 138–
    139
  jury selection, 80–82
  number and types of jury trials, 9, 10,
    32–33
  as obstacle to reasonable decision mak-
    ing by juries, 5, 162–163
  opportunities for improving, 5, 31
  origins and development of jury trial,
    6, 7
  tort case example, 16–18
  use of damages schedules, 181–183
  videotaped jury deliberations, 163
  See also Instructions to jury
Juror characteristics and behavior, 47
  attitudes and beliefs, 89–92, 93–94
  attorneys' theories of, 80–82
  in bifurcated trial, 185–191
  demographic variables, 82–83, 87, 93
  economic status, 84–85
  educational attainments, 85–86
  effects of blindfolding, 167–173
  expectancies, 92–93
  gender, 81, 85–86
  influence of extralegal factors, 26–27,
    47–49, 54, 61–62, 63–66, 77
  interpretation of evidence, 97–99, 142,
    143
  juror–litigant similarity, 87–89, 93
  in jury deliberations, 163–167
  jury simulation methodology, 26–27,
    68, 82, 117, 163, 204

obstacles to determining damage
    awards, 13, 14–15, 202
  political beliefs, 85
  psychological factors, 10–11, 82
  public perceptions of, 4, 7–8, 21–23
  research needs, 204–205
  self-concept, 88–89, 93
  significance of, in awards determina-
    tions, 79–80, 93–94
Jury selection, 80–82

Kalven, Harry, 9–10, 15, 41, 42, 157–
    158, 206
Ku Klux Klan, 63

Lawyer's fees, 169–170
Libel cases, 12
Limits on award amounts, 155–156,
    177–178
  assimilation and contrast effects, 150–
    151
  compensatory damages, 155, 156, 179–
    181
  in damages schedules, 182
  effectiveness, 196–197
  effects on jury decision-making, 179–
    181
  forms of, 177
  jury instructions regarding, 178
  pain and suffering awards, 31, 179
  of punitive damages, 160, 177, 178,
    179–181
Litigant status and conduct
  corporate vs. individual, 38, 53, 65–
    72, 77
  juror–litigant similarity, 87–89
  significance of, in jury decision mak-
    ing, 47, 48, 98–99, 143
  social status, 68–69
  as verdict determinant, 33
  See also Defendant characteristics;
    Plaintiff characteristics
Locus of control beliefs, 82
Lost enjoyment of life, 110

Malpractice. See Medical malpractice
    cases
Medical expenses, 12

Medical malpractice cases, 33, 35, 36
  caps on damages, 179
  comparative negligence in, 74
  consideration of defendant's conduct
    in, 135–136
  equity of compensatory damage awards,
    107
  juror bias in, 72–73
  plaintiff characteristics, 53
  punitive damages, 37, 38, 75, 76, 118–
    119, 202
  trial outcomes, 72–75, 201–202
Model Punitive Damages Act, 192–193

Negotiated settlements, 9
Normative judgments
  commonsense justice concept, 39
  consideration of defendant's financial
    well-being in, 39–41
  in determination of damage amounts,
    30, 39–42
  economic calculations and, 21
  independence of damages determina-
    tion from liability determination,
    41, 42–43
  scope of, 39

Omission, injury by, 119–120

Pain and suffering awards
  components of, 109–111
  criteria for assessing injury severity in,
    112–113
  effects of jury deliberations, 166–167
  evidence for, 114–115
  instructions to jury regarding, 113–
    114, 167
  limits on, 31, 179
  litigant conduct as factor in, 98
  noneconomic compensation and, 110,
    111
  plaintiff characteristics as factor in, 52
  quantification, 13, 108, 113–116
  rationale, 13, 107–108
  severity of injury and, 98, 104, 106
  typicality of injury as factor in, 121
  without evidence of physical injury,
    111–112

Pepper, Jon, 22
Plaintiff characteristics
  age, 58–59
  comparative negligence contributing to
    injury, 127–133, 139–141
  diversity of, 51–52
  gender, 55–58
  geographic location of trial, 59–60
  individual injury claims, 53
  juror–litigant similarity, 87–89
  race, 54–55
  significance of, in jury decision-mak-
    ing, 54, 61–62
  size of plaintiff population, 60–61,
    161–162
  See also Litigant status
Political beliefs, 85
Preponderance of evidence, 17
Pretrial instruction, 5, 31
Pretrial publicity, 138
Products liability cases, 24
  consideration of defendant's conduct
    in, 135–136
  corporate risk assessment, 25
  punitive damages, 37, 75, 76
  trends, 33, 35, 36
  trial outcomes, 73, 75
Property disputes, 32
Property liability, 33
Protective shield effect, 69
Punitive awards, 3, 11
  amount of compensatory damages re-
    lated to, 37
  based on defendant's ability to pay,
    37–38, 39–41, 65–70, 72, 75–77
  in bifurcated trial, 184, 188–191
  caps on, 155–156, 177, 178, 179–180
  comparative negligence and, 140–141
  defendant behavior as factor in, 134–
    139
  defendant characteristics as factor in,
    75–77
  descriptive analysis, 36–39
  determination of amount, 15–16, 37–
    38
  effects of jury deliberations, 165–166
  historical development of legal con-
    cept, 6, 7
  included in compensatory damage
    awards, 159–160, 179–181
  instructions to jury on, 19–20, 68
  judge-imposed, 195–196

litigant conduct as factor in, 98
paid to government, 193–194, 196
rationale, 15, 116
severity of injury as factor in, 101–102, 116–119, 201
size of plaintiff population as factor in, 60–61
trends, 36, 37, 75, 134
unpredictability of, 24–25, 38, 201

Quadriplegia, 112

Race/ethnicity
    of defendant, 65
    of jurors, 81
    of plaintiff, 54–55
Reagan administration, 8
Rehnquist, William, 194
Remittitur, 18
Remorse, 138–139
Responsibility, 102
    defendant's acceptance of, 138–139
Rhetorical asymmetry, 165–166
Risk assessment, 25
Roman law, 6

Schedules of damages, 181–183, 195, 196
Self-concept of jurors, 88–89, 93
Seventh Amendment, 7
Severity and nature of injury
    attributions of responsibility and, 102
    case type and, 103–104
    cause of injury, 119–123

compensatory damage awards and, 103–116, 201
consideration of defendant's conduct and, 136–137
criteria for assessment of, 112–113
defendant liability and, 102
delay between cause and effect, 123–124
equity of damage award and, 24, 51, 107, 125
as factor in liability verdicts, 184, 185
pain and suffering compensation and, 107–116
punitive awards and, 101–102, 116–119, 201
shared liability of plaintiff and defendant and, 139, 140
significance of, in jury decision making, 97–98, 101–103, 124–125
typicality of injury, 120–123, 125
use of damages schedules in assessing, 182
various degrees of injury among multiple plaintiffs, 161–162
Severity shift, 165–166
Special verdict forms, 132–133, 158, 202–203

Tobacco industry cases, 24
Total justice, 40, 131, 141–142

Vertical equity, 24, 104, 125, 201
Vidmar, N., 26, 34

Wite, 6

ABOUT THE AUTHORS

Edie Greene earned her PhD in psychology and law at the University of Washington in 1983. She is currently a professor of psychology at the University of Colorado in Colorado Springs. From 1994 to 1995, Dr. Greene was a Fellow in Law and Psychology at Harvard Law School. In 1999, she received her college's award for Outstanding Research and Creative Works, and in 2001 she was honored with the campuswide research award. She has been invited to lecture at the National Judicial College and at continuing legal education programs nationwide. Dr. Greene has received several federally funded grants to support her research on jury decision making and eyewitness memory. She consults with lawyers on various trial-related issues, including trial strategies and jury decisions, and has, on numerous occasions, testified as an expert witness on jury behavior and eyewitness memory. She is the author of many articles and book chapters and coauthor of *Psychology and the Legal System* (2002). Away from work, she plays the piano and enjoys doing chamber music with her family. She likes to ski, hike, and mountain bike.

Brian H. Bornstein earned his PhD in psychology from the University of Pennsylvania in 1991 and a Master of Legal Studies from the University of Nebraska in 2001. He has been a faculty member and associate director of the University of Nebraska's law–psychology program since 2001, where he is an associate professor in the Department of Psychology and College of Law. Before he came to Nebraska, he was on the faculty at Bucknell University and Louisiana State University. He teaches courses in cognitive psychology, psychology and law, and the history of psychology. Dr. Bornstein's research interests focus on jury decision making and eyewitness memory but also include medical decision making, lay notions of justice, and basic memory phenomena. He has received federal funding for his research, has published dozens of articles, and is a Fulbright award recipient. He also consults on issues of jury selection and trial strategy, has served as an expert witness regarding eyewitness memory and decision processes, and is on the editorial board of *Law and Human Behavior*. In his free time, he enjoys relaxing with his family, reading, cooking, and engaging in various sporting activities.